REMEMBERING
EAST GERMANY

FROM OBERLIN TO EAST BERLIN

RICHARD A. ZIPSER

Elizabeth C. Hamilton

Spring 2015

[*Elizabeth Hamilton's essay on Richard Zipser's book and career was published in the Fall 2015 issue of the Polyglot, the newsletter of the Department of Languages, Literatures and Cultures, University of Delaware, pp. 13-14.*]

ISBN: 978-1-66780-748-5 (Paperback)

First printing edition 2021.

Printed by BookBaby Publishing
7905 North Crescent Boulevard
Pennsauken Township, NJ 08110

www.richard-zipser.com

CONTENTS

PREFACE 1

INTRODUCTION 4

ZIPSER BECAME A "PERSON OF INTEREST" TO THE STASI IN THE FALL OF 1975

OPENING REPORT IN MY STASI-FILE: JUNE 6, 1973 8

BACKGROUND: 1969 – 1975 9

MEETING AT THE GDR WRITERS' UNION: SEPTEMBER 11, 1975 11

CONNECTIONS AND PREPARATIONS 14

LIST OF WRITERS 16

PERSON OF INTEREST 18

FIRST REPORT FROM IME "DICHTER": NOVEMBER 25, 1975 18

FIRST REPORT FROM IMV "KURT": NOVEMBER 25, 1975 21

IMV "KURT" AND IMV "JULIA" 22

SECOND REPORT FROM IMV "KURT": DECEMBER 11, 1975 23

HE IS INTERESTED IN "LONG-TERM CONTACTS" WITH THE GDR

INFORMATIONAL REPORT: JANUARY 26, 1976 25

CONTACT WITH STEFAN HEYM: FEBRUARY, 1976 26

FRIEDRICHSHAIN MUNICIPAL HOSPITAL: MARCH/APRIL, 1976 30

THIRD REPORT FROM IMV "KURT": JUNE 4, 1976 31

FIRST REPORT FROM IMV "UWE": JUNE 4, 1976 32

EBERHARD SCHEIBNER'S REPORT: JUNE 18, 1976 38

VISIT WITH KONRAD REICH IN ROSTOCK: JUNE 20, 1976 40

INFORMATIONAL REPORT: JULY 22, 1976 51

DECISION NOT TO INCLUDE WOLF BIERMANN 56

PROJECT STATUS: SUMMER/FALL, 1976..57

EXPATRIATION OF WOLF BIERMANN: NOVEMBER, 1976..58

PRESENTATION AT THE MLA CONVENTION: DECEMBER 27, 1976 59

PERSONS PURSUING IDEOLOGICAL SUBVERSION: DECEMBER, 1976 62

SECOND REPORT FROM IMV "UWE": FEBRUARY 11, 1977......................................65

CONTRACT WITH NORDLAND PUBLISHING COMPANY: JANUARY, 1977 66

RETURN TO DERLIN: JUNE, 1977..66

FOURTH REPORT FROM IMV "KURT": JUNE 8, 1977..68

RETURN TO EAST BERLIN AS AN IREX SCHOLAR: OCTOBER, 1977 71

FIRST REPORT FROM IM "DÖLBL": OCTOBER 19, 1977.......................................73

ZIPSER IS TO BE PUT "UNDER INVESTIGATION"

INVITATION TO JUREK BECKER (1)..77

MARITAL PROBLEMS CAUSE BRIEF SETBACK..79

SECOND REPORT FROM IM "DÖLBL": DECEMBER 1, 1977 79

FIFTH REPORT FROM IMV "KURT": DECEMBER 2, 1977 93

SIXTH REPORT FROM IMV "KURT": DECEMBER 9, 1977 98

FAREWELL DINNER PARTY / FIRST SURVEILLANCE REPORT: DECEMBER 13, 1977 105

FIRST REPORT ON FAREWELL DINNER PARTY BY IMV "KURT" 115

SECOND REPORT ON FAREWELL DINNER PARTY BY IMV "KURT" 118

SECOND REPORT FROM IME "DICHTER": DECEMBER 30, 1977 124

INVITATION TO JUREK BECKER (2)..126

HE CAN ADAPT HIMSELF TO THE MOST DIVERSE CONVERSATIONAL PARTNERS

NFORMATIONAL REPORT: JANUARY 7, 1978...126

JUREK BECKER IN OBERLIN: FEBRUARY – MAY, 1978......................................139

RETURN TO EAST BERLIN AS AN IREX SCHOLAR: MAY, 1978................................144

FIRST REPORT FROM IMV "JULIA": MAY 25, 1978..144

SECOND SURVEILLANCE REPORT: MAY 25, 1978...150

SECOND REPORT FROM IMV "JULIA": JUNE 6, 1978.......................................170

ASSERTIONS ABOUT RICHARD ZIPSER 176

ANTHOLOGY OF CONTEMPORARY EAST GERMAN POETRY: A NEW PROJECT 178

REPORT ON VISIT WITH KITO LORENC IN WUISCHKE AM CZORNEBOH: JUNE 3-4, 1978 180

REPORT ON MEETING WITH STUDENTS ON JUNE 15-16, 1978 183

TOP SECRET INFORMATIONAL REPORT: JULY 17, 1978 184

TOP SECRET INFORMATIONAL REPORT: AUGUST 4, 1978 187

POSSIBLE DENIAL OF RE-ENTRY INTO THE GDR 189

8TH GDR WRITERS CONGRESS: MAY 28-31, 1978 190

HE MADE AN AFFABLE AND APPROACHABLE IMPRESSION

FRITZ RUDOLF FRIES: IMS "PEDRO HAGEN" 197

FIRST REPORT IN THE FILE LABELLED "PEDRO HAGEN" 199

REPORT ON MAY 24, 1978 MEETING: IMS "PEDRO HAGEN" AND HIS STASI-HANDLER 203

REPORT ON MAY 29-30, 1978 MEETINGS: IMS "PEDRO HAGEN" AND HIS STASI-HANDLER 205

REPORT DATED JUNE 27, 1978 206

NEXT TWO YEARS AT OBERLIN COLLEGE: 1978 TO 1980 209

PROPOSAL FOR ANOTHER PROJECT: ANTHOLOGY OF LITERATURE BY YOUNG GDR WRITERS 213

YEAR AT THE HOOVER INSTITUTION: AUGUST, 1980 – AUGUST, 1981 217

TWO NEWSPAPER ARTICLES OF INTEREST 217

REVIEW OF STEFAN HEYM'S *DIE SCHMÄHSCHRIFT ODER KÖNIGIN GEGEN DEFOE* 223

NINE WRITERS EXPELLED FROM GDR WRITERS' UNION: JUNE, 1979 226

IMB "PEDRO HAGEN" PLANS TO VISIT RICHARD ZIPSER IN CALIFORNIA 230

REPORT ON MARCH 12, 1981 MEETING: IMB "PEDRO HAGEN" AND HIS STASI-HANDLER 234

REPORT ON MAY 13, 1981 MEETING: IMB "PEDRO HAGEN" AND HIS STASI-HANDLER 237

IMB "PEDRO HAGEN" REPORTS ON HIS VISIT WITH RICHARD ZIPSER IN CALIFORNIA 240

FRITZ RUDOLF FRIES'S IMAGINATIVE ESSAY ON HIS VISIT TO SAN FRANCISCO 245

CREATING A NETWORK OF GDR SYMPATHIZERS AT US UNIVERSITIES 246

IMB "PEDRO HAGEN" FINDS A GDR SYMPATHIZER IN MINNESOTA 247

IMB "PEDRO HAGEN" REPORTS ON NORDLAND PUBLISHING 250

PROBLEMS WITH NORDLAND PUBLISHING: 1980-1982 253

IT COULD BE SAID SPECULATIVELY THAT "ZIPSER DID NOT INTEND TO PREPARE A BOOK"

STASI CORRESPONDENCE ON RICHARD ZIPSER: MAY/JUNE, 1981 256

IMB "PEDRO HAGEN" RECEIVES A PRESENT FROM RICHARD ZIPSER 258

IMB "PEDRO HAGEN" PLANS A SECOND TRIP TO THE UNITED STATES 259

BERND JENTZSCH IN OBERLIN: FEBRUARY – MAY, 1982 260

IMB "PEDRO HAGEN" CULTIVATES A GDR SYMPATHIZER: JULY, 1982 263

REQUEST FOR SURVEILLANCE OF RICHARD ZIPSER: JANUARY 26, 1983 266

NO SIGN OF RICHARD ZIPSER OR HIS BOOK 268

A PUBLISHER FOR *DDR-LITERATUR IM TAUWETTER* 271

PROMOTION TO FULL PROFESSOR AND NEW POSITION: 1985 – 1986 272

INVITATION TO HELGA SCHÜTZ 273

ZIPSER IS CONSIDERED TO BE AN "ENEMY OF THE STATE"

RETURN TO EAST GERMANY: MARCH, 1985 279

CYNTHIA MILLER'S INVITATION TO A RECEPTION IN HONOR OF RICHARD ZIPSER 280

IMB "PEDRO HAGEN" REPORTS ON THE RECEPTION AT CYNTHIA MILLER'S RESIDENCE 282

MORE REPORTS ON THE RECEPTION AT CYNTHIA MILLER'S RESIDENCE 288

BOOK FAIR IN LEIPZIG: MARCH, 1985 293

FINAL REPORT IN THE FILE LABELLED "PEDRO HAGEN": MARCH 18, 1985 301

RE-ENTRY BAN: JUNE 11, 1985 304

FINAL COMMENTS ON INFORMANT/WRITER FRITZ RUDOLF FRIES 305

KARL-HEINZ JAKOBS IN OBERLIN: FEBRUARY – MAY, 1986 308

NEW HAMPSHIRE SYMPOSIA FOR THE STUDY OF THE GDR 310

FINAL REPORT IN MY STASI-FILE: AUGUST, 1986 313

REVIEW OF **STUDIES IN GDR CULTURE AND SOCIETY 6**: AUGUST, 1987 314

DDR-STUDIEN/EAST GERMAN STUDIES 319

FINAL ENTRY TO MY STASI-FILE: MARCH 17, 1988 319

AFTER THE DEMISE OF THE GDR

FALL OF THE BERLIN WALL: NOVEMBER 9, 1989 320

PROJECT ON LITERARY CENSORSHIP IN THE GERMAN-SPEAKING COUNTRIES: 1987 – 1990 322

LAST TRIP TO EAST BERLIN: JULY, 1990 325

REUNIFICATION OF GERMANY: OCTOBER 3, 1990 326

FRAGEBOGEN: ZENSUR / QUESTIONNAIRE: CENSORSHIP 328

THREE LETTERS AND A RESPONSE FROM UWE BERGER: 1993–1994 337

IN SEARCH OF MY STASI-FILE (1) 340

JOACHIM WALTHER'S *SICHERUNGSBEREICH LITERATUR / SECURITY ZONE LITERATURE* 341

US GERMANISTS IN THE INDEX TO JOACHIM WALTHER'S BOOK 345

IN SEARCH OF MY STASI-FILE (2) 346

ARRIVAL OF MY STASI-FILE: JANUARY 22, 1999 347

COMING FULL CIRCLE 348

IN SEARCH OF MORE INFORMATION IN THE STASI-FILES OF OTHERS 348

IN RETROSPECT 349

ADDENDUM 351

AFTERWORD 359

TRIBUTE 366

PREFACE

Remembering East Germany. From Oberlin to East Berlin is a documentary memoir that is based primarily on the 396-page file the East German secret police or Stasi compiled on me between 1973 and 1988, when I was travelling and working on a number of scholarly projects in that country. The reports in the file provide a kind of factual foundation for the memoir, as do reports about me found in the files of others, various printed materials, letters I wrote and received, and some memories as well. The book does not have chapters, it has sections—114 in all, some short, some long—that are devoted to all sorts of topics and events that I consider significant. The narrative proceeds chronologically for the most part, starting in 1973 and moving forward in time to 2002, with the occasional flashback.

When presenting the individual reports from my Stasi-file, I have tried to create a framework that will introduce the reader to the material and make it comprehensible. I have also tried to reproduce the reports as accurately as possible in English translation, so readers will be able to see what such reports look like, how they are structured, and what sort of information and commentary they contain. I have elected to include entire reports most of the time rather than excerpts or a summary of the content. This leads to some redundancy, but that is also the actual nature of the file, since information in one report may be repeated verbatim or in a slightly different way in subsequent reports. This is especially true in the informational and summarial reports written by Stasi officers, which were meant to update the file from time to time.

The original version of this book is titled *Von Oberlin nach Ostberlin. Als Amerikaner unterwegs in der DDR-Literaturszene.* It was published in 2013 by the Ch. Links Verlag, a highly regarded commercial publisher in Berlin, Germany. It is written entirely in German and is somewhat shorter in length than the English version that follows. I am grateful to Christoph Links for allowing me to publish an edition for the English-speaking world. Many persons—friends, colleagues, acquaintances—who are unable to read German have encouraged me to translate *Von Oberlin nach Ostberlin* into English, and I decided to undertake this project during my retirement.

An author should record his gratitude to those who assisted him, which I am pleased to do here. I am deeply indebted to my friends and colleagues, theater director/professor Heinz-Uwe Haus and writer/professor Gabriele Eckart, both of whom grew up and spent much of their lives in East Germany. Their insightful and detailed critiques of my first draft were immensely help-ful and improved the book greatly. Let me also mention Christine Becker, widow of prominent prose writer Jurek Becker, who brought my book proj-ect to the attention of its German publisher, Christoph Links. I am grateful to Christoph Links and my copy editor, Jana Fröbel, for their many helpful stylistic reformulations and revisions in the original German manuscript. Finally, I want to acknowledge the outstanding work carried out by Rae Stabosz, who as Project Manager oversaw the production of *Remembering East Germany* in 2021. Her contributions as tech editor, interior text format-ter, and proofreader were, in a word, invaluable.

I would be remiss if I did not mention how much the support of my wife, Ulrike Diedenhofen, meant to me throughout the writing of this book and the period leading up to its publication in April 2013, and more recently during the process of translating it into English. She provided needed encouragement, an open ear whenever I needed a listener, and she helped me in countless other ways. To her I say "thank you," knowing that these words are not a sufficient expression of my thanks.

Lastly, I want to express sincere appreciation to the University of Delaware for granting me a sabbatical leave in 2010-2011. I am particularly grateful to George Watson, then Dean of the College of Arts and Sciences, for arranging the combined sabbatical/administrative year of leave that enabled me to complete the German version of my book without financial hardship.

INTRODUCTION

Stasi, an abbreviation for Staatssicherheit (literally: State Security), is what the secret police of East Germany were commonly called. The Ministry for State Security (MfSS) was responsible for both domestic surveillance and espionage in the Soviet-occupied German Democratic Republic (GDR). At its peak, it employed 90,000 officers full-time. With the help of approximately 190,000 informants, it monitored East German citizens and conducted covert operations in West Germany, West Berlin, and elsewhere in the West, including the United States. Headquartered in East Berlin, in the very building that today houses Berlin's Stasi Museum, the MfSS was widely regarded as one of the most effective and repressive intelligence and secret police agencies in the world. The Stasi was formed in 1950 and dissolved after German reunification in 1990. In 1991, the government of newly reunified Germany passed the Stasi Records Law, under which former GDR citizens and foreigners were granted the right to view their Stasi-files. By the early 21st century, more than 1.5 million individuals had done so. I, Richard Zipser, am one of those persons.

I remember vividly when the Stasi-file arrived at my home, in late January 1999, around the time of my 56th birthday. The bulky, innocent-looking package filled the mailbox; according to the label, the sender was Der Bundesbeauftragte für die Unterlagen des Staatssicherheitsdienstes der ehemaligen

Deutschen Demokratischen Republik (The Federal Commissioner for the Records of the State Security Service of the former German Democratic Republic). This federal commission with the unwieldy name was informally called the Gauck-Behörde (Gauck Agency) for short, after Joachim Gauck, the East German Lutheran pastor who served as the first Federal Commissioner from 1990 to 2000. The agency commonly refers to itself and is also known as the Stasi-Unterlagen-Behörde (Stasi Records Agency).

What a surprise! After six years of waiting impatiently, after writing countless letters to the Stasi Records Agency, most of which went unanswered, there it was! And I was more than curious to see what was inside that package. Upon opening it, I found a cover letter explaining that research in the Stasi archives in Berlin and Leipzig had led to the discovery of my file. Also, that as of December 3, 1982, my file had been labelled "KK-erfasst." "Karteikartenerfassung" (recorded on index cards) was the designation the Stasi used for potential enemies of the state, "for persons who from the State Security Service's perspective had given indications of hostile activity." The letter went on to explain: "Main Department XX was responsible from 1964 on for securing and controlling the state apparatus, culture, and opposition. Department 7 of Main Department XX was responsible for securing and controlling culture, art, and literature." And finally, it stated that the names of innocent third parties had been blacked out to protect their privacy, in accordance with German law. I discovered that holding pages under a strong light so as to read the blacked-out names was a futile exercise, for the original document had first been photocopied by a case worker, then the names had been blacked out, and then a copy of that copy had been made for me. Still, using context and memory as my guides, I was able to fill in most of the blanks without difficulty.

My file is almost 400 pages long. It is filled with information the East German secret police compiled on me in the 1970s and 1980s. The file is not a chronological or linear narrative; it is a haphazard compilation of reports containing information about my personal life, my personality, my academic background, and the nature of my work and activities in the GDR and elsewhere. There is speculation about the "real" purpose of my visits to the GDR, how these visits were financed, and the damage my publications on East German literature might cause the GDR state. The most fascinating sections are the reports written by or based on debriefings of informers, all identified with code names, who were providing the Stasi with detailed information derived from their contacts and conversations with me. The file spans a period of fifteen years, beginning in the summer of 1973 and concluding in the spring of 1988. Most of the information and reports are from the period 1975 to 1978, when I was living off and on in the GDR and working on three book projects. My file is considered to be a victim's file ("Opferakte"), which means that only I and the case worker who read it have had access to it.

There are reports from five types of secret informers in my file; each has a code name preceded by one of the following acronyms: IM, IME, IMV, IMS, and IMB. The acronym IM stands for "Inoffizieller Mitarbeiter" (unofficial collaborator), the most common type of informer in the GDR. These persons usually were not on the Stasi payroll, but often received favors or privileges in exchange for the information they provided. IME stands for "Inoffizieller Mitarbeiter im besonderen Einsatz," i.e., collaborators with special assignments. IMV is short for "Inoffizieller Mitarbeiter, der unmittelbar an der Bearbeitung und Entlarvung im Verdacht stehender Personen mitarbeitet;" these were the upper echelon of informers, individuals the Stasi trusted and deployed to gather information directly from potential enemies of the state. IMS and IMB were the highest level of informants, individuals whose loyalty and trustworthiness had been tested and proven beyond a doubt. IMS is the acronym for "inoffizieller Mitarbeiter zur politisch-operativen Durchdringung und Sicherung des Verantwortungsbereichs." Informants so designated were assigned to gather information and report on suspicious activities in workplaces or areas considered important to state security, such as the cultural sphere. IMB is short for "inoffizieller Mitarbeiter der Abwehr mit Feindverbindung bzw. zur unmittelbaren Bearbeitung im Verdacht der

Feindtätigkeit stehender Personen." These informants were often in direct contact with persons considered to be enemies of the state, not only in the GDR but occasionally in foreign countries as well.

The file reveals that there were nine unofficial collaborators of one sort or another who reported on my GDR-related activities and gathered information on me for the Stasi. Three were writers: IME "Dichter" (Poet), Paul Wiens, a well-known, well-connected poet and communist party loyalist; IMV "Pedro Hagen," the prominent prose writer and opportunist, Fritz Rudolf Fries; and IM "Uwe," the poet Uwe Berger, a cunning opportunist motivated more by careerism than ideology. Two informers were good acquaintances, a married couple I got to know while living in East Berlin: IMV "Kurt" and IMV "Julia." They were friends of the prose writer, Klaus Schlesinger, who introduced us. Another was a publisher, Konrad Reich, who until the 2013 publication of this book in German had not been outed as an informer. There was also IM "Dölbl," Anneliese Löffler, a professor at the Humboldt University; she was assigned to keep tabs on me while I was working in Berlin as an IREX (International Research and Exchanges Board) scholar. Eberhard Scheibner, a functionary in charge of the international department of the GDR Writers' Union, submitted reports periodically on our meetings and communications. And finally, IM "Frieda," the housekeeper of the GDR's most famous writer, Stefan Heym. There is evidence that two American Germanists, "unofficial sources," informed the Stasi about my GDR-related activities in the United States. Although they are unnamed, I was able to identify them from the information provided. The file also contains four surveillance reports (one stretching over a three day period), which were authorized by the Ministry for State Security and prepared by Stasi operatives. In these I have a code name: "Adler," eagle, the bird of prey.

Most of the reports are poorly written, worse than English 101 compositions. The language is bureaucratic and wooden, laden with Stasi-jargon, marred by misspellings and grammatical errors of all sorts. Since many of the reports were drafted by Stasi personnel, this is not surprising. Some were written by the informers themselves, others recorded on tape and transcribed by Stasi personnel, and others cobbled together from handwritten notes taken in meetings between Stasi officers and informants. A favorite word, one that recurs like a leitmotif throughout the document, is "operative."

OPENING REPORT IN MY STASI-FILE: JUNE 6, 1973

The opening report in my file, dated June 6, 1973, amuses me. It begins with a one-sentence summary: "US-American, who has a doctorate in German studies, intends to spend four weeks as a tourist in the GDR, in order to become better informed in general." As I read through the report, the memory of that border crossing resurfaces from the depths of my mind. I am astonished by the level of detail it contains: factual information about me and my first wife, Marjorie, who accompanied me on this trip, our travel route, and plans to visit friends in Hannover after leaving the GDR. How did they know all of this? According to the report, the border guards gathered details in casual conversation with us, as I was switching license plates, replacing the oval international customs number from West Germany with a rectangular GDR plate.

The report concludes with information about my person: "Zipser speaks good German with a slight accent, makes an intelligent, bright impression, but appears to be somewhat helpless mechanically (inept performance while changing the license plates). He was clean and appropriately dressed for the trip. When asked questions, he provided information readily after a brief hesitation." "Somewhat helpless mechanically!" Should I feel insulted? On the contrary, I am delighted to read that I needed help switching license plates, for now I have written proof of my notoriously poor mechanical ability which has always been a joke among family members and friends.

BACKGROUND: 1969 – 1975

Before I provide more excerpts from my Stasi-file, I should explain how I came to have one. During the 1970s, when I was teaching at Oberlin College, I spent a lot of time in the GDR, travelling and working on various projects involving writers. In those days, very few scholars from the United States were able to do research in the GDR, and no scholars from West Germany were permitted to work there. For most Westerners the GDR was a closed society, and it remained that way until everything collapsed in the fall of 1989. I first visited East Germany for two weeks as a tourist in 1969, because I was curious to see what the other Germany was like (to my surprise, mention is made of this trip in the initial report in my file); in the summer of 1973, I toured that country for an entire month. In 1975-1976, I had a sabbatical leave and spent much of it in the GDR working on a book project. In the fall of 1977 and spring of 1978, I spent several months living in East Berlin, supported by an International Research and Exchanges Board (IREX) grant. During this period and during my earlier sabbatical leave, I was able to travel freely throughout the GDR and interview some 45 writers for a three-volume book entitled *DDR-Literatur im Tauwetter: Wandel – Wunsch – Wirklichkeit* (*GDR Literature During the Thaw: Change – Desire – Reality*). In 1985, I was invited by the USIA (United States Information Agency), to attend the Leipzig Book Fair and preside over an exhibit entitled "America's Best: Prizewinning Books 1983-1984." This was my final stay in the GDR before the Berlin Wall came tumbling down.

My interest in GDR literature was awakened in the spring of 1974, when prominent East German prose writer Christa Wolf spent six weeks in Oberlin as German writer-in-residence. She was accompanied by her husband Gerhard, a well-known literary scholar and editor with connections to many contemporary GDR writers and publishers. I spent a lot of time with the Wolfs while they were in Oberlin, and they introduced me to the GDR literary scene through selected readings and conversations. The Wolfs encouraged me to think about doing a sabbatical project on GDR writing in the 1970s and promised to assist me. In the spring of 1975, another prominent East German writer—Ulrich Plenzdorf—came to Oberlin as writer-in-residence. Plenzdorf and I became good friends that semester, and he helped me finalize plans for my sabbatical leave, a good portion of which I intended to spend in the GDR.

According to the plan I had developed with the Wolfs' and Plenzdorf's help, I was to prepare a book that would explore and document how GDR writing had been evolving during the regime of Erich Honecker, who in 1971 had replaced Walter Ulbricht as General Secretary of the ruling Socialist Unity Party. Amazing as it seems today, given what we remember about Honecker's hard-line pronouncements and crackdown on writers in the late 1970s and 1980s, he ushered in a short-lived period of liberalization for literature and the arts in the GDR. The first five years of his regime, the "no taboos" period before the infamous expatriation of dissident writer/singer Wolf Biermann in November 1976, may well have provided a model for Mikhail Gorbachev and the policy of *glasnost* (openness) he initiated in the Soviet Union in the mid-1980s.

The objective of my book was to introduce readers to the leading East German writers of the day, especially to those who were shaping the new sociocritical direction of writing during the 1970s. Each author would be introduced by a bio-bibliographical sketch, photograph, and a personal statement about his or her goal as a writer; this would be followed by a representative text—a short story, poems, essay, or chapter from a novel—a text focusing on some problem in GDR society that was of concern to the writer as a writer; and finally, there would be an interview based on a questionnaire designed to elicit each writer's responses to issues in contemporary GDR society. The literary texts and interviews would become a cause for concern among GDR authorities.

MEETING AT THE GDR WRITERS' UNION: SEPTEMBER 11, 1975

Early in 1975, after my sabbatical leave had been approved, I followed the Wolfs' advice and wrote to the First Secretary of the GDR Writers' Union, Gerhard Henniger. In this letter I outlined the project I proposed to carry out in the GDR, while on sabbatical leave; I also requested assistance from the Writers' Union and authorization to proceed. Eventually, I received a response to my letter from Eberhard Scheibner, the person in charge of their International Relations Department. His letter was short and noncommital, little more than an acknowledgment of my inquiry. He offered to meet with me and advise me regarding the selection of authors, if I were to visit East Berlin. The last thing I wanted, of course, was to have Writers' Union functionaries tell me which GDR authors should be included in my book.

I travelled to East Berlin in September 1975 and met with Scheibner and other functionaries at the Writers' Union headquarters. My file contains a report with detailed information on that meeting and the nature of my undertaking. The author of the report is Captain Rolf Pönig, at that time an intelligence officer in the branch of the Ministry for State Security with responsibility for monitoring the cultural sphere of activity in the GDR. The report notes that I requested the following by way of assistance from the Writers' Union: first, a document authorizing me to conduct and tape record interviews with writers of the GDR; second, the use of an apartment in East Berlin, a base from which to carry out the project; and third, the home addresses and telephone numbers of the writers to be included in my book. In the end, the Writers' Union agreed to provide me with one thing only, advice, but it did not attempt to block my project. In other words, I had its tacit support.

However, from Pönig's report it is clear that the Writers' Union functionaries were from the outset wary of me and the possible consequences of my project, over which they had little control. They were very eager to know the names of all the GDR writers I intended to include in my book and pressed me for that information, then asked me to provide them with a list.

According to the report, I was uncooperative and evasive: "In the discussion Dr. Zipser sidestepped all questions concerning which authors he wished to include in his book." Pönig goes on to note for the record: "After the afore-mentioned discussion Dr. Zipser did not return to the Writers' Union and also did not hand over as agreed the list with the names of authors."

From the beginning and concluding sections of this report, I learn just how important Christa Wolf's and Ulrich Plenzdorf's support for my book project had been. Without their involvement and intervention on my behalf, especially at the outset, I doubt that the GDR authorities would have permitted me to proceed with the interviews and gathering of materials for my book, a process that went on for more than three years. In his preamble to the report, Pönig writes:

> On Oct. 13, 1975 the Secretary of the Writers' Union, Comrade Henniger, briefed the undersigned on the following modes of behavior on the part of writers Christa Wolf and Ulrich Plenzdorf:
>
> During her 1974 stay in the USA, Christa Wolf made the acquaintance of USA citizen Dr. Zipser, assistant professor of German at Oberlin College, Ohio USA.
>
> After returning from the USA, she told the Writers' Union about Dr. Zipser and said she had the impression that Dr. Zipser was among the progressive USA citizens. Therefore, it would behoove the GDR to support his project involving the publication of a reader on GDR literature.
>
> As a result of Comrade Henniger's consultation with Comrade Prof. Held, it was decided to grant Dr. Zipser advice and support in accordance with his request, if and when he calls on the Writers' Union. Comrade Henniger also made Christa Wolf aware of this decision.

The concluding paragraphs of Pönig's report contain some surprising and, for me, confusing revelations:

> On Sept. 14, 1975 Comrade Henniger received a letter from the author Christa Wolf, in which she complained that despite its prior promise of support the Writers' Union turned Dr. Zipser away. Christa Wolf sent a carbon copy of this letter of complaint to Comrade Prof. Held and an additional copy to Stephan Hermlin. [*Hermlin, an influential member of the Writers' Union, was one of the most prominent and powerful authors in the GDR.*]
>
> In Comrade Henniger's consultation with Christa Wolf resulting from her letter, Christa Wolf explained that she did not personally speak with Z., but rather the state of affairs described in her letter had been related to her by Ulrich Plenzdorf.
>
> Comrade Henniger explained that Christa Wolf called him several days later and declared that she was retracting the letter of complaint, because the allegations Plenzdorf communicated to her are apparently untrue and do not correspond to the facts.
>
> Since Plenzdorf is currently in the FRG for the purpose of shooting the film version of his play "Die Neuen Leiden des jungen W." ["The New Sufferings of Young W."], it was not possible to have a discussion with him. During his 1975 reading tour in the USA, Plenzdorf spent some time in Ohio USA., among other places.
>
> In the next meeting of the Executive Council, Comrade Henniger intends to announce that Plenzdorf lied to Christa Wolf.

CONNECTIONS AND PREPARATIONS

While in East Berlin, with help from some writers I had gotten to know, I began assembling a list of the home addresses and telephone numbers of the authors I hoped to visit and interview. The Wolfs introduced me to Volker Braun and also paved the way for my meetings with Stephan Hermlin, Sarah Kirsch, and Günter Kunert. Ulrich Plenzdorf introduced me to two writers in his circle of friends, Klaus Schlesinger and Martin Stade, and to his publisher, Konrad Reich. Reich was head of the Hinstorff Verlag, a prestigious publishing house in Rostock known for publishing works by writers who were controversial and trying to push the envelope. Plenzdorf and I had lunch with Reich at Hotel Unter den Linden in Berlin that September, and I was flattered when Reich not only expressed interest in my project but also in possibly publishing it in the GDR, something I had never imagined might be possible. Many GDR writers considered him to be an entrepreneurial spirit, a well-connected mover and shaker who could make the most unlikely things happen. Almost twenty-five years later, with the help of my file, I would learn that Reich had a second identity and a special assignment related to me.

I returned to Vienna, my home base for the sabbatical year, and laid the groundwork for a longer stay in Berlin, during which time I planned to meet with a large number of GDR writers. When I returned to East Berlin on November 10, Ulrich Plenzdorf lent me a portable tape recorder to use for the interviews. Armed with blank cassettes purchased in the West and my list of fifteen questions, I began to visit GDR writers and conduct interviews.

Interview Questions

1. What, in your opinion, is the function of literature and art in the socialist state?

2. Which contemporary social problems are of the greatest concern to you as a writer?

3. Do your writings incorporate the theme of women in society?

4. What influence have the experiences of your childhood had on your literary works?

5. How have you gained experiences with manual workers? What connections do you have to them today?

6. What, in your opinion, are the distinctive characteristics of GDR literature within the German-speaking world?

7. What differences do you see between GDR literature of the 1970s and that of the previous years? Can you provide some examples to illustrate the differences?

8. What do you consider to be the most important works (your own writings aside) in GDR literature of the 1970s?

9. Which more recent works would you characterize as especially forward-looking?

10. Which contemporary USA authors have you read? How do you rate them?

11. What influence, in your opinion, does a society's increasing prosperity have upon literary productivity?

12. How are reading habits in the GDR influenced currently by television?

13. What role, in your opinion, should literature (in comparison to the other media) play in present-day society?

14. What is your perception of light fiction, literature for popular entertainment, and belletristic literature in the GDR?

15. What do you see as the goal of your literary work? Do you think it is attainable?

LIST OF WRITERS

The original list of writers I intended to include in my yet-to-be-titled book had twenty names on it and was assembled with the assistance of Ulrich Plenzdorf and Gerhard Wolf. These were established writers who, for the most part, had both achieved a degree of prominence in the GDR and published some of their writings in West Germany as well. Between 1975 and 1978, the list would gradually grow from twenty to forty-five, as I was persuaded by some writers on the original list and functionaries at the GDR Writers' Union to add more and more names. In the end, the writers listed below were included in *DDR-Literatur im Tauwetter*. As one can see from the birth dates, these were representatives of the older, middle, and younger generations of GDR authors, the oldest being Anna Seghers (b. 1900), and Thomas Brasch (b. 1945) the youngest.

Erich Arendt (b. 1903)
Jurek Becker (b. 1937)
Uwe Berger (b. 1928)
Thomas Brasch (b. 1945)
Volker Braun (b. 1939)
Jurij Brězan (b. 1916)
Günter de Bruyn (b. 1926)
Heinz Czechowski (b. 1935)
Adolf Endler (b. 1930)
Elke Erb (b. 1938)

Fritz Rudolf Fries (b. 1935)

Franz Fühmann (b. 1922)

Günter Görlich (b. 1928)

Peter Hacks (b. 1928)

Stephan Hermlin (b. 1915)

Stefan Heym (b. 1913)

Karl-Heinz Jakobs (b. 1929)

Bernd Jentzsch (b. 1940)

Hermann Kant (b. 1926)

Uwe Kant (b. 1936)

Rainer Kirsch (b. 1934)

Sarah Kirsch (b. 1935)

Wolfgang Kohlhaase (b. 1931)

Günter Kunert (b. 1929)

Reiner Kunze (b. 1933)

Kito Lorenc (b. 1938)

Karl Mickel (b. 1935)

Irmtraud Morgner (b. 1933)

Heiner Müller (b. 1929)

Erik Neutsch (b. 1931)

Eberhard Panitz (b. 1932)

Siegfried Pitschmann (b. 1930)

Ulrich Plenzdorf (b. 1934)

Benno Pludra (b. 1925)

Hans Joachim Schädlich (b. 1935)

Klaus Schlesinger (b. 1937)

Rolf Schneider (b. 1932)

Max Walter Schulz (b. 1921)

Helga Schütz (b. 1937)

Anna Seghers (b. 1900)

Martin Stade (b. 1931)

Erwin Strittmatter (b. 1912)

Eva Strittmatter (b. 1930)

Paul Wiens (b. 1922)

Christa Wolf (b. 1929)

In the ensuing pages, the names of many of the above-cited writers will appear in various contexts.

PERSON OF INTEREST

The evidence in my file indicates that I became a "person of interest" to the Stasi in the fall of 1975. Their initial interest in me probably resulted from an understandable uneasiness about my project, since it brought me into direct contact with writers of all political persuasions, including dissidents, and it was difficult for anyone to monitor my activities closely. What were the writers telling me in the interview sessions, what sort of literary texts were they giving me for publication in my book, and how was I going to package and present all this material back in the United States? Was I a friend or an enemy of the GDR? Their answer to the last question is, of course, to be found in my file.

FIRST REPORT FROM IME "DICHTER": NOVEMBER 25, 1975

The first informant's report on my activities during this time period is dated November 25, 1975. The report focuses on my activities during the month of November 1975, when I was visiting and interviewing GDR writers while staying at the Hotel Berolina in East Berlin. It was prepared by Captain Pönig and based in part on information he had received from IME "Dichter," who as I mentioned earlier was a poet by the name of Paul Wiens. I first met Wiens while visiting his wife, the prominent feminist prose writer Irmtraud Morgner. He was present and listening attentively during our preliminary conversation and the taping of the interview. Morgner, obviously embarrassed that I had contacted her but not approached Wiens in connection with my project, insisted that I include him, which I readily agreed to do. Excerpts from this lengthy report follow:

> Since Sept. 11, 1975, Dr. Zipser has appeared at the Writers' Union a number of times with the following official concerns:
>
> He intends to publish, in the USA, a book on GDR writers and to this end would like to conduct personal conversations and interviews with GDR writers. Dr. Zipser requested written permission from the Writers' Union for the making of these tape recordings.
>
> After Dr. Zipser refused in the initial discussion to state the names of GDR authors, in the subsequent discussions he disclosed the names of 30 GDR writers whom he intended to interview and provided a written questionnaire for these conversations (see attachment).
>
> In the GDR Writers' Union the following agreements were reached with Dr. Zipser:
>
> 1. The interviews and conversations with GDR authors are to be conducted without a sound recorder.
>
> 2. The texts from the interviews and conversations that are conducted are to be authorized by the GDR writers before their publication.
>
> 3. The publication of texts by GDR authors has to be carried out in compliance with the copyright laws of the GDR.
>
> 4. The GDR Writers' Union named the following writers, in addition to the persons Dr. Zipser had named, for inclusion in his proposed undertaking.

Hermann Kant

Günter Görlich

Max Walter Schulz

Jurij Brězan und

Erwin Strittmatter

In the interest of a sound collaboration, Dr. Zipser was asked to inform the GDR Writers' Union about the results of his conversations with GDR authors at the conclusion of his stay in the GDR.

By means of operative surveillance measures that were initiated, it was learned that Dr. Zipser had asked specifically—in the interviews already conducted with Christa Wolf und Gerhard Wolf, Plenzdorf, Schlesinger, Becker, Fühmann, Hermann and Uwe Kant, Mickel, Morgner, Hacks and Panitz—whether they favored the inclusion of Wolf Biermann in his project. Eight of the authors named above answered this question in the affirmative. [*At that time, the famous dissident writer/singer Biermann was living under house arrest in East Berlin and was not permitted to publish or perform in the GDR. A year later, he would be expatriated, and the short period of liberalization in the cultural sphere would gradually come to an end.*]

Plenzdorf has generously placed a portable tape recorder at his disposal. In order to avoid possible difficulties at border controls, Dr. Zipser indicated that he could have the tape recordings sent to the FRG via his embassy.

At the conclusion of Pönig's report, I learn that the GDR authorities were debating whether or not to allow me to return to East Germany early in 1976 and continue work on my ambitious project.

Dr. Zipser intends to remain in the GDR until Nov. 30, 1975.

At the GDR Writers' Union Dr. Zipser requested permission to reenter the GDR in February 1976, in order to conduct interviews with those GDR authors he cannot speak to before Nov. 30, 1975, presumably due to insufficient time.

The Cultural Division of the Central Committee of the SED (Socialist Unity Party of Germany) was informed of Z.'s intention by Comrade Henniger, Secretary of the GDR Writers' Union.

FIRST REPORT FROM IMV "KURT": NOVEMBER 25, 1975

IMV "Kurt," who today is a practicing lawyer and notary in Berlin, contributed more reports to my file than any other informant. It is clear that he was assigned to gather information on me following my return to East Berlin in November 1975. Kurt's first report is a transcription of a tape recording he submitted to a Stasi officer, First Lieutenant Gerd Paulitz. Kurt begins: "I became acquainted with Zipser at Klaus Schlesinger's apartment on Nov. 11, 1975. In the course of numerous conversations that resulted from this first get-together, I was able to find out the following." Kurt proceeds to provide general information on my academic background, the nature and purpose of my book project, the financing of my sabbatical leave, my contacts with the GDR Writers' Union, and then the interview questions: "In our conversations Zipser admitted to me that his questions are deliberately presented in a way that does not guide the writer in a particular direction, but rather lets the writer answer the questions based on his own stance.... Zipser intends to publish the interviews verbatim in connection with excerpts from these writers' works. The individuals he has interviewed to date willingly provided him with these texts, according to Zipser." Kurt then provides a list of seventeen writers I am intending to interview and notes: "There were additional names on the list (ca. 30), but no sign of Biermann." Finally, he comments on the goal of my project, repeating accurately what I had told him:

Z.'s objective, according to his account, is to publish for the first time ever in the USA a multi-volume book that deals with the GDR literary scene. He has determined that so far very little is known about GDR literature in the USA and wants to close the existing gap. The book is aimed primarily at Germanists, literary scholars, and students. In addition to the items already mentioned, he also plans to publish short biographies of these writers. In his own words, he does not intend to comment and state his position on issues, but wants to impart an objective view of GDR writers' lives and literature in the GDR in general. For information only, he plans to prepend an introduction to the book.

IMV "KURT" AND IMV "JULIA"

I first met Kurt's wife IMV "Julia" in Altrosenthal, a country village near Frankfurt an der Oder where three writers (Plenzdorf, Schlesinger, Stade) and their physician friend (Stefan Schnitzler, son of the infamous SED-propagandist Karl-Eduard von Schnitzler) had purchased a cluster of four farm houses they used mainly as weekend and vacation retreats. Not far from this settlement, Kurt and Julia had a dilapidated farm house that they were in the process of renovating. Their apartment in Berlin, also in a state of disrepair, was located in the Prenzlauer Berg district, not far from the apartments occupied by the Plenzdorfs, Klaus Schlesinger, and his wife Bettina Wegner, the dissident songwriter/singer and political activist. On the weekends, which they liked to spend in the country, they would all gather for coffee and cake or a cookout, usually at the Plenzdorfs' house, which was the largest and nicest. On one such occasion, on my first visit to Altrosenthal, I got together with Kurt and Julia along with their friends from West Berlin, Brigitte and Hellfried Kellner. The Hotel Berolina, where I stayed in November 1975, was located not far from Prenzlauer Berg. Kurt and Julia invited me to their apartment for dinner now and then, and I occasionally would meet Kurt at a nearby pub for a bite to eat and a beer in the evening. Perhaps I should have suspected, since both were evasive about their line of work and alluded vaguely to SED Party connections, that they might somehow be involved with the Stasi.

SECOND REPORT FROM IMV "KURT": DECEMBER 11, 1975

The next report on my activities shocked me when I first read it. The source of the information is again IMV "Kurt." His report is dated December 11, 1975. The subject is Richard Zipser, American Germanist. The topic is transporting tapes with interviews to West Berlin.

> Z. called on me on Thursday, Dec. 4, 1975, at around 4:45 p.m., and asked me to drive him in Klaus SCHLESINGER's automobile to the avenue Unter den Linden; there he would give the tape recordings he had made on cassettes to someone who would bring them to Berlin West for him. When I asked him why he hadn't taken them to Berlin West himself in his automobile, he said that would probably work with two or three cassettes but not with 15. We then went to see Klaus SCHLESINGER, who gave me his car keys and handed ZIPSER the cassettes which were in a plastic bag (5:00 p.m.). Klaus SCHLESINGER was storing the cassettes for Zipser, since he (Zipser) had in the meantime been staying in Westberlin.

> During our ride in the direction of the Brandenburg Gate, I asked Zipser if this method was certain; in response he said he assumed so, but preferred not to comment further so no one would get in trouble. Without being asked directly, ZIPSER said he had been in the USA-Embassy to ask if they could possibly transport the cassettes to Westberlin. His request was rejected with regrets because the embassy is not permitted to provide assistance of that sort. However, they did give him a tip, the name of a person to contact, someone who was now waiting

for him and prepared to take delivery of the cassettes. When I observed that he would surely know tomorrow if it had worked out, ZIPSER said he would not be certain until Saturday. We drove along Unter den Linden, across the Friedrichstrasse, and up to the parking place in the sketch on the other side of the page.

[A detailed sketch showing streets, buildings—including the American Embassy, and where the car was parked, is attached to this report.] ZIPSER showed me the way as we drove and also told me where to park and wait for him. He reckoned it would not take a long time.

I waited for about 20 minutes, from 5:15 to 5:35 p.m. ZIPSER returned from the same direction. We drove back to Klaus SCHLESINGER's place and dropped off his automobile. Vis-à-vis SCHLESINGER, ZIPSER also avoided saying anything about the transport of the cassettes. To the following question from Klaus SCHLESINGER, ". . . in the consulate was it. . .," Zipser fended him off rather decisively by interrupting and saying something like: ". . . no, no, not at all, completely different. . ." Then ZIPSER bade farewell to SCHLESINGER until April 1976. We returned to my place. ZIPSER stayed until 8:00 p.m.

During this time the topic outlined above resurfaced only once. I affirmed to ZIPSER that embassies as a general rule refuse to do a thing like that, whereupon ZIPSER once again stressed that I needn't give this matter any more thought, because it really had nothing to do with the embassy or consulate. He bade farewell to me as well until April 1976.

1. Based on my feeling, I would say that it really is about going through the embassy or consulate:

2. ZIPSER's rather strong defensive reaction when I began speaking about this possibility.

3. ZIPSER's reaction vis-à-vis Schlesinger.

Position of the automobile and ZIPSER's chosen path, whereby I am making the assumption that this path led inevitably to the embassy district on the rear side of the Polish People's Republic Embassy and the Hungarian People's Republic Embassy. Unless, ZIPSER made a decisive detour intentionally, in order to head in another direction beyond my field of vision. Also, the time of just 20 minutes, if one considers that during the handover ZIPSER still had organizational matters to discuss about the receipt in Westberlin. I think it is very important to realize that only ZIPSER and I are informed about the entire course of events. Klaus SCHLESINGER only knows the context relating directly to him, and for that reason only ZIPSER, Klaus SCHLESINGER and I are aware of this.

INFORMATIONAL REPORT: JANUARY 26, 1976

The next document in my file bears the title "Informational Report" and "Main Department XX" appears in the upper left corner. It is a three-page summary of my principal activities in the GDR during the fall of 1975. From the following entry, I learn how concerned the authorities were about the possible inclusion of Wolf Biermann in my book:

> By means of operative surveillance measures that were initiated, it was learned that Dr. Zipser had asked specifically—in the interviews already conducted with Christa WOLF and Gerhard WOLF, PLENZDORF, SCHLESINGER, BECKER, FÜHMANN, Uwe KANT, MICKEL, MORGNER, HACKS and PANITZ— whether they favored the inclusion of Wolf BIERMANN in his project.

Eight of the authors named above answered this question in the affirmative. According to Dr. ZIPSER's comments, the majority of the GDR writers were with that response standing by Biermann. If additional GDR authors should speak out in Biermann's favor, Dr. ZIPSER intends to seek permission from the Writers' Union to include Biermann in his undertaking.

In addition, it was learned unofficially that Dr. ZIPSER—according to his own statements—is very close friends with Christa and Gerhard Wolf, Schlesinger, and Plenzdorf. In conversations with the writers just mentioned he was advised not to forget to include Heym in his book. [*The reference is to perpetual dissident writer Stefan Heym.*]

CONTACT WITH STEFAN HEYM: FEBRUARY, 1976

The next report, dated March 12, 1976, is labelled "Information" and signed by Lieutenant Colonel Müller. Main Department XX/OG [*Operative Group*] appears in the upper left corner. The topic is my attempt to arrange a meeting with Stefan Heym, East Germany's most famous writer.

From a reliable unofficial source, it was learned that the American Germanist

Dr. Richard ZIPSER
current residence: Vienna, Hörlgasse 11/6

made contact by letter with Stefan HEYM in the beginning of February 1976. ZIPSER told HEYM that he is currently preparing teaching materials on GDR literature for universities in the USA and, beyond that, seeking to obtain GDR writers for lectures at universities of the USA.

In addition, ZIPSER disclosed that he would again be staying in the capital city of the GDR, from 3/28 until 4/9/1976, and would like to use this opportunity to meet with HEYM. By means of operative surveillance measures that were initiated, it was determined that HEYM responded to ZIPSER promptly on 2/5/1976, indicating that he would be pleased to greet ZIPSER at his home in the beginning of April 1976.

From HEYM's letter it is obvious that he is ready to answer ZIPSER's questions and thereby support his undertaking.

Reading this report, I learn for the first time that I actually had been carrying out my project with the official approval of the Writers' Union in coordination with the Central Committee of the SED Party, a body that had enormous powers.

Regarding Richard ZIPSER: It is known that Richard ZIPSER was already staying in the GDR and conducting interviews with various GDR writers in October 1975, with the official approval of the GDR Writers' Union, in consultation with the Central Committee of the SED. . . . He tape recorded some of these interviews, even though he had not been granted permission to work with sound recording equipment.

The IM further reported that in the beginning of February HEYM received a letter from a Dr. Richard ZIPSER, from Vienna, Hörlgasse 11/6. In this letter ZIPSER reports that he is presently engaged in preparing teaching materials on GDR literature for universities in the USA. Furthermore, ZIPSER is trying to obtain GDR writers for lectures on GDR literature at universities of the USA. In this connection he mentions that writers Christa and Gerhard WOLF and Ulrich PLENZDORF had expressed special interest in such lectures. In addition,

ZIPSER told HEYM that he would be in the capital city of the GDR from 3/28 until 4/9/1976 and would like to use this opportunity to meet with HEYM.

IMV "Frieda" [*Heym's housekeeper*]

The final two pages of the report contain a photograph of the typewritten letter that Heym sent me on February 5, 1976, inviting me to visit him in early April. There is also a photograph of the envelope addressed to me in Vienna, with three postage stamps and Heym's return address on it. Due to an illness, I was unable to visit Heym in April 1976, but did meet with him at his villa in Berlin-Grünau in June of that year.

Heym, an internationally prominent German-Jewish writer, was at that time living under open Stasi surveillance. A secret police vehicle occupied by at least two officers was always parked on the street in front of his house, so he would know they were monitoring the coming and going of all persons to his residence, also to discourage people from visiting him. Inside the house, his informant housekeeper was able to overhear and report on his conversations with visitors, photograph documents that might be of interest to the Stasi, and keep a watchful eye on her employer whose telephone was most certainly bugged. The fact that he was constantly being observed must have bothered Heym, but he seemed to consider it a badge of honor, a tangible sign of his success as a SED regime critic and human rights advocate.

Heym had led a most unusual and eventful life. Born in Chemnitz in 1913, he fled the Nazis in 1933, moving first to Prague, and from there emigrating to the US in 1935. He completed his education at the University of Chicago, where he received a Master's degree, and then for two years was editor-in-chief of the German-language weekly, *Deutsches Volksecho* (*German People's Echo*). From 1939 to 1942, Heym worked as a printing salesman in New York City while trying to establish himself as a freelance author, writing in English. His first novel, *Hostages* (1942), was a bestseller, and his novel *The Crusaders* (1948) climbed to sixth place on *The New York Times* list of best sellers. He became a US citizen and served in the US Army during World War II. For his meritorious service as Technical Sergeant in 1944 and 1945, he was awarded the Bronze Star Medal. In 1952, he wrote a letter to President Eisenhower, protesting the Korean War and the fascistic policies of the American government. Heym claimed to have sent the Bronze Star and his US Army commission to Eisenhower, but he remained a US citizen. He moved back to Prague with his wife and requested asylum in communist East Germany, where he hoped to find the personal rights that he said were lacking in the US. In 1953, the GDR government restored his former German citizenship, enabling him and his wife to move to Berlin, where he had been a student in the early 1930s.

SED Party officials would soon come to regret their decision to repatriate Heym, as he would demonstrate time and again to their chagrin that he was a rebellious, fearless dissident, a thorn in the side of the government. His first major conflict with the GDR authorities occurred in 1956 when his novel about the June 17, 1953 mass uprising of workers in East Berlin, *5 Tage im Juni* (*5 Days in June*), was rejected for publication in the GDR. The novel was published in West Germany and in English translation, but the fact that it was banned in East Germany underscored how dangerous Heym's fictional recounting of history was in the minds of GDR leaders.

Heym began publishing his books in the West, both in German and in English, and these publications earned him large sums of hard currency that GDR officials were eager to share in accordance with a formula the state had established. Heym resisted, and in 1969 he was convicted of violating the GDR's currency exchange regulations after publishing his novel *Lassalle* in West Germany. In 1979 he was again convicted of breaching the GDR's currency exchange regulations, this time in connection with the publication of his novel *Collin* in West Germany. This violation ultimately resulted in his expulsion from the GDR Writers' Union and a major confrontation involving several other writers that will be discussed later on.

Heym had written many of his works in English and welcomed the opportunity to converse with me in that language when we met. He told me proudly that he subscribed to *The New York Times* and read it every day. Unlike other East German writers, Heym as a US citizen was able to leave the GDR and take trips abroad, such as his two-month visit to the US in 1978. He was pleased when I invited him to visit and give a talk at Oberlin College as part of his lecture tour. He came to Oberlin for two days and on November 17, 1978, he gave a memorable hour-long lecture to a huge audience on the inherent conflict between writers (he called them "practitioners of literature") and cultural policymakers in the GDR.

FRIEDRICHSHAIN MUNICIPAL HOSPITAL: MARCH/APRIL, 1976

According to the visa in my passport, I returned to East Berlin on March 22, 1976, with the intention of staying there until April 13. For this visit, I had booked a room in Interhotel Berolina, where I had resided in November 1975. This hotel was centrally located and had convenient parking, which made it an ideal place to stay while carrying out the next stage of my project. However, due to illness I had to cancel most of my appointments with writers and return to Vienna prematurely. At the beginning of June 1976, I would return to East Berlin and resume work on my project.

I have very unpleasant memories of this visit to East Berlin. When I became ill, I foolishly continued working on my project, which caused my health problem to worsen rapidly. Eventually, the Plenzdorfs took me to the emergency room of nearby Friedrichshain Municipal Hospital for treatment. After examining me, the doctor recommended that I be admitted immediately to the hospital, since I needed an operation and was not strong enough to drive back to Vienna. What a situation! I had no choice in the matter, so I entered the hospital without returning to my hotel and remained there for a week.

Three writers were especially kind to me in this time of need. Ulrich Plenzdorf let Christa Wolf and Jurek Becker know that I was in the hospital, and he also called all the writers I was scheduled to visit and cancelled the appointments. Christa Wolf went to Interhotel Berolina and was permitted to pack my clothes and belongings, which the hotel stored in a secure place. A week later, when I was feeling somewhat better, Jurek Becker came to the hospital and drove me to Hotel Berolina, where I settled my bill, retrieved my belongings, and then headed for West Berlin. In West Berlin, I stayed with a relative for a few days before driving back to Vienna, where I would soon undergo an operation.

THIRD REPORT FROM IMV "KURT": JUNE 4, 1976

ZIPSER called me on 6/1/1976 at around 6:20 p.m. and informed me of his presence. We arranged to meet on 6/3/1976. He called at around 11:30 a.m. from Ulrich PLENZDORF's and came to see me at around 6:30 p.m. From our place we drove to have dinner at Hotel "Stadt-Berlin," where he is also staying.

He told me he wants to stay in Berlin until 6/11/1976 or so, and then stay until 6/15/1976 or so in Hotel "Warnow" in Rostock.

With regard to his intentions, I am aware that he wants to continue with the interviews he began doing in fall 1975. I do not know the date of his entry.

From his comments I was able to learn that he had contact up to now with

Sarah KIRSCH
Volker BRAUN
Klaus SCHLESINGER
and Ulrich PLENZDORF.

He is entertaining the idea of going to visit Ulrich PLENZDORF, etc., at his country cottage in [*blacked out*], on the weekend of 6/5-7/1976.

He was planning to do an interview with Volker BRAUN on 6/4/1976, around midday, and to dine with Ms. Sarah KIRSCH in "Ganymed" on 6/5/1976.

D. Zipser commented on the 10th Parliament to the effect that he finds it beyond belief to see so many police and Free German Youth [*socialist youth organization of the GDR*] marshals on all street corners. He observed that, if we can manage to carry out such an elaborate operation, we probably have too large a workforce.

FIRST REPORT FROM IMV "UWE": JUNE 4, 1976

Below is the complete text of a five-page report, prepared by the poet Uwe Berger, on my June 2 meeting with him at his home. "Main Department XX/7" appears in the upper left corner.

During the visit I had today (June 2, 1976) from Dr. Richard Zipser, assistant professor of contemporary German literature at Oberlin College, Ohio, USA, I was able to obtain some information and disclosures.

With regard to his current project, Zipser told me this: He wants to present 35 GDR authors in a publication containing an introduction, biographies, original texts in German (generated after the 8th Party Congress), and interviews. Originally, he only wanted to include 10-20 authors, but after consultation with our Writers' Union he had to enlarge the circle. Literally: "What kind of consultation is that anyhow, with persons who know virtually nothing about literature and are not writers. All right—I will let them advise me and then do what I want."

Zipser was cautious, but I got him to divulge what he meant by that. His book is not supposed to include assessments and judgments. But some authors—he did not want to name them, apparently prose writers Scheibner recommended like Görlich and Neutsch—had given him such bad, boring texts that these instantly stood out. He also talked about the wide variety of responses to his questions and described this as something positive, but I perceived his effort to focus here on deeper contradictions. Of course, everything without any evaluation on his part, just in the words of the authors, purely documentary, etc.

By the way, tips from authors about their peers have been very valuable to him, as with Schlesinger and me (from Sarah Kirsch).

On June 3, Zipser plans to meet with Volker Braun and Stefan Heym. Furthermore, he intends to have conversations with Christa Wolf, Günter Kunert, Rolf Schneider and other writers. He has surely already spoken with Berger, Fühmann, Hermlin, Jakobs, R. Kirsch, S. Kirsch, Kunze, Mickel, Morgner, Neutsch, Panitz, Plenzdorf, M. W. Schulz, Schütz, Wiens and Gerhard Wolf, who is making an original contribution—an essay on GDR poetry in the 1970s (so, evaluation after all). [*Gerhard Wolf is not among the authors included in this book.*] In addition, the names Becker, Claudius, Endler, Görlich, Hacks, Kant, H. Müller, Pitschmann, Schlesinger, Seghers, Erwin and Eva Strittmatter were mentioned.

Zipser said he wanted to find a publisher in the USA for his book, possibly a publisher associated with a prominent university (Harvard). If that doesn't work out, he will approach a publisher he knows in Switzerland. The FRG is out of the question. I said that I am confident he will prevail. He murmured: "That could become difficult." He immediately revoked that comment: apparently, he regretted having made it.

Zipser brought up the 9th Party Congress early on, when he spoke about the time frame of his publication. I asked if he had been able to concern himself with that as yet and what his impression was. He replied that he was only able to read up on it in the *Spiegel*. [*This is a German news magazine that was published in West Germany and not available in the* GDR.] However, in conversations with a number of GDR citizens, and not just writers, he encountered disappointment and resignation. People assume that their standard of living will not continue to develop as it has in the last ten years and above all, to be specific, because this does not please the Soviet Union which commands stiff prices from the GDR for energy. That causes "frustrations" and, consequently, conflicts. GDR citizens may be proud of their socialism, but they still have remained quite German, hardworking and proficient. And they don't want to be cheated out of the fruits of their labor. For Zipser, the solid German way of doing things and this East European brand of socialism are also incompatible. The Germans have to remember who they are.

Zipser spoke as if he had not yet read my responses to the questionnaire he sent me some weeks ago. I replied to him in a soft voice and friendly way, seemingly thinking more about his tirades, that it remains to be seen how the standard of living will progress. Also, saying that one could view socialism in the GDR as a successful experiment for socialism in a Western European country. There are conflicts and disparities in the level of development in the capitalist world as well, so that is probably a principle of life. And by the way, I am against German isolation, this nationalism we had pushed to such an extreme in the past, and also against isolation toward the West (this last assertion to win him over again). Later Zipser declared that Helsinki was detrimental. I asked innocently, why; after all, Helsinki was positive. Zipser: "In and of itself, yes. But the

Eastern Bloc exploits Helsinki, does not adhere to it, seeks to gain advantages for itself." I showed my lack of understanding and Zipser backed off, apparently regretting that he had revealed so much. [*Regarding the references to Helsinki above: The Helsinki Final Act, Helsinki Accords, or Helsinki Declaration was the final act of the Conference on Security and Cooperation in Europe, held in Helsinki, Finland, between July 30 and August 1, 1975. Thirty-five states, including the United States, the Soviet Union, the Federal Republic of Germany, and the German Democratic Republic, signed the declaration in an attempt to improve relations between Communist Bloc and Western nations.*]

Of further importance, it seems to me, is what Zipser had to say during our four-hour conversation about Heym's book, *Five Days in June*: namely, it is not a book that confronts the GDR; yes, it criticizes, but provides constructive criticism in terms of socialism; it could foster a "Communication between Top and Bottom" in today's GDR society. Publishing it in the GDR could only stimulate independent thinking.

I replied that we are very in favor of independent thinking. This is a stated pedagogical goal of our school system. In my opinion, real thinking does not end in solipsism, but rather in the perception of what is general and what is common.

Zipser agreed with me, arguing however that one also has to teach young people to have a critical relationship to the world around them. I replied, asking if he does that at his college. Immediately after that came the surprising, rather emphatic answer: "When my students graduate from college, they are thinking human beings who are opposed to the Vietnam War, who say to themselves that one must be in favor of socialism." Prior to this, Zipser had explained to me that in the USA countries like Sweden and Austria are also considered to be socialist countries.

When I asked Zipser for his opinion on why people in the USA, but not in the FRG, were interested in my writings, he avoided answering. The things I write about were difficult to sell and were seldom translated. I expressed my desire to emerge from a certain isolation; even in the Soviet Union none of my books has been translated yet. Zipser replied that, without flattering me, he was surprised to hear that. He had been taken with my writings when he first read them recently and also wants to contribute in a modest way to making them well-known.

Zipser is not an Austrian, he is a native-born US citizen. He speaks very good German with an American accent. I estimate that he is 35 years old. He has studied in Freiburg, Munich [*Mainz, not Munich*] and Vienna. He has a pretty good knowledge of the literature of German-speaking countries and is a relatively serious scholar. His devious propaganda, the direction of which he revealed to me, is therefore all the more forbidding. Not to be underestimated as well, on its own, is the psychological impact when a bright, friendly man "from over there" takes a fervent interest in an author. As he said: "I visited with Rainer Kirsch for days." Or: "Christa Wolf and I always have such pleasant chats that we don't get right down to business." Naturally, the "multifaceted picture of GDR literature" that Zipser wants to present in a nonjudgmental way will not be truly objective. Naturally, he will try to cobble together a broadly-based rebellion, and somehow label those who do not fit in. Nevertheless, the advantage for us would remain having a voice abroad, albeit only in German and thus just for specialists.

We must not attach all too much importance to Zipser's commitment to "fairness," remarkable as it is in itself. Tape recorded interviews were conducted with about 10 authors, among others with Hermlin, Kunze, Wiens, the transcriptions of which are to be presented to the authors. At the end of his visit with me Zipser pointed to his large carryall and remarked that today he also had a tape recorder with him. It is not impossible, it seems to me, that at some time it will be secretly running in somebody's place.

Regarding Oberlin College, I learned additionally that there is a foundation there, which provides funds for inviting writers from German-speaking countries (with one exception up to now they all came from the FRG and Austria). Zipser has, in his own words, "academic freedom," which means that the content of his courses is of his own choosing, not dictated to him, although he has to discuss his general concept with his supervisors.

Zipser didn't want to admit to a special fondness for certain GDR authors, with the exception of Sarah Kirsch and me, which for certain was a tactical act of politeness. In our conversation his affinity to authors at the "right of center" (as Zipser stated at one point) became quite apparent to me, hence to Plenzdorf and the Wolfs, to Rainer Kirsch, Mickel and Endler ("great ability"), Kunert, Kunze ("very interesting"), Hacks and Müller ("pillars of GDR dramatic art"). Personally, he was impressed by Hermlin, Fühmann, Wiens. On the whole, he has a higher regard for the poetry than the prose of the GDR.

signed "Uwe"

Before I departed, IMV "Uwe" gave me a volume of his poetry entitled *Lächeln im Flug* (*Smiling in Flight*, 1975) and inscribed it as follows:

> For Dr. Richard Zipser
> as a memento of
> our meeting,
> which for me was
> very interesting.
>
> 6/2/1976   Uwe Berger

EBERHARD SCHEIBNER'S REPORT: JUNE 18, 1976

GDR Writers' Union functionary Eberhard Scheibner submitted a written report to the Stasi entitled "Memorandum on a Conversation with Dr. Richard A. Zipser (USA) on June 11 in Berlin." The report has three sections, as follows:

I. Re Background:

This section provides information about me, my project, and my contacts with the GDR Writers' Union from the beginning of 1975 to this point in time.

II. Course of the Conversation:

The June 11, 1976 discussion in Berlin, which came about as a result of our initiative, was supposed to produce more detailed information about the views and intentions of Dr. Zipser in connection with the project that has been described. It yielded essentially the following information:

1. Dr. Zipser promised—just like he did in our earlier examination of his work—to give us a list of the authors he has visited along with information on the envisaged literary texts.

2. When asked about his impressions of our literature, Dr. Zipser commented that, despite the complexity and diversity in the literary output and in the aims of our GDR authors, he can perceive at the same time a continuity in the literary design and development. He concurred with my view that the years after the 8th Party Congress in particular have led to a further enrichment of the literary scene in the GDR, the originality of which thereby distinguishes it noticeably from, for example, the literature of the FRG.

3. Without being asked, Dr. Zipser expressed the thought that there was also another way he wanted to act in the future on behalf of GDR authors, so as to make them known in the USA. He considered it quite possible that in the future additional writers could join the ranks of those GDR authors previously invited to universities in the USA (Christa and Gerhard Wolf, Günter Kunert, Ulrich Plenzdorf, Heiner Müller). He would like to try approaching eight American universities, in order to explore their interest in hosting and financing a reading tour of GDR writers; in doing so in that way, he thought that after the first successful attempt up to four GDR writers could be introduced annually in the USA. Dr. Zipser promised to inform us, should the implementation of this project become a possibility.

4. Dr. Zipser commented that he probably would return to Berlin for a while in January 1977, in order to resolve the legal issues related to the texts he had selected.

III. Conclusions:

From Dr. Zipser's statements (he also asked about the possibility of spending some time teaching at a university in the GDR), one can conclude that he is interested in long-term contacts with the GDR, especially in the area of literature and cultural policies. But as long as an end product of his work (like, for example, the publication he has announced) is not publicly available, it is very difficult for us to assess the nature of his activity. We therefore proceeded initially on the assumption that the book project he described, the purpose of which is to popularize GDR literature, could be beneficial. And we have done everything within the confines of the previous consultation sessions to prevent a distortion both of the views of our writers and the portrayal of our literature through the submitted texts (e.g., via instructions to use texts that are already published; to gather authorizable written responses to the questions instead of uncontrollable tape recordings, among other things). In connection with the suggestion Zipser made in II/3 above and to avoid leaving the initiative for possible additional projects up to the USA representative, the question arises whether—as long as there is no evidence on hand of negative activity on the part of Dr. Zipser—we should maintain a loose advisory contact as we have done up to now or whether an attempt ought to be made to reshape the present noncommittal contact into a stronger influential contact that is in our interest and have the Writers' Union play a more active official role with proposals and demands from our side. (Irrespective of that, we have already submitted proposals to the GDR Embassy in Washington for initiatives of our own concerning the stimulation of invitations to GDR authors.)

We request, as a matter of principle, clarification of this question: What position is the Writers' Union to take vis-à-vis "private" USA contacts who show up, in the interest of preserving optimally our ability to exert influence in the future.

[*initialed*]
Eberhard Scheibner

VISIT WITH KONRAD REICH IN ROSTOCK: JUNE 20, 1976

Next is a ten-page document labelled "IM-Report," Rostock, June 23, 1976. "Department XV" appears in the upper left corner. It begins: "Dr. Richard Zipser visited me in my apartment on Sunday, 6/20/1976. I already provided information previously on what this is about." Reading on, I quickly realize that the author of this document is none other than the head of one of the

GDR's most prominent publishing houses, the Hinstorff Verlag. Konrad Reich prefaces the report to his Stasi-handler with the following information about me, my activities in the Rostock area, and my travel plans:

> He was in fact compelled to leave the country back then in order to have an operation.

> He has now finished his first stay in Berlin and afterwards visited me.

> I would like to say in advance that his visit with me was just one part of his program.

> On Saturday, he conferred the entire day with the writer Siegfried Pitschmann here in Rostock and on Monday with Martin Stade.

> He drove in his automobile to Rerik and spent the night at Stade's place. I had asked him to pass through Rostock again on his way back and stop by, so I could hear what things had emerged during his conversations with Stade.

> However, he then drove on the direct route to Berlin, via Schwerin I think, because he had to be back in Vienna (his place of residence for the past year) by a certain point in time. He will be staying on in Vienna until 7/21/1976 and then will return to America.

Recalling our conversation, Reich then launches into a discussion of my project, its purpose and potential for harming the GDR, and my person.

<u>Re the matter at hand:</u>

He has interviewed 35 GDR writers. These 35 GDR writers had received advance information from him in the form of a questionnaire, which he recited from memory. I made a mental note of such questions as:

What do you consider to be the most important example of GDR literature in recent years?

How do you relate to the socialist society of the GDR?

What do you derive from the working class?

What sort of connections do you have with factories, agricultural production cooperatives, or other producers of goods?

What role does the relationship between emancipated women and society play in your writing?

How is the set of problems related to youth reflected in your writing?

What are you working on now?

What is your basic aesthetic concept?

What is your view on political interference in the area of literature?

Tell me about your projects for the coming years.

The wording of the questions may deviate here and there, but that of the last question is absolutely accurate. I formulated the exact sense of each question from memory because these are all things that are familiar to me.

In addition, the authors were all called upon to select a prose text or poetic work which could be taken as evidence of their theoretical position or as a particularly typical example, about which the author himself is convinced that it is a typical example of his literary potential.

The authors have complied with his request, generally with published works that already have appeared in the GDR. But 10 authors, among others Günter Kunert, who gave him 12 poems to choose from, Sarah Kirsch—poems, Bernd Jentzsch—poems. So poets especially, as one can see, have sent unpublished texts to him in Vienna, which he can then use later on.

These 35 authors—Stade and Pitschmann were the most recent—have answered all the questions and, to be precise, not in writing (except for the literary documents); on the contrary everything was tape recorded. Still not participating is Erwin Strittmatter, the only writer up to now who has refused to be interviewed, but Zipser is going to try again to win him over in Berlin. All in all, more than 80 tapes have been recorded. Some of these conversations and interviews lasted for more than 2½ hours.

Dr. Richard Zipser is basically a very pleasant-natured person, but I am unable to say anything about his mission (later I will say something more about him as a person). He told me, in an extremely triumphant manner, that all of the authors more or less indicated explicitly that they were interacting more openly with him as an American than they would with someone who came from a socialist country or the GDR. He told me that the material he had was nothing less than sensational because the writers spoke out without restraint, to some extent even about their own colleagues; and also because, of course, in a tape-recorded conversation so much more emerges through the oral communication than would if one only provided written answers to questions 1-10.

I believe that this can become a document that will cause us more problems than all the cultural-political trouble some people stirred up in recent years.

Zipser also came up with an interesting idea. His book will have 800-900 pages; in America that will be 2 large volumes, each with 400-450 pages. The format of this edition will be as follows: Zipser will introduce all 35 authors with a short biographical sketch and analysis. Photos of the authors will then be presented along with the literary texts that the authors have selected. In the second part of the book all the authors' answers to each question will be listed separately and in alphabetical order, showing how each one answered question 1) and then question 2), etc.

This method is tremendously underhanded. But what is even more interesting is the material that we have handed over here to a young American literary scholar, which apparently has enormous firepower and explosive force.

Reich's comments on our acquaintanceship reveal his enormous ego and sense of self-importance. Note that he makes reference to the luncheon we had (together with Ulrich Plenzdorf) at Hotel Unter den Linden in the fall of 1975, at which time he expressed interest in possibly publishing my book.

Zipser has a great deal of trust in me. That results from the following:

1. Adopting the perspective of many different types of GDR writers, he recognizes me as a publisher who in his entire behavior is never deceitful, who prefers instead to part company with someone if a political or ideological concept does not suit that person.

2. Obviously, persons such as Plenzdorf or Schlesinger must have said positive things about me, e.g., that one can get along with me, even though it may go against the grain sometimes, because my views—as everyone knows—don't always coincide with many of the views prevalent in the GDR, at least within these circles.

3. I have the impression that he also values my opinion somewhat and has respect for me. Such things really happen in life!

4. He was pleased when I told him, back then at our first meeting in "Linden"—I informed you about this—that I would be interested in making something like that happen [*Reich refers here to the publication of my book in the GDR*], but said that this idea ought to remain between the two of us.

5. As instructed, I showed my loyalty somewhat. For example, when Zipser related that he had visited [*blacked out*] and [*blacked out*] asked him if Erik Neutsch was also included, and he said "yes," and then was asked if Hermlin also was included, and then he again said "yes," whereupon [*blacked out*] remarked: amazing, amazing Mr. Zipser, what you are doing, neither the one nor the other is a writer.

Well, when I hear something like that I would normally make a rather annoyed face because

1. Neutsch and Hermlin are not comparable and

2. that is a really stupid comment by this arrogant [*blacked out*], who otherwise is indeed a very good writer, but a terribly arrogant man.

But here I joined in laughing.

[*I am certain that Peter Hacks is the author whose name is blacked out in section 5 above—and Reich is right, Hacks was very arrogant.*]

Sequence of Events:

He plans to finish writing Part I, which I spoke about earlier, by the summer of 1977.

By the spring of 1977 all of the tapes are supposed to be transcribed in America and available as typewritten material.

In the second half of 1977 the tapes are going to be edited down and, accordingly, the transcribed versions of the tapes will be sent back to the authors—our authors—and then put together in the first half of 1978 so that both volumes of the book can be published in the second half of 1978.

I told Zipser once again that I am interested, from the standpoint of a publisher, in his entire undertaking, but that my interest has to be kept under wraps.

If I am telling you that here, we also have to consider—for example—whether or not I report that to my Main Directorate.

That's how I expressed my interest to him, however for the purpose of our GDR security, not because I am interested from the publishing standpoint.

After that he explained that in February or March he will be coming to Vienna or the GDR with at least 2/3 of the entire manuscript, and he asked me if we could meet for two or three days, in order to go through everything together. I am supposed to read everything and might possibly receive copies, but by summer 1977 I will definitely receive the entire manuscript which as yet no one has gotten to see.

I asked him whether he has done the following: For instance, if when he was visiting Günter Kunert, he revealed to him what Schlesinger had said.

As a matter of principle, he did not do that, since that would of course be very dishonest. He can not afford to do that because the entire group of writers would then be at his throat, and he also assured me emphatically that up to now no one, not even his wife, knows or has seen anything. He wants to give me the first look in the spring and the whole thing by summer 1977. He said he would need my advice in order to bring the project to completion. And that very important advice would be on the Wolf Biermann problem.

He has therefore not visited and not interviewed Biermann. He explained, however, that he cannot publish this book in America with 35 of the best known and most distinguished GDR authors, if Biermann is missing.

I can understand the predicament of publishing such a book in the midst of the sensational and politically adversarial tendencies of American publishing houses. For them, a person like Biermann, particularly since his recordings are being sold everywhere in America, is of course a tremendous drawing card. Zipser would not be able to find a capitalist publisher for his book, if Biermann is not included. Then he asked me, what he ought to do. I'll now repeat what he had to say: He could write a foreword and in it explain that the GDR is quarreling with

Biermann at present and has been for a long time for whatever reasons, and therefore he didn't feel obligated to include Biermann—that wouldn't work.

What would then happen is that the book would not be accepted for publication in America.

The second thing is that none of the GDR writers has asked him if Biermann is being included.

By the way, one needs to think about this comment for a moment, because it actually means that no one was alert enough to consider the company he would actually be in with the interview.

According to Zipser, whenever he had been asked, he had always said, he was still contemplating that but didn't know for certain.

And then he asked me if it would be all right for him to say vis-à-vis the GDR—until all his work is finished and to secure permission to re-enter the country and do other things—that Biermann is not being included, but in the meantime do an interview with Biermann and then, when all work on the project here in the GDR has been completed, include him in the book without informing the GDR.

To be sure, it is not necessary for me to comment on that.

I told him without hesitation, because my loyalty could only extend so far, that I consider that wrong as a matter of principle and indeed from moral points of view, such as that of telling lies, falseness, underhandedness, political conspiracy, etc.; but then I told him that I would think about everything, whereupon he said repeatedly that this was just between ourselves, of course, and when we see each other in February or March I can tell him how he ought to proceed, and he gave me his word that he would not do anything as far as Biermann is concerned between now and February/March.

I don't know if he will keep that promise. But since he drove right back to Berlin from Stade's place, and wanted to try to get hold of Strittmatter from Berlin, and then immediately head for Vienna and in the last ten days of July (i.e., July 21, 22, 23) depart for home, and not return again until February/March of next year, I assume that in the meantime nothing can go wrong.

Reich then speculates on the damage my project, once published, could do to the GDR: "For me the whole thing was interesting only insofar that I just now realize that here the GDR, with grandiose vigilance, has latched onto something that makes everything previously written look like hymnbooks versus what is playing out here." He is exaggerating, of course, but his assessment reflects the paranoia that pervaded GDR society, at every level.

How is he financing his stay?

After waiting seven years, he received a one-year paid leave from his university where he has a regular appointment as assistant professor, in order to carry out this project. The reason he gave for this is that in America, after a seven-year affiliation with a university, professors receive a paid one-year sabbatical leave. Using this money, he has rented an apartment in Vienna for his wife and himself (he does not have children) and is financing his travels and his stay. Just to test him, I offered to cover his overnight stay here. But he apparently prepaid everything in West German marks through a tourist agency.

He brought along and dropped off this movie actress from Berlin, Evelyn Opyschinski [*Opoczynski*], who once made a film with Manfred Krug and is now doing something or other for GDR television. I don't know if he's having an affair with her.

His stay in Vienna is being financed by his university in Oberlin, Ohio.

Reich concludes his report with this commentary on my person.

Personal information:

He is about 30 years old, doesn't belong to any political group, presents himself as very left-progressive, which doesn't really mean anything. That is only meaningful in comparison to the rather stupid and rigid American literary scholarship, which to a certain extent is utterly reactionary, apart from a few exceptions.

His demeanor is quite unassuming.

For as long as I have known him, he has been running around in the same jeans outfit and pullover sweater.

He doesn't smoke, drinks moderately, and makes a kind of solid citizen impression—very pleasant-natured, really nice, not at all provocative or argumentative.

So I would say, if one knew precisely who this person is, a likable fellow. But even if one doesn't know that, he has a genuinely modest, reserved character, which apparently really impressed the GDR authors.

But it is interesting that his demeanor was so laid back that in the end almost every writer said he was the right interview partner. With a different person, someone from the socialist countries and the GDR, the writers never would have been able to connect in the way they had done.

At the foot of the final page of Reich's report, one sees "gez. IM" (signed by unofficial collaborator), confirming that he was an informant and secretly providing information to the Stasi. However, in contrast to the other informants who contributed to my file, no code name appears—and he may not have had one. But the title of this document, "IM-Bericht" (IM-Report), his use of the word "auftragsgemäss" (as instructed) which clearly indicates he was carrying out a special assignment, and the reference he makes to his "Hauptverwaltung" (Main Directorate), lead me and should prompt others also to conclude that Reich was indeed a high-level collaborator.

After reading this report, I could not help but wonder if Reich informed on writers whose books he published during his many years as head of the Hinstorff Verlag. And if he did, why was he not outed as so many other collaborators were in the 1990s? How did he manage to conceal his connection to the Stasi?

In my mind's eye, I try to picture Reich. While I have only a hazy memory of him from our two meetings, I somehow am able to bring him clearly into focus, especially after seeing photos of him on the internet. As regards his personality, I recall that he was a confident, self-assured, expansive, take-charge, can-do person. Plenzdorf, who liked and admired him, called him a "Macher," a person who gets things done, a real rarity in the bureaucratic GDR. Today, I know just who and what Konrad Reich really was—an informant and imposter.

INFORMATIONAL REPORT: JULY 22, 1976

The next report bears the title "<u>Information</u> on the second stage of interview activity in the GDR by USA citizen Dr. Richard ZIPSER," and "Main Department XX/7" appears in the upper left corner. The report is a five-page summary and analysis of my project-related activities in the GDR during the month of June 1976, based on information the Stasi had gathered from various unnamed (with one exception) sources. Without calling me an enemy of the GDR state, the report asserts that I was using the interviews to encourage GDR writers, particularly those who did not have strong political and ideological views, to take positions that were critical of socialism and the SED Party. At this point in time, the Stasi had clearly concluded that I was a provocateur and possibly an operative.

> Through unofficial sources it became known that Dr. Zipser, the American professor for contemporary German literature, carried out the second phase of his interview activity with GDR writers in the first two weeks of June after receiving official permission to do so from the leadership of the Writers' Union.

> During this time period Zipser interviewed these writers: Volker Braun, Stefan Heym, Christa Wolf, Günter Kunert, Martin Stade, Uwe Berger.

> Worthy of note is the systematic, uniform way Dr. Zipser proceeds by asking his interview partners questions that are similar with regard to content. Moreover, this process involves the same 15 questions he sent to the writers he had selected for his project, to be answered in writing, and also submitted prior to that to the Writers' Union. In each individual instance, Zipser pays very close attention to the writer's state of mind; in questions on details he concentrates on the weak points he knows about that particular interview partner. By proceeding in this manner Zipser automatically forces the person being interviewed to take a stand on problems in the development of the GDR in cultural, political, and ideological spheres.

> By connecting the author's personal views to general problems of development within GDR society Zipser manages, by the time the interview is finished, to present a fairly comprehensive picture of the author, the content of which is distinguished by the author's point of view on our society, on the working class, on the SED Party, and on the overall development of society.

The personalized portrayals of GDR writers prepared by Zipser enable him to detect leverage points for individual authors, in order to take advantage of writers who are politically uncommitted and engage them in antisocialist activities. By holding out the prospect of various types of offerings such as guest lectureships at universities, reading tours, publications in the USA with the accompanying reviews, and the awarding of prizes to GDR writers, Zipser is bound to have a greater harmful political-ideological influence than before on GDR authors, in an effort to bring about confrontations with the Party.

Zipser aims to figure out the extent to which GDR authors exert influence on the development of society with their writings. He pays special attention to the investigation of motif complexes in written materials.

Zipser's method of posing questions is aimed at swaying writers whose political views are not firmly formed to adopt a class-neutral stance when responding. This determination is especially obvious in the interview Zipser conducted with Martin Stade.

In response to Zipser's question about the function of literature and art in socialist countries, Stade stated that he was of the opinion that "literature has no function whatever. The goal of writing in socialism is the same as in a capitalist social system. The writer zeros in on something and just writes about it. He writes because he is moved to do so." In this connection Stade comments further that "he considers it his duty to criticize weaknesses in the socialist social system as sharply as possible. Socialist literature does not have a particular role to play." (Stade is a member of the SED.)

During a conversation Zipser had with Comrade Scheibner, Secretary for International Relations in the Writers' Union, about his activity in the GDR, Zipser remarked that "his interview activity in the GDR would serve to promote the spread of GDR literature in the USA to a much greater degree." Zipser commented that he was in contact with eight universities in the USA regarding the publication of his project and also that he would be receiving financial support from highly regarded American publishers. [*This last assertion is wholly inaccurate.*]

Through his approach and demeanor, Zipser was able to give each of the interviews an individually personalized touch. This led some of his interview partners to confide in him very trustingly.

As Zipser commented to an unofficial source, the trusting relationship GDR writers had to him was strengthened by the fact that he had received official permission to do his work and been announced to the authors by the GDR Writers Union.

During his interviews, as well as in the personal conversations related to them, Zipser adhered painstakingly to the extensive review of the 15 well-known questions he has presented.

Noteworthy, it appears, is that during conversations with his interview partners Zipser often highlights the broadness of his contacts among the GDR writers, in order to bring about the most confidential rapport possible and to dispel any potential reservations.

Zipser also conducted interviews and had informatory conversations with writers Günter Görlich, Hermann Kant, and Erich Neutsch, among others, whose contributions were completely positive. [*These are some of the* SED *Party loyalist authors the GDR Writers' Union functionaries had added to my list, knowing that they would respond in an appropriate—i.e., politically correct manner.*]

In this connection it has been determined unofficially that Zipser is especially interested in such authors as Sarah Kirsch, Ulrich Plenzdorf, Klaus Schlesinger, and Martin Stade, among others, persons who harbor wavering, negative, and to some extent hostile views with regard to the cultural policies of the GDR. Zipser made a proposal to the GDR Writers' Union, offering to invite GDR authors on a regular basis to give readings and lectures at universities in the USA, in order to contribute in this way to the promotion of GDR literature in the USA and to satisfy the interest of many USA citizens who want to become acquainted with GDR literature.

The purpose of the abovementioned is clarified by a statement Zipser made vis-à-vis an unofficial source, as an explanation: "The selection of the writers to undertake reading tours in the USA will of course be made by the appropriate institutions in the USA and not determined by the GDR Writers' Union. Participation by the GDR Writers' Union in the decision-making process is ruled out." Zipser confided in the unofficial source, informing this person of his intention to include Wolf Biermann in his publications and asking the source to maintain strict silence about this.

Zipser has concealed this intention from all the GDR authors he has interviewed to date because he feared that a large number of writers would cancel their participation in his book project upon learning of his intention, especially those writers with close ties to the Party and government.

Furthermore, Zipser is aware that if his intention is made known the GDR Writers' Union probably will not continue to permit him to do his work.

Since Zipser is worried that the quality of his book will suffer due to insufficient participation by internationally known writers, he plans to conduct an interview with Biermann during the very last part of his stay in the GDR. More precisely, he thinks it will be possible to conduct this interview when the other manuscript already has been completed. He tries to play down this undertaking by maintaining that "a publication on GDR literature will assuredly find a better market with Biermann."

It was possible to expand the contact to Zipser by means of an unofficial source [*Konrad Reich, obviously*], to whom he will deliver the manuscript of his publication in due time.

DECISION NOT TO INCLUDE WOLF BIERMANN

It is interesting that the report above indicates with certainty that I <u>would</u> be interviewing Biermann and including him in my book, even though I had not actually decided to do that. Ultimately, I decided not to include Biermann and explained my decision in the introduction to *DDR-Literatur im Tauwetter: Wandel – Wunsch – Wirklichkeit* (*GDR Literature During the Thaw: Change – Desire – Reality*), 1985.

Many readers will wonder why Wolf Biermann's name does not appear in the table of contents. The explanation is quite simple. It would have been impossible to carry out a project of this kind without at least the unofficial approval of the GDR Writers' Union. The Writers' Union would undoubtedly have rejected any proposal for a book that included SED regime critic Biermann. When I met with functionaries of the Writers' Union in the fall of 1975, I was asked on various occasions: "You are surely not intending to visit Biermann?" or "Biermann will not be represented in your book, isn't that so?" A number of the authors I visited later on asked me similar questions. In this way and in other ways I was given to understand clearly that the Writers' Union would block my project if I were to visit Biermann. In the final analysis it came down to Biermann *or* the book. I opted for the book. Later on, when all the interviews were in my possession and Biermann was living in West Germany, I could of course easily have included him. But since I had agreed to do the book without Biermann, it would have been—for the reasons I have cited—a questionable move to incorporate him ex post facto. (Vol. I, 11-12)

PROJECT STATUS: SUMMER/FALL, 1976

My three-week stay in the GDR was very productive, but much work remained to be done on my book project and my sabbatical leave was coming to an end. The tape-recorded interviews needed to be transcribed and then authorized by each writer for publication in my book. I also had to gather a text from each author, along with permission to publish that text from either the author or his/her publishing house, and I also needed a portrait photograph of each writer. In addition, I had many more authors to visit and interview, since my list had grown from 30 to 45, the number of writers actually represented in the three-volume book, *DDR-Literatur im Tauwetter*. My original idea had been to do a single volume with 20 writers, but the project mushroomed in size as GDR writers on the original list and the GDR Writers' Union recommended the inclusion of other authors they considered important. It threatened to overwhelm me, but I was determined to complete my work and publish a comprehensive documentary of the period of thaw in GDR cultural policies that soon would come to an end.

I returned to Vienna in the final week of June 1976, and then in late July flew home to Ohio, back to my full-time job at Oberlin College. In the fall and winter of 1976, I did two things related to my project: first, I gave a 20-minute presentation at the December Modern language Association Annual Convention on the work I had been doing in the GDR; second, I applied for an International Research and Exchanges Board (IREX) grant, so I would be able to return to the GDR in the fall of 1977 and continue work on my half-finished project. Fortunately, my IREX application was successful and enabled me to spend three more months in the GDR. If I had not been awarded this grant, I doubt that the GDR authorities would have permitted me to continue interviewing writers and gathering materials in the GDR.

EXPATRIATION OF WOLF BIERMANN: NOVEMBER, 1976

The expulsion in November 1976 of famous dissident writer/singer Wolf Biermann triggered events that brought the period of liberalization and intellectual optimism to its unofficial end. The GDR government had permitted Biermann to embark on a concert tour in West Germany that November. While he was on the tour, they "expatriated" him and did not allow him to return to his home in East Berlin. This unexpected and cruel solution to the Biermann problem prompted outrage among GDR writers and artists. Twelve of the GDR's most distinguished authors (Erich Arendt, Jurek Becker, Volker Braun, Franz Fühmann, Stephan Hermlin, Stefan Heym, Sarah Kirsch, Günter Kunert, Heiner Müller, Rolf Schneider, Christa Wolf, and Gerhard Wolf) and a prominent sculptor—men and women who had previously pushed for more liberal cultural policies from inside the system—reacted by publishing in the West a letter asking the regime to reconsider its decision. In the days that followed, more than a hundred other writers and artists added their names to the petition. The leaders of the SED Party, at first surprised by this unusual display of opposition, soon returned to the offensive. The loyalist/opportunist majority within the GDR Writers' Union was mobilized to condemn independent-minded colleagues, many of whom were then expelled from the Party. Those protesters who refused to recant were publicly denounced, encouraged (directly or indirectly) to leave the country, or even placed under arrest, as in the much publicized case of Jürgen Fuchs. By the end of 1977, such talented younger writers as Bernd Jentzsch, Thomas Brasch, Reiner Kunze, Sarah Kirsch, Hans Joachim Schädlich, and Jurek Becker had departed for the West. The GDR authorities, aware that the Biermann case had precipitated a major human rights crisis, insisted repeatedly that this confrontation would have no important consequences, that the less restrictive cultural policy endorsed by SED Party First Secretary Erich Honecker in 1971 would continue to obtain. A few concessions were indeed made, but in May of 1978 seven leading authors (Franz Fühmann, Stefan Heym, Günter Kunert, Ulrich Plenzdorf, Klaus Schlesinger, Rolf Schneider, and Christa Wolf) were excluded from participation in the national GDR Writers Congress in Berlin, evidently to prevent them from speaking out. In June 1979, nine "rebellious"authors (Kurt Bartsch, Adolf Endler, Stefan Heym, Karl-Heinz Jakobs, Klaus Poche, Klaus Schlesinger, Rolf Schneider, Dieter Schubert, and Joachim Seyppel) were reprimanded and expelled from the Writers' Union. In addition, they were barred from making public appearances and from publishing their work either in the GDR or in the West—i.e., deprived of all means of earning their living as writers. And with the departure of Günter Kunert for West Germany in the fall of 1979, the list of GDR authors living in exile grew even longer. [*For more information on the Biermann crisis, its major causes and effects, see William Treharne Jones's review-article, "East German Literature, Problems of Communism (March/ April 1978), 71-77, which I have cited in the section above.*]

PRESENTATION AT THE MLA CONVENTION: DECEMBER 27, 1976

The paper I presented at the annual meeting of the Modern Language Association, in a special session on GDR Prose Fiction: Critical Approaches and Model Analyses, was entitled "Contemporary GDR Prose Writers and Their Society: Perspectives from Within." Imagine my surprise when I read the following report, prepared in Berlin and dated April 21, 1977, on my MLA talk. The report is titled "**Information**: References to GDR Writers during the annual conference of the Modern Language Association (MLA) USA." "Main Department XX/3" and "Top Secret" appear in the upper left corner of the first page.

Unofficially, it became known that Richard A. Zipser, Oberlin College, Ohio spoke on the topic "Contemporary GDR Prose Writers and Their Society" at the annual conference of the MLA. His presentation was based on interviews that Z. had conducted with 35 writers in the GDR in conjunction with his private visits in 1976.

The following authors responded to Z.'s interview question, "Which contemporary social problems are of the greatest concern to you as a writer?": Jurek BECKER, Günter de BRUYN, Fritz Rudolf FRIES, Franz FÜHMANN, Stephan HERMLIN, Stefan HEYM, Karl-Heinz JAKOBS, Hermann KANT, Günter KUNERT, Irmtraud MORGNER, Erik NEUTSCH, Eberhard PANITZ, Ulrich PLENZDORF, Klaus SCHLESINGER, und Rolf SCHNEIDER (Answers given by the abovelisted writers and the interview questionnaire are in the attachment).

Furthermore, it became known that Joan GLICK (now HOLMES, because divorced) was present at the conference just mentioned and read a paper on "The 9th Party Congress and Cultural Policies in the GDR." The person referred to above is still in the GDR as a result of a private extension of her stay at the Humboldt University of Berlin for academic purposes, within the framework of the agreement with the International Research and Exchanges Board (IREX) based in New York. IREX considers itself responsible for the exchange of scholars from the USA and socialist countries at the university level.

[*Joan Holmes received her Ph.D. in German literature from The Johns Hopkins University in 1976. Her dissertation was entitled "Portrayal of Tragic Conflicts in the Drama of the German Democratic Republic." In the fall of 1975, she was in the first group of IREX scholars from the United States conducting research in the GDR, where she was able to remain until 1977.*]

The next page of this report contains a list of the fifteen questions I had been using to interview GDR writers. The names of fifteen GDR authors appear on this sheet, which was actually a handout I had distributed to everyone attending the MLA session. Then, on the next page, the following paragraph from my talk is quoted verbatim:

> In the second section of my paper, I should like to cite the responses of several well-known GDR prose writers to one of the more topical questions I posed: "Which contemporary social problems are of the greatest concern to you as a writer?" Since none of this information has been published as yet, I wish to anticipate and avoid any possible difficulties which could result from quoting at this time. Thus, I have elected to name the responding authors, then to list their answers in random order. For the purposes of this paper, it is only important to know what the individual responses were, not who said what, and I hope my reluctance to reveal the latter information will be understood. The writers in question are: Jurek Becker, Günter de Bruyn, Fritz Rudolf Fries, Franz Fühmann, Stephan Hermlin, Stefan Heym, Karl-Heinz Jakobs, Hermann Kant, Günter Kunert, Irmtraud Morgner, Erik Neutsch, Eberhard Panitz, Ulrich Plenzdorf, Klaus Schlesinger, and Rolf Schneider. The answers they gave to the above question (which in many instances have been edited, in order to shorten them) were as follows: [*The next five pages of this report contain fifteen answers, which were taken directly from the handout I distributed to everyone attending the MLA session.*]

How did all this information wind up in the hands of the Stasi and eventually find its way into my file? I have reason to believe that an American Germanist in the audience sent it to a writer-friend in the GDR who was a SED party loyalist, and that he in turn passed it along to a high-level functionary at the GDR Writers' Union. Of course, since the writers names were not linked directly to the responses on the handout, the GDR authorities also were unable to know who said what. However, the information on the handout gave them a good idea of the kind of material I had been gathering in the interviews.

PERSONS PURSUING IDEOLOGICAL SUBVERSION: DECEMBER, 1976

I next turn my attention to a bound 27-page attachment to my file, the cover page of which bears the following stamps: "Original received," "Ministry for State Security/General Repository for Individuals," and "Closed Filing," indicating that it was a top secret document. The first page in the attachment is a letter, written on December 3, 1976, from Generalmajor Paul Kienberg, Director of Main Department XX in the MfSS, to the Director of Department X in the same building. In this internal communication, Kienberg instructs his colleague to request information from the state security agencies of other socialist countries on a number of persons considered hostile to the GDR. Attached to this letter is a list of nine persons, all of them foreigners from Western nations—England, the Netherlands, and the United States, who purportedly have been engaging in subversive activities in the GDR. The names of these persons and the personal information about each are blacked out on my copy—with one exception, which shocks me. That person is none other than

Dr. ZIPSER, Richard
Born on 1/23/1943 in Baltimore
Residence 102 Shipherd Circle/USA
Oberlin/Ohio
Assistant Prof. of German Literature
Oberlin College/Ohio/USA
USA Citizen

A MfSS stamp on the letter, signed by Colonel Willi Damm and dated December 4, 1976, acknowledges receipt of this order and the information-gathering process begins that day.

The attachment also contains letters from Oberst Willi Damm of the Stasi to the Ministry of the Interior, which was ultimately in charge of state security, in the following communist countries: Hungary, Poland, Bulgaria, and Czechoslovakia. The letters were written in the first week of December 1976. They are virtually identical, so I am reproducing just one as an example:

. . . .

December 1976

Persons, who carry out ideological subversion	U/	/7

<u>PERSONAL</u>　　　　　　　<u>TOP SECRET</u> !

Ministry of the Interior
Hungarian People's Republic
Comrade Lieutenant
Colonel DACZI

<u>Budapest</u>

Esteemed Comrade Daczi!

I am contacting you to request that you have reviews undertaken on the persons named on the enclosed list with attention to the following:

> Have the named individuals previously entered the Hungarian PR?

Where applicable, when and for what purpose did these entries occur?

Have any of these individuals previously surfaced as operatives and is there possibly evidence of their connections to hostile agencies and intelligence services?

The named individuals became known to the MfSS in connection with its work on hostile entities in the GDR in the category of political-ideological subversion.

I thank you in advance for your assistance.

With socialist greetings
[signature]
Damm
Colonel

Enclosure

. . . .

The responses from the four state security agencies to Oberst Damm's inquiries arrived at MfSS headquarters in late January/early February 1977; they were promptly translated into German and forwarded to Generalmajor Kienberg for evaluation. In my case, reference is made only to trips I had taken as a tourist to Hungary in 1969 and to Czechoslovakia in 1973 and 1975. The information on the nine foreigners thought to have been carrying out subversive activities in the GDR, a total of 79 pages in a bound volume, was archived on March 16, 1988.

SECOND REPORT FROM IMV "UWE": FEBRUARY 11, 1977

There is a considerable amount of trivial information in the file, along with information that could be considered important. Uwe Berger's second report, to Captain Pönig in Main Department XX/7, is a good example of the former.

Information

In a meeting on 2/9/1977, IMV "Uwe" reported that he had received a phone call on 2/4/1977 from a female person who spoke with an English accent. This female person introduced herself using the name Holwers (or something like that). She explained that she came from the USA and is an American.

At present she is staying in the capital of the GDR, she says, and has been asked by Dr. Richard Zipser to convey greetings to his friends living here.

At the same time she is supposed to inquire if the source has received the poetry magazine Zipser promised to send. The source confirmed receipt to the caller and promised her that he would soon inform Zipser of this via a letter

The caller did not show any interest in meeting in person. She stated that she is very busy, whereupon the source asked her to give Dr. Zipser his kind regards, which the caller promised to do. In all probability Mrs. Dr. Holwers is identical to the person named Dr. Holmes, who contacted Sarah Kirsch. [*Indeed, this was IREX-scholar Joan Holmes, who had participated with me in the MLA special session on GDR literature in late December, then returned to East Berlin to continue her research.*]

CONTRACT WITH NORDLAND PUBLISHING COMPANY: JANUARY, 1977

On the 28th of January, 1977, I signed a contract with Nordland Publishing Company, Inc., to publish "DDR-Literatur im Tauwetter" in a single edition of 1,500 copies, the number stipulated in my agreement with GDR publishing houses and writers. Nordland was a small press based in Belmont, Massachusetts, which specialized in publishing academic books. A colleague and good friend recommended that I consider this press, mainly because his brother-in-law was Executive Vice President of the company. I would come to regret my decision to publish with little-known Nordland, as the company encountered financial difficulties around 1980 and eventually went bankrupt. This resulted in a five-year delay in the publication of my three-volume book, a delay in my promotion from associate to full professor, and it caused me considerable financial hardship, as well as a great deal of frustration and embarrassment.

RETURN TO BERLIN: JUNE, 1977

In early June 1977, shortly after the conclusion of Oberlin College's spring semester, I returned to Berlin for a week. I stayed with friends in West Berlin, Brigitte and Hellfried Kellner, who kindly let me use the guest bedroom in the basement of their lovely villa in the district of Lichterfelde. During this time, I made several day trips to East Berlin, where I visited some friends and writers. A report in my file dated June 6, 1977 refreshes my memory of this visit and its purpose. According to the Stasi, I was interested as an operative or provocateur in meeting with GDR writers they viewed as enemies of the state.

Unofficially, it became known that the USA citizen

Dr. ZIPSER, Richard
born: 1/23/1943
residence: Oberlin, Ohio 44074 (USA)
employed as: Assistant Prof. German Dept.

Oberlin College
known operatively as active contact of hostile-
oppositional GDR writers

who for about a week now, since 6/4/1977, has been staying with
the KELLNER family (Tel. [*blacked out*]) in Westberlin, is trying
to set up meetings with GDR writers

Jurek BECKER
Ulrich PLENZDORF and
Sarah KIRSCH.

On 6/5/1977 ZIPSER got together with Sarah KIRSCH in
her apartment.

ZIPSER has arranged to meet with Ulrich PLENZDORF on
6/6/1977, at noon, in the capital of the GDR.

The specific reason for ZIPSER's discussions with Sarah KIRSCH
and Ulrich PLENZDORF could not be determined.

ZIPSER wants to invite Jurek BECKER to visit the USA in 1978
and have preliminary discussions about that now.

[…]

A get-together with Jurek BECKER is scheduled for the
afternoon of 6/9/1977.

In addition to that, Dr. ZIPSER contacted Gerhard WOLF and
arranged to meet with him as well on 6/9/1977.

FOURTH REPORT FROM IMV "KURT": JUNE 8, 1977

Main Department XX/Operative Group   Berlin, 6/14/1977

Ta.

Transcript of tape recording

Source: IMV "Kurt"

received: First Lieutenant Paulitz on 6/8/1977

ZIPSER, Dick – USA Citizen: Germanist

On 6/6/1977 ZIPSER called me from Plenzdorfs' place and said that he wanted to visit me with Helga PLENZDORF.

Around 7:00 p.m. he arrived at my place with Helga P. and her daughter Ulrike.

Shortly after his arrival he made a telephone call from my place to a citizen of Westberlin

KELLNER, Hellfried
born on [*blacked out*] 1942 in Berlin
resident of Westberlin, [*blacked out*]
construction engineer

and to a GDR citizen

Christa or Christine – ca. 35 years old
employed: GDR television

Christa met ZIPSER in Hotel "Berolina"
during his last stay in the capital of
the GDR.

After he informed KELLNER that he would be not be coming back to his house until after midnight (ZIPSER is staying with KELLNER), he asked Christa to make her way to the PLENZDORFs' place, so they could spend the evening together following his return.

At 8:45 p.m. we picked up Christa at the Plenzdorfs' and headed over to Hotel "Berolina," in order to have supper together in the cellar restaurant. At around 10:00 p.m. Ulrich PLENZDORF joined us there.

At 11:15 p.m. ZIPSER and Christa left the restaurant after announcing their intention to walk together to Güst Friedrich-Zimmer-Street, from where ZIPSER would leave for Westberlin. ZIPSER declined Helga PLENZDORF's offer to drive him to the border in her car.

[…]

According to ZIPSER's account, he has been in Westberlin since Saturday, 6/4/1977, and plans to travel to Austria on 6/11/1977, in order to arrange a talk or series of talks in Vienna. [*On June 16, 1977, I gave a talk in Vienna on "Literatur der DDR heute" (Contemporary GDR Literature), as part of the Literary Quarter lecture series, sponsored by the Vienna Art Association.*]

ZIPSER did not comment on the specific reasons for his stay in Westberlin. It appears that he is using the transit journey as a week-long opportunity to call on friends and acquaintances in Westberlin and in the capital of the GDR.

ZIPSER mentioned that he met with Sarah KIRSCH on Sunday, 6/5/1977, and on Monday with Ulrich PLENZDORF, at whose home he also got together with Martin STADE.

I know that STADE was in Berlin on 6/6/1977. That afternoon Ulrich PLENZDORF drove him to Altrosenthal. Moreover, on the way to Hotel "Berolina" Zipser was carrying the book *19 Fische* [*19 Fish*, a volume of short stories by Stade].

ZIPSER reported that his book on GDR literature would soon be published.

Furthermore, he has received a new fellowship from his university [*a reference to the grant I received from IREX*] and intends to return to the GDR in October 1977 and spend two months here as a resident. He did not comment on the specific nature of his activity here. It appears, however, that he plans to concentrate further on GDR literature. According to his own account, he frequently listens to the tape recordings he made a while ago with GDR writers.

In addition, ZIPSER reported that on 6/7/1977 he plans to meet with

Thomas BRASCH

in Westberlin. Supposedly, ZIPSER got to know BRASCH only now in Westberlin.

Personal Information

ZIPSER has an excellent command of the German language. According to his own account, he began learning German in the 10th grade and spent a year in the FRG [*Federal Republic of Germany*] as a college student. At age 20, he first began to read books in German and since that time has devoted himself intensively to German literature.

His demeanor is characterized by an unassumingness that one cannot fail to notice. For example, ZIPSER refuses to use his academic degree (Dr.) with his name when reserving a table in Hotel "Berolina."

ZIPSER is able to adapt himself perfectly to his conversational partners and participate with concentration as the discussion progresses. Also, these behavioral patterns don't change when he is under the influence of alcohol. Because of his adaptability, he quickly engages his contact partners in unrestrained discussions on diverse topics and thereby becomes a "sympathetic conversational partner" in relatively short order.

As I read the last two paragraphs of IMV "Kurt's" report, with his comments on my person, I am reminded of Hinstorff publisher Konrad Reich's observations about me in the "Personal Information" section of his report dated June 23, 1976. It is interesting to know how the informants perceived me way back then, and what I read in these reports pleases me.

RETURN TO EAST BERLIN AS AN IREX SCHOLAR: OCTOBER, 1977

The IREX grant I was awarded in the spring of 1977 enabled me to return to the GDR for three months, in order to complete the work on my book project that had to be carried out in the GDR. IREX officials allowed me to divide my stay into two parts, as follows: two months in the fall/winter of 1977, and one month in the spring/summer of 1978. I was worried that I would not be able to accomplish everything that still needed to be done in the GDR in a single three-month stay, hence my request to spend two months there initially and then return for one month a half year later. As it turned out, this plan worked out very well.

On October 15, 1977, with the approval of the GDR Ministry of Higher Education and sponsorship of the Humboldt University, I returned to East Berlin as an IREX scholar. The Humboldt University provided me free of charge with a very modest studio apartment in a dreary highrise building in a settlement known then as the "Hans-Loch-Viertel." The Hans-Loch-Quarter, named after the former GDR Minister of Finance, was situated in the locality of Friedrichsfelde, in the district of Lichtenberg, not far from the Friedrichsfelde Zoo. This neighborhood was not very close to the center of East Berlin, Berlin Mitte, but the Friedrichsfelde subway station was nearby and I had wisely purchased an older Volkswagen in West Berlin, so I would not be dependent on public transportation. In accordance with their exchange agreement with IREX, the GDR provided me with a stipend in the amount of 700 East German marks per month. There was a bugged telephone in my apartment, which I could use free of charge for calls within the GDR. I also had a special multiple-entry visa, which as an IREX scholar I received free of charge, that permitted me to go back and forth as often as I wished between East and West Berlin. This enabled me to visit friends in West Berlin now and then, also to go shopping for myself and for my East German friends who needed or wanted items that were not available in the GDR. Some of the items I procured for others were jeans, fresh fruit (especially bananas), white asparagus, smoked eel, wines from France, books by West German and US authors, replacement parts for appliances that had been manufactured in West Germany, and even toilet paper (which now and then was in short supply in the GDR).

As an IREX scholar, I was assigned a "Betreuer" or minder by the name of Anneliese Löffler, a professor of GDR literature at the Humboldt University and an opportunistic SED Party loyalist. Löffler (code name IM "Dölbl") was rumored to have close ties to the Stasi, and several writers warned me to be careful in conversations with her and not to trust her. When the Stasi archives were opened in the 1990s, the exact nature and extent of her involvement with the secret police became known—and it was substantial. In order to advance her career, Löffler became an important source of information for the Stasi in the early 1970s. She informed on and denounced many GDR writers, carried out special assignments for the Stasi, and also used her influence as book reviewer ("Gutachterin") to prevent literary works she considered politically incorrect from being published; hence, she wielded a lot of power and influence. Her assignment this time was to keep a watchful eye on me and find out as much as possible about my book, also to get a look at the manuscript. The Stasi would rely heavily on her to assess the potential damage my book could do to the GDR's image when published. I purposely had very little contact with Löffler during my two-month stay in East Berlin, and her reports to the Stasi reflect a great deal of frustration.

FIRST REPORT FROM IM "DÖLBL": OCTOBER 19, 1977

Professor Löffler made her first report orally, in a meeting with her Stasi-handler two days after we had dinner together at Hotel Unter den Linden, where I had been her guest. It appears below in its entirety.

Main Department XX/7   Berlin, 10/19/1977
                                                      Ti/Lü

Information

IM "Dölbl" reported at our rendezvous on 10/19/1977 that the USA citizen

> Z i p s e r, Richard
> born: 1/23/1943
> Professor at Oberlin College Ohio/USA

has been staying in the GDR again, since 10/15/1977, now within the framework of an exchange agreement with the Ministry of Higher Education.

For the entire duration of ZIPSER's 8-week stay in the GDR, IM "Dölbl" is assigned to be his contact person with regard to all questions related to his work opportunities at the Humboldt University. So far, in an initial conversation with Zipser on 10/17/1977, the unofficial collaborator was able to find out the following about what ZIPSER intends to do during his stay in the GDR:

At the Humboldt University, Zipser wants to familiarize himself with the way students are trained in the field of German language and literature, with overall problems in German studies, and with GDR literature. With this in mind he is participating in courses (lectures and seminars, colloquia, etc.) and having conversations with faculty members.

Furthermore, ZIPSER intends to complete the scholarly project on GDR literature that he already began during his previous stays in the GDR. For this purpose he had selected and interviewed 35 GDR authors, asking all of them the same questions, during earlier visits to the GDR. ZIPSER tape recorded the responses to these questions. Up to now ZIPSER has mentioned the following authors' names to the unofficial collaborator:

Stephan HERMLIN	Peter HACKS
Christa und Gerhard	WOLFPaul WIENS
Franz FÜHMANN	Irmtraud MORGNER
Günter KUNERT	Max-Walter SCHULZ
Jurek BECKER	Erik NEUTSCH
Ulrich PLENZDORF	Uwe BERGER
Volker BRAUN	Eberhard PANITZ
Erich ARENDT	Günter GÖRLICH
Klaus SCHLESINGER	Benno PLUDRA
Martin STADE	Hermann KANT
K.-H. JAKOBS	Uwe KANT

Heiner MÜLLER

Rainer KIRSCH

Karl MICKEL

The first of the questions ZIPSER asked is: "Where do you stand with regard to the SED Party and GDR State?" [*Actually, the first question was: What, in your opinion, is the function of literature and art in the socialist state?*]

ZIPSER emphasized in the presence of the unofficial collaborator, by way of example, that BECKER, PLENZDORF and SCHLESINGER insisted that ZIPSER return the answers they had already submitted and gave him new answers. In the new answers, according to ZIPSER's account, the prevailing tone that was originally optimistic and affirmative with regard to socialism has changed to one of deep resignation over the alleged lack of prospects for the development of socialism in the GDR. According to Zipser's statements, BECKER, PLENZDORF and SCHLESINGER are now placing all their hope in young people growing up in the GDR.

With regard to the format of his book on GDR literature, ZIPSER commented that he plans to begin with his own assessment of GDR literature, which will be approximately 10 pages in length. That will be followed by texts, completely new ones for the most part, written by the 35 selected writers; these are supposed to impart a picture of GDR literature.

A short biographical introduction will then be provided for each of the selected writers. ZIPSER's interviews with the GDR writers will be included as well. The 35 authors' answers to each individual question will appear one below the other.

In ZIPSER's opinion, as expressed to the unofficial collaborator, the authors' answers are astonishingly varied and repudiate the notion prevailing up to now that GDR literature is characterized by "uniformity."

The unofficial collaborator observed additionally about ZIPSER that he posed rather tightly focused questions to members of the faculty at the Humboldt University of Berlin.

Furthermore, the unofficial collaborator described as extraordinary the fact that ZIPSER has a disproportionately long time at his disposal for the work he is doing on GDR literature. While it is customary for faculty employed at colleges in the USA to be granted a one-semester leave every 5 years for the purpose of studying abroad, ZIPSER has already required more than 3 semesters for his project. When the unofficial collaborator asked him how this is possible, ZIPSER said that he is handling things privately, without any financial support from the college.

During his stay in the GDR, ZIPSER is living in a Humboldt University of Berlin apartment in Berlin Friedrichsfelde, Volkradstrasse.

On 10/15/1977 a representative of the Humboldt University met and welcomed ZIPSER at the Friedrichstrasse train station. In the process, the assigned representative ascertained that a friend of Sarah KIRSCH,

W a r d e t z k y, Jutta
born: [blacked out] 1939
residence: 104 Berlin, [blacked out]

was also waiting for ZIPSER.

ZIPSER greeted WARDETZKY with these words: "Best regards from Sarah! Everything is going well." WARDETZKY also drove ZIPSER to his quarters in her automobile.

From 10/18/1977 until the weekend ZIPSER is staying at Plenzdorf's countryside cottage in [*blacked out*].

INVITATION TO JUREK BECKER (1)

As I mentioned earlier, Oberlin College had a German writer-in-residence program which enabled us to invite a writer from a German-speaking country to spend a good portion of the spring semester in Oberlin. Since our experiences with Christa Wolf and Ulrich Plenzdorf had been such positive ones, the German faculty decided to invite another East German author for the spring 1978 semester. The writer we selected was Jurek Becker, one of the most prominent and outspoken writers in the GDR, who had told me he was very interested coming to Oberlin. Becker had achieved international recognition through the publication in 1969 of his first novel, *Jakob der Lügner* (*Jacob the Liar*), which had been translated into many languages and made into a motion picture with the same title. The letter of invitation was being sent to me at the US Embassy in East Berlin, where I picked up my mail periodically, so I could hand-deliver it to Becker. This would prevent the GDR authorities from intercepting the invitation and enable Becker to seek permission for his stay as guest writer in Oberlin without delay. The next report in my file, reproduced in its entirety below, is mainly concerned with the invitation to Becker.

Main Department XX/7   Berlin, 10/21/1977

Ti/Lü

Information

about activities of USA citizen Richard ZIPSER during his
current stay in the GDR

Unofficially, it became known that ZIPSER called on the GDR
writer Jurek BECKER on 10/16/1977. In ZIPSER's company
was a person known to be closely connected to Sarah KIRSCH

> W a r d e t z k y, Jutta
> born: [blacked out] 1939 in Leipzig
> residence: 104 Berlin, [blacked out]

ZIPSER informed BECKER about the length of his stay in
the GDR and about the handling of the formalities which he,
ZIPSER, has taken over for BECKER in preparation for the
journey to the USA BECKER has planned for the spring of
next year. ZIPSER plans to give BECKER the invitation and
the contract with Oberlin College in the state of Ohio, USA, in
the coming week. As for the term of BECKER's residency in the
USA, ZIPSER suggested the time period from 2/25/1978 until
5/10/1978.

ZIPSER presented BECKER with a prospective program for his
stay at Oberlin College: he would give a 1½-hour lecture course
at least once a week, hold readings on 10 predetermined free
days, and devote the remaining time to his own writing.

ZIPSER let BECKER know that in the coming days he is
expecting to receive a letter for BECKER from the USA, which
will contain the supporting documents for BECKER's 1978
trip to the USA. ZIPSER thought it would be unsafe to have
the letter sent directly to BECKER. ZIPSER intends to use the

same method to convey BECKER's response to Oberlin College. ZIPSER mentioned additionally that he is well acquainted with a former staff member at the USA embassy in the GDR, KLEIN.

BECKER intends to stay in the USA beyond the time period ZIPSER proposed. Subsequent to his stay at Oberlin College, he said, he plans to spend approximately 2 months living in a friend's house in a suburb of San Francisco.

BECKER was of the opinion that the outbound trip to the USA would be approved without any difficulties because the state-run agencies wanted nothing more at the moment than to be rid of him for a long time.

MARITAL PROBLEMS CAUSE BRIEF SETBACK

During the second week of my stay in East Berlin, two letters from my wife who was still in Oberlin arrived at the US Embassy. She informed me that she had rented an apartment in the nearby city of Lorain, would be moving out of our house and taking half of our furniture and other belongings with her. Although we had been experiencing marital problems for around two years, as I recall, this news took me very much by surprise and—as the saying goes—threw me for a loop. I wanted to return to Oberlin, but my wife urged me not to do that. I decided to stay in the GDR, press forward with my project to the best of my ability, and make the best of a situation that was very distressing. I lost momentum for a couple of weeks, but somehow managed to accomplish most of what needed to be done during the remainder of my stay.

SECOND REPORT FROM IM "DÖLBL": DECEMBER 1, 1977

The next report on me, containing information from Anneliese Löffler, is nine pages long, single-spaced. There are two sections: 1) a three-page preamble labelled "Report" that appears to have been written by her Stasi-handler,

Captain Joachim Tischendorf, who specialized in cultural issues, and 2) a six-page report entitled "Prof. Zipser's Project," which appears to have been composed and typed by Löffler. A cover page bears the following heading:

Main Department XX/7   Berlin, 12/1/77

Collaborator/Source:
Captain Tischendorf / "Dölbl"

And there is a notation indicating that the source of the information has been checked ("überprüft") and is reliable ("zuverlässig"). Below are the two documents:

R e p o r t

In accordance with the assignment that was given, IM "Dölbl" had arranged a get-together on 11/28/1977 with USA citizen Dr. Richard ZIPSER, who is currently residing in the GDR. In the course of this meeting the unofficial collaborator was able to gather a considerable amount of information about the content, goal, and political aspects of ZIPSER's book on GDR literature. The attached report, which the unofficial collaborator prepared, summarizes this information.

The unofficial collaborator pointed out the politically explosive effect that would result from the publication of ZIPSER's book, which now comprises around 800 pages in manuscript form. This explosiveness stems from the fact that the answers of the 38 GDR writers ZIPSER interviewed, to each individual question the unofficial collaborator cited in the report, are reproduced one after another without the name of the respondent being mentioned again. Hence, by way of example the answers from KUNZE could appear beside those of Günter GÖRLICH or Hermann KANT. [*Reiner Kunze was a dissident writer who at the time of the interview was not permitted to publish in the GDR. Günter Görlich and Hermann Kant were writers loyal to the SED Party.*]

Even more dangerous, in the unofficial collaborator's opinion, is the fact that—aside from a few exceptions—the answers give voice to a collection of alleged conflicts, unresolved problems and difficulties in the GDR, especially in the development of literature, which in their totality present a completely distorted picture of the Party and State cultural policy.

In addition, the unofficial collaborator pointed out difficulties in gaining access to ZIPSER's manuscript on the basis of the exchange agreement, since there is in fact no provision requiring ZIPSER to allow perusal of the manuscript.

The basis for ZIPSER's recurring stay in the GDR is an existing agreement between the GDR and the USA, within the scope of the UNESCO Organization IREX, regarding the exchange of scholars. [*UNESCO is the United Nations Educational, Scientific and Cultural Organization.*] The Ministry of Higher Education is responsible for ZIPSER's support and care and the regulation of all organizational aspects of his residence in the GDR. ZIPSER's intention to write a book on GDR literature is set forth in the existing related contract with him.

The unofficial collaborator was able to find out from ZIPSER that

> W a r d e t z k y, Jutta
> Research Associate at the
> Academy of Arts

who is known to have a connection to Sarah KIRSCH, is carrying out a portion of the organizational tasks for ZIPSER (clerical work, among other things) without any authorization to do so from the State. [*I did not receive any assistance from Jutta Wardetzky and have no idea how Löffler arrived at this conclusion.*]

The unofficial collaborator was instructed to communicate the established facts as regards ZIPSER's project at the next executive board meeting of the Berlin Writers' Union, making reference to the political consequences that would follow the publication of his book, in order to precipitate a discussion among the positive forces participating in ZIPSER's project, the goal of which is to demand access to ZIPSER's complete manuscript. The further participation of these authors in ZIPSER's book project should be made contingent on that. Furthermore, measures to prevent the publication of this book with its present hostile bias should be initiated. [*The GDR Writers' Union had insisted that I include in my book some writers known to be party loyalists; these are the "positive forces" Tischendorf refers to above. If those writers had withdrawn from the project, my book would have lacked balance and presented a more negative and potentially damaging portrayal of the GDR state and its cultural policy. Only one writer—Siegfried Pitschmann—withdrew from the project after agreeing to participate, and I do not think the Writers' Union officials encouraged him or any other authors to do so.*]

In addition, the unofficial collaborator was instructed to review the existing contract IREX and the Ministry of Higher Education have with ZIPSER, to see if legal grounds for gaining access to the complete manuscript might be worked out.

Prof. Zipser's Project

1. Zipser began his work in 1975. According to his own statements, the following induced him to undertake his current project:

a.) the need, in the interest of his own professional reputation, to begin working on a new and extremely appealing project;

b.) the intellectual stimulation resulting from a stay in the GDR that he carried out while residing in Austria;

c.) the advice he received from Gerhard Wolf, who spent half of a semester in Oberlin (USA) with his wife Christa Wolf. Reportedly, the format of the planned book is for the most part his idea.

2. In 1975 he held preliminary discussions with Comrade Scheibner from the Writers' Union. He gave him a list of writers' names he had prepared with Gerhard Wolf, which Scheibner supplemented. Zipser is not prepared to say who was on the list prior to that and who was added later on. His response: "Oh, you know, that has changed so many times." I know that the names of 38 authors are now on the list. I was able to identify the following: Jurek Becker, Uwe Berger, Volker Braun, Juri [*sic*] Brězan, Günter de Bruyn, Adolf Endler, Elke Erb, Karl-Heinz Jakobs, Fritz L. [*sic*] Fries, Franz Fühmann, Günter Görlich, Peter Hacks, Bernd Jentzsch, Benno Pludra, Rainer Kirsch, Sarah Kirsch, Rainer [*sic*] Kunze, Heiner Müller, Rolf Schneider, Paul Wiens, Irmtraud Morgner, Karl Mickel, Stefan Hermlin, Stefan Heym, Eberhard Panitz, Klaus Schlesinger, Martin Stade, Ulrich Plenzdorf, Günter Kunert, Hermann Kant, Christa Wolf, Gerhard Wolf, Uwe Kant. As Zipser said, he would also have placed importance on the opinion of Anna Seghers and Erwin Strittmatter, but both have been unwilling to provide him with information. When asked about the reason for this selection,

he said that he had picked those authors who played a role in literary proceedings after 1970 (the first draft of his proposal stated: authors who attained prominence after 1960!). When I said to him that subsequently completely different names had come under discussion, he narrowed the focus to the period after 1970.

3. The format of his book looks like this:

a.) introduction by Zipser on the development of literary activity in the GDR over the past 15 years, i.e., since the beginning of the 1960s;

b.) biographical sketches of writers which for the most part are drawn from relevant reference works;

c.) brief personal statements about writing, focusing on the questions: What goals have you set for your artistic work and do think you can achieve them?

d.) the statements that were provided through the interviews and, to be specific, presented in this format: At the beginning of each set of questions the names of the authors who responded to that question appear and then comes a series of answers (without the names being cited again). It is not possible to discern who has given which answer to a particular question. Since the answers remain anonymous in each sequence, basically only someone who knows the authors can figure it out. [*It seems that Löffler misunderstood what I had told her. In the volume containing the interviews, each author's name always appears before his/her answer to a given question.*]

e.) a literary text of approximately 10 to 15 pages in length for each author appearing in the book;

f.) Zipser's commentary on these texts, the main purpose of which—according to him—is to clarify for the reader unfamiliar information and connections in the content of these works.

4. The questions for the authors are of a social nature. Just in case they are not known, I am listing them below. [*A list of the interview questions follows*].

5. Upon his arrival Zipser explained that he had completed the most important preliminary work, especially on the interviews, back in 1975 and 1976. His main concern now is to have the writers authorize the interviews. I asked if I could take a look at the manuscripts; at first he said he didn't have them with him. When I pointed out that this could not be possible because ultimately one cannot secure permissions to publish without the manuscripts, he referred to the incomplete state of the project and the possibility of viewing it at a later point in time.

6. Zipser stated emphatically that he is focusing for the most part on texts written in 1975 [*actually, between 1971 and 1976, the first five years of the Honecker era*]. He claims that the authors presently have a completely different attitude toward the texts they wrote during the earlier 1970s, as a result of the events that occurred in November 1976. [*This is a reference to the expatriation of dissident writer/singer Wolf Biermann that precipitated massive protests on the part of GDR writers and artists.*] Prior to that a very optimistic mood still prevailed, Zipser says, but now he senses that just the opposite is the case. Many writers have expressed a desire to give him new written material for his book. He says he urged the writers to allow him to use the texts from the earlier 1970s, because their significance as part of a historical document would otherwise be lost. When asked which authors he had interviewed most recently, he replied: Christa Wolf, Volker Braun, Heiner Müller,

and Peter Hacks. Moreover, all four agreed to give answers based on statements that reflect the perspective they had in 1975, so they would not stand out in contrast to the others. When asked why the authors were viewing everything differently today, he replied: after the 8th Party Congress [*June 1971*) a new cultural policy and a new freedom for the arts came into being; however, this freedom was curtailed at the 9th Party Congress [*May 1976*] and in the past year it was eliminated completely.

7. Issues Related to Zipser's Stance:

   a.) His stance on GDR literature stems from his close friendship with Christa Wolf and Ulrich Plenzdorf, who both (Christa Wolf with her husband) spent a half year in Oberlin. Plenzdorf and Becker (who is going to Oberlin next year) have for the most part smoothed the way for him here. A woman who works in the Academy of Arts, a friend of Sarah Kirsch, has been carrying out organizational tasks for him.

   b.) Zipser emphasizes his friendly attitude toward GDR literature and his indifferent attitude toward the GDR in general. He says that a project like the one he is doing could not have originated in the FRG (West Germany) because there ideological reservations would come to the fore. With him, he asserts, everything is being organized without prejudice; as a result, his book will be genuine publicity for GDR literature. Besides, so he says, he can proceed in an uninfluenced manner because—although he has in fact been interested in GDR literature for a long time—he had not been fully cognizant of how many works and authors this literature has to offer.

c.) Zipser pretends to be remarkably naïve and reticent; he gives the impression that with him it is all about a friendly scholar who comes to a foreign country without any preconceived notions and observes with wide-eyed amazement everything that is going on there. Here is what seems questionable to me:

his in-depth knowledge of GDR literature and the completion of a project that one individual <u>cannot</u> possibly complete without assistance;

the possibility of receiving free time and money, over and above what is legitimately due him, which actually guarantees that he can accomplish his work. He always downplays this question, i.e., the question about the value of his project for the government agencies in the USA or even for the general public. He says he cannot expect success in the public sphere or even public recognition, since no more than 1,500 copies of his book will be printed and these are certain to be purchased by libraries only. However, this information actually makes the <u>extraordinary</u> sponsorship even more questionable. Basically, what remains is merely the still unanswered question about the significance of his project for the GDR, which is becoming increasingly serious.

d.) Zipser maintains that the length of his stay is barely sufficient for the completion of his work. Hence, he needs to concentrate entirely on his work with the writers and is unable to be involved with the university. He is indeed very interested in this activity (i.e., active involvement with the university), but he has to put every available minute into completing his project. In response to the objection that he is after all a guest of the university, he said the following: yes, but as stipulated in the agreement, for the purpose of completing a project the university knew about and the goals of which were presented ahead of time. This also conforms to the terms of the IREX agreement. University staff members would also not be able to help him because basically everything has already been set in motion and now only needs to be completed. What remains to be done is a question of organization and mutual understanding with the writers as regards the manuscripts. His <u>own</u> foreword has not yet been completed; he has not yet begun working on it, but plans to write it in January and then will gladly consult with me in May. His initial avowed desire to participate in seminars and possibly some lectures at the university also cannot be put into practice, since he was confronted with problems related to his divorce during the first weeks of his residence here. On October 26 he received two letters (from his wife) which suddenly put him in this situation and really threw him for a loop; as a result he was also unable to work. Things will be different next year, he says, since he will establish close contact with the university.

e.) Informal meetings with students:

Zipser has had two informal meetings with students from the group of degree candidates in their fourth year of study. The participants were: Gregor Edelmann, his wife, Tatjana Rese, Doris Stauffenberg, Andre Baulgart, and some other students who were present only at the first gathering. According to the students' statements, the conversations were concerned with the following topics:

His most recent problems with GDR writers which he generally just called "problems," without making any distinctions. He expressed annoyance with the GDR writers a number of times, because of all the difficulties they were causing him due to their unreliability.

The bureaucracy of GDR agencies, especially the International Office at the Humboldt University and the Ministry of Higher Education.

Ways of life in the GDR, housing and living conditions, opportunities for higher education, types of jobs at the university level, etc.

The next section of the report focuses on a presentation I gave on November 28, 1977, at Löffler's insistence, to a small group of German literature professors from her department at the Humboldt University. Since I had been avoiding Löffler during my two-month stay, and since I had not accepted any of her invitations to visit with her at her weekend cottage in the country, I felt I had to comply with this request. The problem I faced was how to give detailed information on my project, including an interesting sample of the interview material, without revealing too much.

My talk amounted to a report on the nature and goal of my book project combined with some information I had gathered through interviews with GDR writers to be represented in it. To give an example, I distributed a sheet to everyone present with sixteen answers to one of the questions I had asked GDR writers: "Which contemporary social problems are of the greatest concern to you as a writer?" I listed the authors who had responded in alphabetical order, without linking any one of them to a specific answer; the answers to the question were listed randomly. The Germanists in the room, all of whom were conversant with contemporary GDR literature, were invited to match the names of authors to answers, which of course no one would be able to do. Löffler was not amused by my impish game and, when we were alone following my presentation, she proceeded to scold me. I was delighted to read her lengthy report on this gathering of professors.

8. Meeting at the German Studies Department of the Humboldt University. Participants: Prof. Löffler, Prof. Eva Kaufmann, Dr. Hörnigk, Dr. Karin Kögel, Dr. Brigitte Stuhlmacher.

I had asked Mr. Zipser to present his project in as much detail as possible, and asked my colleagues to ask as many questions as possible about the project.

The Outcome:

a) Presentation by Zipser which did not divulge more than has been stated in sections 1 to 4 of this report.

b) The presentation and reading of answers to the question cited in section 4 b). [*Which contemporary social problems are of the greatest concern to you as a writer?*]

And here is where the problem with this book begins: only two of the answers went into social progress in the GDR, and they came across—whether as a result of editing or due to inadequate ability on the part of the respondents—as exceptionally banal and vacuous. All of the other answers delved into 'hot' problems and conflicts: questions of power—i.e., how does power manifest itself for the individual person, questions of democracy, the achievement principle, young people's problems, problems in general education, the dubiousness of societal advancement, if at all. Aside from a few answers, I can easily imagine that to an individual author an individual answer might not seem very problematic—and probably in isolation it also is not. In the aggregate, however, the compendium must come across as a unique collection of concerns which right now, on top of that, are not voiced and discussed in the GDR. I asked him afterwards what the answers look like in the other sets of questions. He gave a vague answer, but I could definitely tell that it will for the most part be even more problematic; for example, in the section on trivial literature where—so he told me—the entire body of literature published by the Military Press is designated as trivial. Probably the authors had a false conception of trivial literature, he says, and he will make some changes there.

In any case: if this conglomeration of answers—even if presented in an anonymous format—were made public here in <u>our</u> country, this would <u>have</u> to have the effect of a major blow, objectively speaking, since people would immediately say: that is what our writers are saying about the realities of the GDR when they are allowed to express themselves 'freely', and that is what they said in 1975, so what would they have to say <u>today</u>?

Furthermore, the situation is such that we are certainly going to be surprised by the outcome in its entirety, since no one will see the manuscript as a whole prior to its publication. There is no way for us to compel him to hand it over. I have requested that he do so many times; each time he pointed to the incomplete state of the project and to the fact that every text will have been written and authorized by an author residing in the GDR, so therefore any misgivings are totally out of place, and he would show me his foreword in May of next year. Apart from that he says his book will definintely promote the cause of GDR literature; any excessively glowing presentation would only be in conflict with this goal.

c) The entire meeting did not proceed in the way it potentially might have gone. In order to clarify this disclosure, I would like to quote an opinion expressed by Dr. Hörnigk, who on the evening of the day our meeting took place (11/28/77) told me this: He and Eva Kaufmann had left the room on the pretext that they had an appointment with the department head, because they perceived themselves as incapable of questioning a man who was doing a project that actually we should be doing but would not be permitted to do.

The question-and-answer game proceeded in a corresponding manner. Zipser explained the nature and purpose of his undertaking, adding to the already mentioned reasons for it that GDR scholars were after all not always able to write what they want. Also approvingly received was his opinion that GDR literature, as a result of its strong social ties to the reality of the GDR, has decidedly provincial traits. When I asked him what his conception actually was of worldliness and world literature, he pointed to Christa Wolf and her novel *Nachdenken über Christa T. (The Quest for Christa T., 1968)*, and Frank Hörnigk then commented that Heiner Müller was an author pursuing worldwide prominence, also right now an author of international importance.

In addition, he was asked about how he was going to handle Bernd Jentzsch, Sarah Kirsch, and Reiner Kunze. [*These three disaffected authors had recently resettled in the West. Earlier in 1977, Kirsch had been granted an exit visa and was living in West Berlin. The GDR regime had expatriated Kunze in April of that year, whereupon he moved to West Germany (Bavaria). Jentzsch, who had become involved in the furor surrounding the expatriation of dissident writer/singer Wolf Biermann in 1976, decided not to return from a trip to Switzerland so as to avoid imprisonment.*] In response he said that he could not eliminate them; after all, vis-à-vis all the other authors who wanted to revise their texts under the shadow of the current situation, he would react by referring to the historical importance and authenticity of their texts from the year 1975. But that would also mean that he would have to treat all the authors who were living in this country at that time as GDR authors.

There was further discussion about the view that the 8th Party Congress ushered in a new cultural policy. Many authors were indeed of this opinion, Zipser said, but ultimately they were not right. As a result the insistent reference to continuity of cultural policy through the 9th Party Congress has been combined with a process of disillusionment for most of the authors. The emphasis was on the relationship of cultural policy and the development of the arts after 1961, together with all of the contradictions and conflicts.

Following this detailed recounting of the question-and-answer period, Löffler concludes her report. Her frustration and anger are evident:

> Afterwards, in a private conversation between Zipser and me, I urged him strongly to take seriously the collaboration with the partner institution that under the terms of the contract is making his residence in the GDR possible. He asked once again for my understanding of his precarious situation, claiming that he was at his wit's end as a result of his divorce and would barely be able to complete the most essential tasks during the time remaining to him. He likewise made reference to the difficulty of working with the authors, but seemed surprised when I asked him what difficulties he had apart from that.

FIFTH REPORT FROM IMV "KURT": DECEMBER 2, 1977

On December 2, IMV "Kurt" submitted another tape-recorded report on my activities and contacts to his Stasi-handler. The transcript of the report, which was added to my file on December 3, appears below.

Main Department XX/Operative Group   Berlin, 12/3/1977

Pa/Ha

Tape-recorded report

Source: IMV "Kurt" on 12/2/1977

Received: First Lieutenant Paulitz

ZIPSER, Dick, USA Citizen

ZIPSER has been staying in Berlin again, since around the middle of October. Within the context of official contacts between his college in Oberlin (USA, State of Ohio) and the Humboldt University in Berlin, Department of Literary Studies, ZIPSER is spending 3 months in the GDR's capital city for academic purposes. ZIPSER is being taken care of directly by the department of the Humboldt University mentioned above. He has a female contact person (doctor, name unknown), who is said to be a member of the Department of Literary Studies.

During his stay he is living in a high-rise apartment building on Volkradstrasse, close to the Berlin-Friedrichsfelde Passageway. In this apartment house ZIPSER got to know a Chilean (first name Carlos), who is a doctoral candidate at the Advanced School of Economics "Bruno Leuschner." As ZIPSER explained to me, while here he is receiving a high stipend in GDR currency [*East German marks, see below*] from the Humboldt University. He stressed that he had in his possession a considerable amount of our currency and therefore was being careful about spending his Western currency [*West German marks and US dollars*], which he could put to better use elsewhere. Also, he didn't want to support the "Intershop business" [*see below*] in the GDR, since he disapproves of it.

[**The East German mark (M)** *was officially valued by the East German government at parity with the West German mark (DM). However, because it was not readily convertible and because the GDR's export market was restricted, it was practically worthless outside East Germany. On the black market the exchange rate was about 5 to 10 M for 1 DM. In the 1970s and 1980s, one could easily visit foreign currency exchange offices in West Berlin or Vienna and purchase East German banknotes at the rate of approximately 8 (East) for 1 (West). However, the GDR forbade the import or export of GDR currency into or out of the GDR. Penalties for violating this law ranged from confiscation of smuggled currency to imprisonment. The East German mark could not be spent in Intershops to acquire Western consumer goods; only "hard currencies" such as West German marks and US dollars were accepted. The only legal ways for East Germans to acquire hard currency were as gifts from relatives living in the West or from wages earned for work in Western countries.*]

[**Intershop** *was a chain of government-run retail stores in the GDR, in which only hard currencies could be used to purchase high-quality goods that had for the most part been imported from Western countries. The East German mark was not accepted as payment. Intershop was originally oriented toward visitors from Western countries; it later became an outlet where East Germans could purchase goods they could not otherwise obtain. The selection included food, alcohol, tobacco, brand-name clothing, toys, jewelry, cosmetics, watches, technical devices, musical recordings, appliances, and even Western-made automobiles, such as Volkswagen and Volvo. With the arrival of the first Interhotels, which were intended to house Western tourists, Intershops began appearing in these Western-oriented hotels, the most upscale of which also had fancy restaurants that accepted payment in hard currencies only. Many East Germans came to view the Intershops as a key driver of inequality in the GDR.*]

His activity here is focused on the completion of his project on GDR literature, for which purpose he has already visited the GDR a number of times. He is polishing up the interviews with GDR writers as regards the content of their statements and is translating them. According to his own account, the Humboldt University Berlin has provided him with secretarial assistance to facilitate this.

He revealed additionally that he sees no value in being under direct supervision all the time, since he would prefer to do some things on his own now and then.

Among his closest contact persons are

Klaus SCHLESINGER

Ulrich PLENZDORF

in part   Martin STADE (at present abroad)

Jurek BECKER

with whom he has been invited to dine several times, as well as the female persons who were already mentioned earlier

Christa (GDR television) and

Evelyn OPOCZYNSKI
(maiden name, now married)

For the purposes of his stay in the capital city of the GDR, ZIPSER is using an automobile with a West Berlin license plate, which Mr. Hellfried KELLNER (further personal information known) purchased. The vehicle is registered to K.'s wife, Brigitte

KELLNER. Once a week or so he drives this vehicle over to West Berlin, where he visits a female person (name unknown) and stays overnight as a rule with the KELLNERs.

Zipser declared that he actually no longer wants to continue working on his project, but having invested so much time in it, he now has to bring this difficult undertaking to completion. He hopes to publish his book in 1978.

[*At this point in time, my enormous undertaking had truly begun to overwhelm me. I realized that I would need to find a colleague in the United States who would be willing to step in and help me finish the project. Löffler was right when she asserted that the project was too big for one person to carry out by himself.*]

Concentrated work on the book is also limited as a consequence of a letter he received about 4 weeks ago from his wife, in which she informed him that she is getting a divorce.

In addition, I learned that GDR writer Jurek BECKER, in response to an invitation from Oberlin College, is planning a trip to the USA.

In the evening hours of 12/2/1977 there will be a celebration in the Artclub "Möwe" (birthday party for Ingrid STRASSENBERGER—personal information known), to which the following persons have been invited:

> STRASSENBERGER family
> Ulrich PLENZDORF
> Hellfried KELLNER, West Berlin
>
> Brigitte KELLNER, West Berlin
> ZIPSER, Dick and feminine person
> Stefan SCHNITZLER and wife.

[*How did IMV "Kurt" know who would be coming to Ingrid Strassenberger's birthday celebration? Dirk Strassenberger, Ingrid's husband, would surely have known who was on the guest list. Is it possible that he was IMV "Kurt" and she IMV "Julia?"*]

signed: "Kurt"

F.d.R. Paulitz, First Lieutenant [*with signature*]

SIXTH REPORT FROM IMV "KURT": DECEMBER 9, 1977

I discover, to my surprise, that the next report in my file is also from IMV "Kurt." Since this report provides some information about aspects of my book project, and since it was submitted just one week after his previous report, I surmise that "Kurt" had been asked to find out as much as possible about the content of my manuscript and interviews with writers before my mid-December departure. This would have been a logical next step, since—as IM "Dölbl" indicated in her report dated December 1—she had been unable to gain access to portions of the manuscript or extract any useful information from me. The transcript of "Kurt's" tape recorded report appears below. Be sure not to overlook the reference to his December 2 report and Ingrid Strassenberger's birthday gathering in the private Artclub "Möwe".

Main Department XX/Operative Group   Berlin, 12/13/1977

Ha/Pa

<u>Tape-recorded report</u>

<u>Source:</u>   IMV "Kurt"

<u>Received:First</u>   Lieutenant Paulitz on 12/9/1977

<u>ZIPSER, Dick USA Citizen</u>

The book project, which according to ZIPSER is going to be finished in 1978, can be traced back to a private initiative on ZIPSER's part. In its present state, enough work has been completed to warrant the award of a stipend for a three-month stay in the GDR; because of this, he has been residing here since September [*actually, since October*].

The book will consist of:

short stories and/or excerpts from narratives or books by the individual authors.

commentaries which he has prepared on the writers in question.

interviews which he has conducted with each individual author.

According to him, this will make it possible for the interested reader to acquire a multifaceted picture of the writer's personality as well as of his or her literary activity.

The above-mentioned texts may either be published or unpublished works; that will be left up to each writer.

ZIPSER stated additionally that at least for now he is not going earn anything with this book; rather, he will have to cover the cost of the first edition himself. When that has been sold, his money will be refunded. The primary consideration for him is to become well known in the USA as a specialist for GDR literature.

At the same time, ZIPSER is working on a second project. He has prepared an American textbook edition of U. Plenzdorf's novel

"Die neuen Leiden des jungen W."
[*The New Sufferings of Young W.*, 1973]

which is intended to help advanced students of the German language learn and understand colloquial speech, including slang expressions in German, among other things. This book is going to be published by a USA publishing house in New York (name unknown, but according to ZIPSER a very well-known and large publisher). Meanwhile, he knows that the book has been accepted. In this regard there are connections with the

Hinstorff Publishing House
Rostock

which has granted the USA publisher a license for the printing of this book (the processing of the text based on the content of this book). ZIPSER maintains that he is not going to earn much by doing this; the main thing is that his name will become known, since U. PLENZDORF will appear as author and D. ZIPSER as editor. The USA publisher is also not going to make a financial profit on this; rather, the publisher is seeking to enhance its image.

The rationale behind this is that a USA citizen who is seeking specific literature from the GDR will always know to turn to this particular publisher, which will have created a niche for this special area.

ZIPSER says the Hinstorff Publishing House is the first publisher in the GDR to have a contract with a USA publisher. The project mentioned above is going to benefit Hinstorff most of all in terms of

a.) its publicity in the USA

b.) the financial gains that will result from this contract.

[*Ulrich Plenzdorf's "Die neuen Leiden des jungen W." was first published as a screenplay in "Sinn und Form" (March 1972), the leading literary journal in the GDR. The stage version that followed was performed to full houses in Eastern and Western Europe, and the film version was also a tremendous success in the German-speaking world. Plenzdorf wrote a prose version as well, which was published in East Germany by the Hinstorff Publishing House (1973) and in West Germany by the Suhrkamp Publishing House (1976). By the mid-1970s, mainly as a result of this work's popularity, Plenzdorf had become the most discussed, reviewed, and performed GDR writer since the death of Bertolt Brecht in 1956.*

Plenzdorf, accompanied by his wife Helga, spent April and May 1975 at Oberlin College where he was Max Kade German Writer-in-Residence. The Plenzdorfs lived and took their meals in a dormitory, along with the students. During his stay in Oberlin, Plenzdorf visited German language and literature classes on all levels and participated actively in my Intermediate German course, where he discovered how passionately involved American students had become in "Die neuen Leiden des jungen W." Upon his return to the GDR, he helped me secure permission from Hinstorff for a textbook edition of his famous work.

I began preparing the textbook edition in the fall of 1976, after returning from my sabbatical leave, and completed work on it during the summer and early fall of 1977. It was published by John Wiley & Sons in 1978 and remained in print for about fifteen years. It was the only work by an East German author to be published in its entirety, in a special textbook edition, in the US.]

As regards the safeguarding of his manuscripts and the written materials he is working on at present, it has not been possible to gather any information up to now.

Always available to Zipser is the opportunity to store materials in West Berlin, for example at the home of the KELLNER family which has already been mentioned several times.

> KELLNER, Hellfried
> [*blacked out*], 42 in Berlin
> 1 Berlin 48, [*blacked out*]
> ID card no. [*blacked out*]
> Issued on [*blacked out*]
> by Police Headquarters of Berlin
> KELLNER, née [*blacked out*], Brigitte
> [*blacked out*] 1949 in Neuwied
> resident: same as above
> [*blacked out*]
> ID card no. [*blacked out*]
> Issued on [*blacked out*]
> Police Headquarters of Berlin

I am aware that ZIPSER has his mail—from the FRG, the USA, and other countries—sent to KELLNERs' address, and he picks it up there when goes to West Berlin.

He hardly ever mentions anything pertaining to the actual content of his conversations with the writers who play a role in his book. When I raise questions about this in conversations, he doesn't always refuse to discuss it or become evasive, but instead usually proceeds to make sweeping generalizations.

ZIPSER had especially positive things to say about

> Jurek BECKER and
> Peter HACKS;

on HACKS, for example, with regard to his exceptional ability as a writer and his quality of life, evidence of which is readily visible in his home. ZIPSER asserts that present-day GDR literature is unable to put forth the name of anyone who would count as a world-class writer. In his opinion, the writers closest to making this claim are

> Christa Wolf – in the area of
> prose writing
> Sarah Kirsch – in the area of poetry

He thinks that the GDR literati focus and concentrate too much on their own country and its problems, and this imparts more than a hint of provincialism to the literature. The problems that are treated are also not apt to stimulate thinking beyond the borders of the GDR, in the way—for example—that Thomas and Heinrich Mann, Brecht and others have done. ZIPSER thinks that GDR literature is completely underprivileged and undervalued in the USA, where there is not a broadly based readership for GDR literature. He hopes to be able to influence that somewhat with his book and the textbook mentioned earlier.

With regard to the gathering in the "Möwe" on 12/02/77, I have the following to relate: all the persons I named in my report of 12/02/77 were present.

The conversations focused above all on ZIPSER's projects, as they have been described by me, and on various matters of personal concern to those present (real estate, automobile, family, etc.), most of the time in dialogues which already are known.

Around the beginning of October I discussed with ZIPSER for the first time the possibility of planning a weekend trip to Hiddensee [a *lovely car-free island in the Baltic Sea*]. He is positively disposed toward this trip and showed strong interest. I said I was prepared to take care of the organizational matters. We agreed on a time in the early summer, when he is back in the GDR or West Berlin. In this connection ZIPSER said that he will consider the month of May, because that will be the conclusion of his residence in the GDR during 1978.

In reference to a farewell party he wants to have before his upcoming departure (departure date Thursday, 12/15/1977), he mentioned this coming Tuesday evening. I am cordially invited, although he cannot say just yet when and where it will be held. He will communicate this information to me by telephone. He was considering the restaurant "Moskau".

The next document in my file is a one-page memorandum dated December 12, 1977, which appears in its entirety below:

Main Department XX   Berlin, 12/12/1977

Memorandum

Prof. Zipser, Richard
born on 1/23/1943 in Maryland
residence 102 Shipherd Circle, Oberlin/Ohio/USA
current residence 1136 Berlin, Volkradstr. 8
Associate Professor at Oberlin College Ohio/USA

Z. is currently residing in the GDR as a guest of the Ministry of Higher Education, due to the establishment of an exchange agreement with the USA under the auspices of the UNESCO Organization IREX. The contract with ZIPSER was first negotiated in 1977. This contract provides for participation in courses as well as discussions with students and faculty members at the Humboldt University of Berlin.

As a sideline, ZIPSER is engaged in completing a book on GDR literature, a project initiated in 1975. It includes interviews with 38 GDR writers conducted on the basis of a questionnaire containing 15 questions.

With this project in mind ZIPSER previously visited and stayed in the GDR, on his own initiative, in September/October 1975 and in June 1976. He secured approval to prepare a book on GDR literature for readers in the USA and to conduct interviews with 38 GDR writers from the GDR Writers' Union, after consultation with the Central Committee's Department of Culture had been carried out. [*Here I learned for the first time that permission for me to carry out my book project and conduct interviews with GDR writers had actually been granted by party officials at the level of the Central Committee of the SED, which was the ultimate authority for cultural-political matters in the GDR.*]

ZIPSER is leaving the GDR on 12/15/77. In May 1978 he intends to return to the GDR for four weeks, in accordance with the existing contract.

FAREWELL DINNER PARTY / FIRST SURVEILLANCE REPORT: DECEMBER 13, 1977

As noted in IMV "Kurt's" last report, I had decided to have a farewell dinner party before returning to Oberlin. The event was held at the new Hotel Metropol, which had an excellent restaurant where I would be able to pay the bill with East German marks. This would be an opportunity to thank and say goodbyc to my GDR writer friends and others who had helped me during my two-month visit. The writers in attendance were Christa and Gerhard Wolf, Ulrich Plenzdorf and his wife Helga, Klaus Schlesinger, and Martin Stade. Willy Moese, a well-known caricature artist was there, as was his wife Maria, a well-known television personality. Also present were Dirk Strassenberger, a lawyer I had gotten to know while living in East Berlin; Helga Schrader, a friend from West Berlin; and Carlos, a Chilean doctoral candidate who was living across the hall from me in the apartment house.

As the file reveals, the Stasi had advance notice of my farewell party and decided to conduct a surveillance operation, beginning at 7:00 p.m. on December 13, and ending shortly after 3:00 a.m. on December 14. This report is supplemented by a long, detailed narrative one of my guests (IMV "Kurt") provided a few days later. When one reads and compares the two reports, it is obvious that the Stasi surveillance team did not know one of my guests was an informant. He has a different alias in their report ("Milan," not "Kurt"), and therefore his identity is protected. All but one of the other guests in the Stasi-report were given ornithological code names— "Blackbird," "Starling," "Titmouse," "Finch," "Raven," "Magpie," "Swallow," and "Siskin," probably so they would not seem out of place at "Eagle's" farewell party. One guest has the code name "Haken" (Hook), which he had been given at an earlier point in time. The event itself is described in considerable detail—from start to finish—in the surveillance report, sections of which I have reproduced below. First comes (A) the approved formal request to conduct the surveillance, which presents the rationale for it, then (B) the surveillance report itself.

(A)

Council of Ministers of the
German Democratic Republic
Ministry for State Security
Registry No. 2395/77
Main Department VIII   Division VIII

Main Department XX/7

Assignment Request – Surveillance

Code name: "Eagle"

[My real name appears beneath the code name, along with my date and place of birth, marital status, home address, profession, etc.]

Goal and Purpose of the Surveillance

The person is to be observed from 8:00 p.m. on 12/13/77 until 3:00 a.m. on 12/14/77.

Where is the surveillance to take place?

> In the Hotel "Metropol" where the person under surveillance is having a get-together with GDR writers on 12/13/77 at 8:00 p.m.

Justification in concrete terms of the necessity and goal of the surveillance that is to be carried out. What specific information is going to be gathered through the surveillance?

> Identification of as yet unknown contacts of the person under surveillance, who are participating in the social event mentioned above.

Assignment request actualized by Main Department VII 3/3.

When: 12/13 -14/77

(B)

VII/3/3   Berlin, December 14, 1977

                                                          Ru/Rei

7352

XX/7

Comrade Gentz

Z i p s e r, Richard   born 01/23/1943

102 Shipherd Circle   Oberlin/Ohio (USA)

"E a g l e"

12/13/1977   from 7 p.m. until 3.05 a.m.

12/14/1977

The target of the search "228507" [Sarah Kirsch] did not show up at the scheduled get-together.

The presumptive rendezvous partners were placed under operative surveillance.

At

7.00 p.m. the surveillance was initiated in the Nationalities Restaurant

                    Hotel "Metropol"
                    Berlin – Mitte [Center]
                    Clara-Zetkin-Strasse

7:52 p.m.   a younger male person, who is being given the code name "Eagle," entered the restaurant, looked around, and then left the premises.

7:55 p.m.   "Eagle," three male persons and two female persons entered the restaurant and seated themselves at a table that was set for 12 persons. One of the male persons was identified as the contact known as "Hook." The remaining persons were given the code names "Finch," "Titmouse," "Siskin," and "Swallow." After everyone was seated at the table, "Hook" directed the serving staff to reconfigure the seating arrangement so as to make it smaller. The servers objected to this because everyone would then be sitting too close to one another. After that they all agreed to remove two tables from the seating arrangement and place the chairs so that 4 persons would be sitting on each of the longer sides and 2 persons on each of the shorter sides. The attendees each ordered an aperitif of their own choosing. Then they began to converse interactively, but in hushed voices.

8:05 p.m.   a female and a male person came to the table. They were given the code names "Blackbird" and "Starling." As they greeted the other attendees, these persons stood up, returned the greetings by shaking hands and in some cases bowing. After that they sat down, also ordered an aperitif and took part in the conversation. The conversation had a superficial nature, since it was carried out in muted voices as all persons conversed with one another. Small conversation groups formed and the conversations took place in very low voices.

8:09 p.m. a male and a female person came to the table. They were given the code names "Raven" and "Magpie." They greeted all the other attendees, who however all remained seated this time, with handshakes. Both of them then sat down, ordered an aperitif and also joined in the conversation.

8:13 p.m. a male person wearing an overcoat and holding a briefcase, who is being given the code name "Milan," came to the table; he greeted everyone briefly by nodding his head and then left the restaurant. After about a minute, Milan reentered the restaurant and sat down at the table. He had stored his coat and briefcase outside. During their stay in the restaurant the conversations were mainly between "Siskin" and "Milan," "Eagle" and "Blackbird," "Finch" and "Titmouse" and "Starling" as well as "Swallow," "Raven" and "Magpie." "Hook" sat there impassively much of the time or joined in the conversation that "Finch," "Titmouse" and "Starling" were having. Everyone ate saddle of veal, which was served from the whole roast, a portion of whipped cream, and drank white wine. From

10:00 p.m. until everyone left the hotel the attendees were no longer being monitored.

11:55 p.m. "Eagle" and [blacked out] left the hotel, walked until they were alongside Café "Metropol," where they stopped, chatted and kissed.

12:00 midnight "Eagle" bid farewell to "Swallow" with a kiss and then returned to the hotel. "Swallow" walked quickly along Friedrichstrasse to the Friedrichstrasse Railway Station and asked something at the rapid transit ticket counters. After that the person on duty at the counter window pointed immediately in the direction of the departure pavilion. "Swallow" walked through the station concourse, searching, and subsequently made her way to the departure pavilion.

12:07 a.m. "Swallow" passed through the Friedrichstrasse border checkpoint and was consigned to Main Department VI for document control.

12:05 a.m. the rest of the persons in the group left the hotel and stood in front of the hotel's main entrance until departing at

12:06 a.m. after a brief conversation "Blackbird," "Starling," "Finch," "Titmouse," "Siskin," and "Hook" said goodnight to "Eagle," "Milan," "Magpie," and "Raven" and were not monitored further.

The last four persons mentioned proceeded directly to Hotel "Unter den Linden" and at

12:15 a.m. entered the lobby bar of the hotel which, however, at this time was filled to capacity. After they had looked around for a short while, they left the hotel and slowly made their way via Unter den Linden and Otto Grotewohl-Strasse to Hermann-Matern-Strasse. On the way, "Eagle" and "Magpie" as well as "Milan" and "Raven" always walked together in pairs and engaged in conversation.

12:34 a.m. the four persons who were to be observed entered the artclub

"Möwe"
Hermann-Matern-Strasse

and were not under surveillance there.

2:35 a.m. "Milan", "Eagle", "Raven", und "Magpie" left the club and climbed into a waiting taxi of the

Make: Wolga
Color: gray
License plate no.: IAT 3 – 16.

The taxi drove these persons to Volkradstrasse, via the most direct route: Unter den Linden, Karl-Marx-Allee, Lichtenberger Bridge, Einbecker-Strasse.

2:50 a.m. "Milan" und "Eagle" climbed out of the taxi and walked, while conversing, to the well-known point of contact

Volkradstrasse No. 8
Berlin – Lichtenberg.

On the way there, "Milan" was overheard commenting to "Eagle" in broken German:

"... Christa was very reticent..."

In addition, one of these persons was overheard saying:

"... I am glad that you included me ..."

3:10 a.m. the surveillance of "Milan" and "Eagle" at the well-known point of contact was terminated.

The taxi drove "Raven" und "Magpie" to Adolfstrasse in Biesdorf via Massower Strasse, the most direct route.

3:05 a.m. both of them entered the well-known point of contact

Adolfstrasse No. 13
Berlin – Lichtenberg

and the surveillance of "Raven" und "Magpie" was terminated.

Descriptions of Persons

"S w a l l o w"

According to information from Main Department VI, identical to:

Last name:	Schrader
First name:	Helga
Born on:	[blacked out] 1945 in Venusberg
Residence:	Hamburg
Passport-No.:	[blacked out]

Age:	ca. 28 years old
Height:	ca. 1.65 meters
Build:	slender
Hair:	light blond, tinted, short, curly
Eyes:	light in color, light blond eyebrows
Clothing:	brown shoes, salt and pepper pants, ¾-length calfskin jacket (brown-white)

"E a g l e" male

Age:	ca. 23 – 28 years old
Height:	ca. 1.75 meters
Build:	slim
Hair:	blond, parted on left side, full, neck-length
Beard:	mustache
Face:	full
Clothing:	light brown sport jacket, brown pants, ¾-length overcoat (brown, woven fabric), white scarf
Accessory items:	light-colored shoulder bag, plastic bag

"M i l a n" male

Age:	ca. 30 – 35 years old
Height:	ca. 1.75 meters
Build:	slim
Face:	oval, haggard, sunken cheeks
Beard:	combination mustache and goatee
Nose:	bridge of nose bent outward, base dips downward, conspicuously large
Hair:	light brown, full, neck-length, groomed
Clothing:	dark brown overcoat, dark blue suit, light blue shirt, dark blue necktie, black shoes
Accessory item:	black executive briefcase

"Blackbird"	female	identical to [blacked out]
"Starling"	male	identical to [blacked out]
"Titmouse"	female	identical to [blacked out]
"Finch"	male	identical to [blacked out]
"Hook"	male	identical to [blacked out]
"Raven"	male	identical to [blacked out]
"Magpie"	female	identical to [blacked out]
"Siskin"	male	identical to [blacked out]

Head of the Department
[signed]
Bestier
Lieutenant Colonel

FIRST REPORT ON FAREWELL DINNER PARTY BY IMV "KURT"

The file contains two more reports on my farewell dinner party, both of which provide some interesting additional information. The first of these, which is dated December 14, 1977, appears in its entirety below. The information in it was provided by IMV "Kurt," who was a guest at the dinner party. The absence of prominent dissident poet/prose writer Sarah Kirsch, who had moved to West Berlin earlier in 1977 and who had accepted my invitation to attend the party, is noted. A memorandum attached to the report indicates that it was prepared by Captain Hans Schiller, Main Department XX/7.

Main Department XX   Berlin, 12/14/1977

Information

about USA citizen ZIPSER's get-together with GDR writers on 12/13/1977 in the capital city of the GDR.

The gathering took place on 12/13/1977, from 8:00 p.m. to 12:00 midnight, in the specialty restaurant of the Hotel "Metropol." The attendees were:

Zipser, Richard	--USA citizen, associate professor at Oberlin College in the state of Ohio, USA, residing at present in the GDR
Wolf, Christa	--writer
Wolf, Gerhard	--writer
Plenzdorf, Ulrich	--writer
and his wife	
Stade, Martin	--writer
Moese, Willi	--caricaturist
Moese, Maria	--television announcer

as well as a male and a female person who have not yet been identified. [*The unidentified persons are Helga Schrader, my guest from West Berlin, and Carlos, the Chilean doctoral candidate who lived in my apartment house. But for some reason IMV "Kurt" does not list two other guests: Klaus Schlesinger, the writer, and Dirk Strassenberger.*]

Sarah KIRSCH, who left and moved to West Berlin, had also been invited to this get-together. She had originally indicated that she was coming, but then did not participate. She did not reenter the capital city of the GDR.

As regards this subject, the following was learned unofficially:

At the beginning of the gathering, ZIPSER pointed out that before returning to the USA he wanted to get together with those friends to whom he owed the most and thank them for their support during his residence in the GDR.

He says the manuscript of his forthcoming book on GDR literature is finished, apart from the foreword he still needs to write, and he expects to receive the galley proofs by the end of 1978.

In this connection, ZIPSER made known his intention to also offer the book he is preparing to a publishing house in the GDR for possible publication when the galley proofs are available.

Gerhard WOLF recommended the publisher Buchverlag "Der Morgen" for this purpose.

ZIPSER mentioned that the head of Suhrkamp Publishing Company in the FRG, [*Siegfried*] Unseld, had already expressed interest in his project on GDR literature.

The attendees approved of ZIPSER's plan to publish his book in the GDR. PLENZDORF, SCHLESINGER and STADE expressed doubts about this manuscript being accepted by a GDR publishing house.

Moreover, it was learned that ZIPSER is intending to include an interview with Erich ARENDT in his book. However, since is leaving the GDR on 12/15/1977 and no longer able to meet personally with ARENDT, he plans to have ARENDT's written answers sent to him in the USA.

In this context, ZIPSER expressed thanks for the support of Gerhard WOLF, who on short notice still was able to put him in contact with ARENDT.

ZIPSER mentioned additionally that he had visited Stefan HEYM last Sunday.

During the remaining portion of the get-together more and more one-on-one conversations among the attendees came about. Topics of conversation at this juncture were Oberlin College, where ZIPSER is employed and about which he made insignificant remarks, Italian architecture about which STADE commented in connection with his recent trip to Italy and passed around a picture with a statue.

It was noticeable that Maria MOESE conversed very intensively with the person not yet identified and Willi MOESE carried on animated conversations with ZIPSER.

SCHLESINGER was relatively isolated. For the most part he did not participate in the conversations and only now and then exchanged a few words with PLENZDORF.

At 12:00 midnight the get-together concluded. The participants said their farewells in front of the Hotel "Metropol" and set off separately for home.

SECOND REPORT ON FAREWELL DINNER PARTY BY IMV "KURT"

Department XV   Magdeburg, 12/16/1977

Control no.:   10/77
Serial no.:   10
Case no.:   XV/3677/74

Distribution list:

1. Ex.:   Main Directorate Dept. IX

2. Ex.:   Main Directorate Dept. XI

3. Ex.:   Main Department XX

Information

Dr. Richard Z i p s e r
(Follow-up information to Control no. 9/77,
Serial no. 9 from 12/6/77)

On 12/13/1977 Dr. Zipser invited the source to participate in
a party he was having at 8:00 p.m. that day. He was inviting a
number of good friends who had frequently invited him, in
order to reciprocate. When the source asked him who would
be there, he only said that Schlesinger is coming, among others,
and that there would be a total of 12 persons.

The party will take place in the Hotel "Metropol."

At approximately 8:15 p.m. the source arrived at the restaurant
in the Hotel "Metropol," where everyone was already seated at
the table in the alcove. In attendance were (listed in the same
order in which they were seated):

Dr. Richard	Z i p s e r
Helga	S c h r a d e r
	(Friend of Dr. Z. from
	West Berlin)
S c h l e s i n g e r	
Martin . . .	Member of the Writers' Union
Maria	M o e s e
	(Television announcer
	– residence: 1138 Berlin-
	Kaulsdorf, [*blacked out*])
Willy	M o e s e
	(Caricaturist – Tel.
	[*blacked out*])
A Latin American man	
Christa W o l f	
Husband of Christa	
W o l f	
Wife of P l e n z d o r f	
P l e n z d o r f	

[*Although IMV "Kurt" provides a list of the guests, he does not include himself on that list, presumably to protect his identity. However, it is obvious that "Kurt" and "Milan" are one and the same person. It is also apparent that the secret police conducting the surveillance were not aware that "Milan" was an informant working for the Stasi.*]

Furthermore, one could see that these persons did not know one another personally; as a result of that conversations arose mainly between

> Plenzdorf – Schlesinger – Martin [*Stade*]
> Plenzdorf – wife of Plenzdorf – Christa Wolf
> Maria Moese – Helga Schrader

Dr. Zipser turned out to be an excellent host (dinner, beverages – wine only) and conversed with each of the participants, one after the other. The source was unable to overhear the content of these conversations. Dr. Zipser had a longer conversation with Christa Wolf. This was primarily about five photos she had brought along for him to include in his book. He disapproved of these photos because she looked very sad in all of them. Christa Wolf looked exceptionally sad and listless all evening long.

At 11:50 p.m. Dr. Zipser took his female friend to the city railway station. He asked Schlesinger to look after the guests during his absence.

At around 12:20 a.m. everyone said their goodbyes in front of Hotel "Metropol." [*Name blacked out*] drove off in his automobile, even though he had consumed about five glasses of wine. Dr. Zipser, Maria und Willy Moese, and the Latin American man then walked together to the "Möwe" where they remained until around 2:45 a.m. [*For some reason*, IMV *"Kurt" does not mention that he accompanied them to this private club.*]

From 3:00 a.m. until 5:00 a.m. the source conversed with Dr. Zipser in his apartment. The invitation to have a nightcap together came from Dr. Zipser. In a conversation presumed to be confidential, Dr. Zipser then made the following remarks:

a.) He emphasized several times that he is not in contact with the American Embassy in the GDR.

b.) He said three fourths of the questionnaires have been answered via interviews, one fourth (i.e., ten writers) have answered in writing.

c.) He had the questionnaire approved by the Writers' Union. They provided him with the names of only fourth- and fifth-level writers to interview. He also gave these writers the questionnaire, of course, and their answers will be compared to those of Plenzdorf, Christa Wolf and Schlesinger.

d.) He emphasized that he is also interested in getting together with writers who are not well known. A friend is supposed to make it possible for him to do that in 1978.

e.) He has <u>intentionally</u> avoided the minder the Humboldt University assigned to him. This person has frequently tried to contact him, but he has managed to become so "elusive" that they have not seen each other.

Dr. Zipser offered the source his unconditional support, in West Berlin as well as in the USA. The source is to procure a visa for West Berlin, without fail, when he returns to the GDR in May 1978. He then wants to bring the source together "with his people." The people in question are not writers though, but rather architects, engineers, and others.

Since the source indicated that an earlier trip to West Berlin might be a possibility, he gave the source the following addresses:

> Ingrid Lechner
> [*blacked out*]
> 1 Berlin 30, Tel. [*blacked out*]

> and

> Helga Schrader
> [*blacked out*]
> 1 Berlin 45, Tel. [*blacked out*]

It should be noted that Schrader plans to get together with Maria Moese soon in the capital city. They were not acquainted previously, but supposedly come from neighboring places.

Dr. Zipser will drive to West Berlin on 12/15/1977 and from there travel back to the USA on 12/18/1977. He said that his project here in the GDR has assumed such proportions that he is now in need of a collaborator. For that purpose he proposes to gain the assistance in the USA of

Christiane Kraus or Krause

(comes from Leipzig, father is supposedly a professor at the "Karl Marx" University, moved to the USA in 1964). She is planning to write a book about art and culture in the GDR.

Dr. Zipser then wrote down his address for the source

Richard Zipser
102 Shipherd Circle
Oberlin, Ohio 44074
USA
Tel. (216) 775-3785
Dept. of German
Oberlin College

As we parted company, he said to the source: "It was a great pleasure for me to get to know you in the GDR. Perhaps you are the right one after all!"

In the source's judgment, Dr. Zipser's basic attitude toward the GDR is distinctly hostile. He has a strong interest in continuing to stay in contact with the source. His overall behavior vis-à-vis the source does not preclude a desire to make use of this person himself or recruit the source for intelligence service.

Also to be noted operatively is that Dr. Zipser was in Cafe Burger four times, together with Schlesinger, where he presumably also got together with Gerd Poppe [*blacked out*]. [*Gerd Poppe was a human rights activist who protested the expatriation of writer/ singer Wolf Bierman. From the late 1970s on, he was an important figure in the opposition movement in the GDR.*]

Evaluation

The source is reliable and has been vetted. The information is not assessable officially, or else the source's identity would be revealed.

The last section of IMV "Kurt's" report is very cleverly written and misleading. He had told me that he was applying for a visa to attend a conference in West Berlin in the spring of 1978 and asked for the names of contact persons. The information I gave him, as well as my offer to be helpful, is presented in a way that makes it look like I was trying to recruit him as an operative. Since his Stasi-handler had no way of knowing what was actually said in our conversations, and since he could not verify most aspects of the report, "Kurt" could easily omit information, misreport conversations, or even fabricate statements (e.g., "Perhaps you are the right one after all!") to suit his own purposes. In so doing, "Kurt" was probably trying to elevate his status and importance as a trusted informant—and he may have thought this would somehow increase his chances of getting a visa for a first visit to West Berlin, something he was extremely eager to do.

As "Kurt" mentions in his report, my project had become so large in scope that it threatened to overwhelm me. I had indeed decided to seek a collaborator, a Germanist with a keen interest in GDR literature who was also a native speaker of German. I first asked Dr. Christina Kraus (University of Pittsburgh) if she would like to work on the project with me, but—after giving the matter considerable thought—she declined. I turned next to Dr.

Karl-Heinz Schoeps (University of Illinois at Urbana-Champaign), who agreed to step in and assist me. We worked well together and in 1980 were able to finalize the manuscript. Without the able assistance of Karl-Heinz Schoeps, I doubt that I would have been able to complete this massive project. My undertaking was far too ambitious for a single person to carry out.

SECOND REPORT FROM IME "DICHTER": DECEMBER 30, 1977

The poet Paul Wiens provided the final report in my file for 1977, based on information gathered in two December meetings with me. A memo attached to the report, dated January 5, 1978, indicates that Stasi officer Rolf Pönig received the information from IME "Dichter," who is known to be a reliable source. The report appears below in its entirety.

Main Department XX/7   Berlin, 12/30/1977
                              Pö/Wa

Report

IME "Dichter" reported on two meetings he had with the American Germanist

> Dr. Zipser, Richard
> residence: 102 Shipherd Circle
> Oberlin/Ohio/USA

on 12/8/1977 and 12/15/1977.

~~During the first meeting ZIPSER asked the unofficial~~ collaborator to review his contribution to ZIPSER's book on GDR literature with regard to its correctness and accuracy in representing the unofficial collaborator's views.

ZIPSER stated to the unofficial collaborator that, as far as possible, he ought not to make any modifications. He said he has experienced major difficulties with a number of writers lately. The reason for this is because he conducted interviews with writers primarily at the end of 1975 and in the first half of 1976. In the aftermath of the Biermann affair many of them now want to rewrite their contributions.

The unofficial collaborator told ZIPSER that he is not one of those persons who change their opinion at every opportunity. If ZIPSER has represented his views correctly, he will not make any changes. It was agreed that ZIPSER can return to pick up the unofficial collaborator's contribution on 12/15/1977, after the unofficial collaborator has reviewed it.

During their second meeting ZIPSER told the unofficial collaborator that he had experienced a series of family problems all the while he was working on the GDR literature and writers project. His wife, from whom he is now separated, did not show any understanding for his work. She is a librarian and archival specialist by profession, and was not able to find a job in this line of work in the places where he had to reside. On top of that, she did not have any interest in accompanying him. She came from a wealthy family and had been completely spoiled. While he was away from home travelling, she consoled herself with another man. In the end, these circumstances led to their separation. Very convenient for the separation, according to ZIPSER's account, was the fact that he and his wife did not have any children.

After that ZIPSER offered the following comments on his literary project: This book will not be published initially in the English language in the USA, but rather in German by a FRG [*West German*] publishing house. In order to finalize the work on this manuscript, he will return to the GDR on 5/15/1978. The unofficial collaborator commented that this ought not be a burden to him and that a serious collaboration also demands a certain honesty, since ZIPSER chose this date in order to be in Berlin during the 8th Writers Congress. After the unofficial collaborator made this direct reference, ZIPSER confirmed that it is his intention to confer with as many GDR writers as possible during the Writers Congress.

ZIPSER mentioned further that Ulrich PLENZDORF has given him much assistance with this book project and that he sometimes stays at his countryside cottage. The working conditions are very favorable for him at PLENZDORF's home in [*blacked out*], he said.

ZIPSER promised to get in touch with the unofficial collaborator in 1978, after he returns to the GDR.

Pönig
Captain

INVITATION TO JUREK BECKER (2)

One of things I managed to accomplish before flying home from Berlin was to give Jurek Becker a formal invitation to spend much of the spring 1978 semester in Oberlin, as Max Kade German Writer-in-Residence. Becker had moved to West Berlin in December 1977, so he did not need to get a special visa from the GDR authorities.

INFORMATIONAL REPORT: JANUARY 7, 1978

The next document in my file is a 15-page informational report, compiled from various sources, which has three attachments. The first attachment is a list of GDR writers (30 of 45) to be represented in my book; the second is a list of the 15 interview questions; the third lists the titles of the literary texts some GDR authors had given me. The report, which appears in an abridged form below, begins with a profile of my person and demeanor, underscoring my effort to appear left-wing progressive.

Main Department XX   Berlin, 1/7/1978

Informational Report

[...]

According to his own account, ZIPSER studied German language and literature in Wiesbaden/FRG and also earned a doctorate there. [*I studied in Mainz, not Wiesbaden, and received my Ph.D. from The Johns Hopkins University.*]

He speaks perfect German with only a slight accent, which does not automatically reveal him to be a foreigner. He is considered to be very intelligent, adaptable, and can adapt himself to the most diverse conversational partners. He always strives, while concealing his own intentions from his conversational partners, to learn as much as possible by asking well-directed questions.

Beyond that, various unofficial sources size Zipser up as follows:

He appears to be a relatively serious scholar with very good knowledge of German literature, especially that of the GDR and the FRG. He stresses that he is positively disposed toward GDR literature.

[...]

In all aspects of his behavior Zipser gives the impression of being a "progressive leftist." This makes him a genial conversational partner and sets him apart from the stupid and predominantly ultraconservative US-American literary scholarship which, however, is completely irrelevant if measured by our political standards. He tries to represent his attitude toward the GDR as indifferent, since the form of real socialism established here does not correspond to his concept of a socialist state.

Zipser pretends to be naïve and reticent, creating the impression that he is nothing more than a friendly scholar who has come to a country foreign to him and observes with wide-eyed amazement everything that is going on there.

He appears modest, extremely polite, open-minded, without prejudices, not at all provocative or argumentative. He doesn't smoke, drinks moderately (at least in public), and tries overall to come across as a sympathetic, tolerant partner—as a solid citizen.

Various sources of information indicate that he is interested in widening the circle of his female acquaintances.

[...]

ZIPSER first attracted attention operatively in 1975.

[...]

Through the mediation of [*children's book author*] Uwe KANT's wife, a teacher at the "Max Planck" High School in Berlin-Mitte [*the center of Berlin*], Auguststrasse, Zipser was able to appear before a group of pupils in the 11th grade on 11/26/1975. In order to give the pupils the opportunity to ask questions and discuss issues freely and informally (without teacher supervision), Zipser's request that he be permitted to appear alone before the class was granted.

ZIPSER's 1975 stay in the GDR coincided time-wise with the activities of SCHLESINGER, PLENZDORF and STADE related to the realization of their anthology project "Berliner Geschichten" [*Berlin Stories*], which was hostile to the SED Party.

[*On November 10, 1975, the Stasi sent a report to SED Party officials at the highest level on a subversive initiative spearheaded by three oppositional writers: Ulrich Plenzdorf, Klaus Schlesinger, and Martin Stade. These writers were quietly and without authorization assembling an anthology of short stories to be published under the title "Berliner Geschichten." Each of the stories was to focus on a societal, political, or other problem that its author was concerned with as a writer. The plan was to offer the anthology to an East German publishing house and to insist that it be published without revisions—i.e., in its original, uncensored form. Further, as I learned from informal conversations with and among the three editors, if the anthology were rejected for publication in the GDR they were prepared to offer it to a West German publisher. Using threats of various kinds, the Stasi and the GDR Writers' Union were able to block this 'dangerous, subversive' initiative. Ironically, I was a beneficiary of their action, since several Berlin writers gave me the short stories they had written for the anthology to publish in my book,* DDR-Literatur im Tauwetter *(GDR Literature During the Thaw). Twenty years later, in 1995, Suhrkamp Verlag in Frankfurt published "Berliner Geschichten".*]

Due primarily to his connection to PLENZDORF and SCHLESINGER, one can assume that ZIPSER has received detailed information on this undertaking. After it was certain that the anthology was not going to come into being, SCHLESINGER demonstratively handed over his contribution to ZIPSER.

According to unofficial reports, PLENZDORF, SCHLESINGER and STADE were arranging reading tours to Austria in January 1976; these had been brokered by ZIPSER.

During his stay, ZIPSER was living at the Hotel "Berolina." However, he did not remain in the capital city continuously from October until November 1975, but rather travelled several times to West Berlin and primarily to Vienna.

[...]

In June 1976 ZIPSER returned to the capital city of the GDR, in order to carry out the second stage of his discussions and interviews with GDR writers.

[...]

After completing this second stage of his undertaking, ZIPSER did not re-enter the GDR until June 1977, according to previous accounts. At that point in time he had meetings with Gerhard WOLF, Jurek BECKER, PLENZDORF and Sarah KIRSCH. Information on the content of their conversations did not come to light.

From 10/15 – 12/15/1977 ZIPSER was again residing in the GDR. This time as a guest of the Ministry of Higher Education due to the establishment of an exchange agreement with the USA under the auspices of the UNESCO Organization IREX. His contract provided for participation in courses as well as discussions with students and faculty members at the Humboldt University of Berlin. For its part, the Humboldt University of Berlin furnished ZIPSER with an apartment for the duration of his stay at

1136 Berlin, Volkradstrasse 8

In addition, he was assigned a minder [*"Betreuer"*] who was supposed to support and assist him. But since ZIPSER was using this stay to carry out the remaining work on his book, he tried to avoid the contact person. He himself remarked that he was quite successful in doing this.

Over the course of his residence, the following observations were able to be made operatively:

ZIPSER met with Jurek BECKER a number of times. On those occasions organizational and substantive questions related to his residence at Oberlin College were clarified. Following ZIPSER's suggestion, BECKER is supposed to give lectures there during the period of time from 2/25 to 5/10/1978. ZIPSER has arranged to have the official invitation from the College and the relevant contract delivered to BECKER.

He met on a number of occasions with the WOLFS, PLENZDORF, and SCHLESINGER, among others, and several times stayed for a while at [*blacked out*].

ZIPSER still maintains close relations to Sarah KIRSCH, who in the meantime has relocated to West Berlin. In addition, he maintains close relations to

WARDETZKY, Jutta
born on [*blacked out*] 1939 in Leipzig
residence: 104 Berlin, [*blacked out*]
Research Associate at the
Academy of Arts
friend of Sarah Kirsch

and

KÖHLER, Renate
residence: 102 Berlin, [*blacked out*]
good acquaintance of [*blacked out*], for whom she
she took care of many and various items of business
in the past ([*blacked out*] also resided at [*blacked out*] before leaving the country).

ZIPSER obviously functioned as a transmitter of information between these three persons.

ZIPSER maintains a connection of an unknown nature to

OPOCZYNSKI, Evelyn
113 Berlin, [*blacked out*]
actress

HÜBSCHER, Gerhard and Edith
Berlin-Johannisthal, [*blacked out*]

STRASSENBERGER, Dirk
Berlin-Prenzl. Berg, [*blacked out*]

SCHNITZLER, Stefan – physician

The stylistic revision of ZIPSER's interview texts during his stay was undertaken by one

LECHNER, Edith
102 Berlin, [*blacked out*]

to whom he also had very close personal contact.

ZIPSER maintains a relationship of an unknown sort to an employee of GDR television whose first name is Christa.

ZIPSER uses the West Berlin residence of

KELLNER, Hellfried
born [*blacked out*] 1942 in Berlin
residence: 1 Berlin 45, [*blacked out*]

KELLNER, Brigitte
born [*blacked out*] 1949 in Neuwied
residence same as husband
[*blacked out*]

as a depository for materials related to his book project and as a mailing address.

PLENZDORF has maintained close contact to both persons for a long time. One cannot rule out the possibility that the ZIPSER – KELLNER association came about due to his facilitation.

ZIPSER's intimate friend in West Berlin is one

[*blacked out*]
born on [*blacked out*] 1945
Hamburg 61, [*blacked out*]re
sidence: 1 Berlin 45, [*blacked out*]

whom he brought along on several occasions to the capital city, thereby enabling her to get to know a number of his contact persons [. . .] [*This person, whose full name has already appeared in this book, was a friend of Brigitte Kellner. I met her while staying with the Kellners in West Berlin. The four of us would go out to brunch or dinner together, to the theater or a concert, etc. We were good acquaintances, nothing more. Since this woman was interested in meeting some East German writers and getting to know East Berlin, I invited her to come for a visit a few times and also to attend my farewell dinner party on December 13, 1977. IMV "Kurt" and the Stasi obviously concluded, wrongly, that she was an 'intimate' friend of mine. I want to set the record straight.*]

ZIPSER also passed along the address of one

> LECHNER, Ingrid
> Residence: 1 Berlin 30, [*blacked out*]
> Telephone [*blacked out*]

to his contact partners.

Whether connections exist between her and the LECHNER, Edith living in the capital city, due to the sameness of their surnames, is not known. [*Ingrid and Edith Lechner are sisters.*]

According to unofficial reports one cannot rule out the possibility that ZIPSER, on visits together with SCHLESINGER to Cafe "Burger" in the capital city, got to know [*blacked out*].

According to his own account, ZIPSER has embarked on a second book project. He has prepared a textbook edition of PLENZDORF's "Die neuen Leiden des jungen W." [*The New Sufferings of Young W.*], which is intended to help advanced students of the German language in the USA learn and understand colloquial speech, including slang expressions, among other things.

A USA publishing house [*John Wiley & Sons*] is committed to the execution of this project and has already procured the necessary publication license from the Hinstorff Publishing House in Rostock. The USA publisher is not going to make a profit on this book, but is seeking to enhance its image, just like ZIPSER who will earn very little from this publication. The main thing for him is to have his name become better known.

On 12/13/1977 there was a gathering in Hotel "Metropol" at ZIPSER's invitation; the attendees, in addition to him, were:

> Christa and Gerhard WOLF
> Ulrich PLENZDORF and his wife
> Martin STADE

Klaus SCHLESINGER

Willi and Maria MOESE

Helga SCHRADER (*blacked out*).

At this gathering ZIPSER emphasized that before returning to the USA he wanted to get together again with those friends whom he owed the most and thank them for their support.

He said that the manuscript of his book is for the most part finished and might appear in print at the end of 1978.

Furthermore, ZIPSER mentioned that the head of the Suhrkamp Publishing Company (FRG), [*Siegfried*] UNSELD, also expressed interest in his manuscript.

ZIPSER stated that he plans to return and re-enter the capital city in May 1978 (the GDR Writers Congress will take place at this time), in order to complete the final tasks related to his book project—e.g., obtain authorization from the GDR writers to publish the interviews.

From the comments he has made up to now, it is not entirely clear who his publisher will be or in which country his book will actually appear in print; he has made contradictory statements about this.

In summary, here is an assessment based on unofficial reports:

From a political standpoint, ZIPSER's manuscript appears to be extremely explosive. By his own account, the answers he received from the 38 writers in all he interviewed, when placed next to each other, make it possible for the answers of Hermann KANT or Günter GÖRLICH, for example, to appear alongside those of persons like SCHLESINGER or Gerhard WOLF. [*Kant and Görlich were party loyalist writers, whereas Schlesinger and Wolf were at this point in time voices of opposition.*]

In this way ZIPSER can construct a collection of alleged conflicts, unresolved problems and difficulties in the GDR, particularly in the development of its literature, which in their totality will present a <u>completely distorted</u> picture of the Party and State cultural policy.

At this juncture it should be noted that, at the annual conference of the MLA (Modern Language Asssociation, USA) in spring 1977 [*actually, it was in late December 1976*], ZIPSER presented a paper on "Contemporary GDR Writers and Their Society," in which he already made use of his interviews and put into practice this method of citing answers next to each other without commentary.

Reference is being made to the difficulty in gaining access to ZIPSER's manuscript because—on the basis of the existing agreements—there are in fact no real legal grounds for demanding to see it.

Consequently, it is not possible at present even to know precisely which 38 writers ZIPSER has included in his manuscript.

During his previous stays in the GDR, ZIPSER had the opportunity to scoop up and collect very diverse and comprehensive information about the cultural sphere in the GDR, and specifically, also after the events surrounding Biermann, which go far beyond the scope of his proposed book. Unofficial sources doubt anyway that he has coped with the work on the manuscript by himself, as he maintains.

ZIPSER's multiple stays in the GDR mark a departure from the way USA universities have typically proceeded in similar cases. Therefore, in comparison to what normally is the case, ZIPSER has had about triple the amount of time at his disposal. ZIPSER himself has provided contradictory information about this.

Furthermore, it is not clear where the funding for his stays is coming from. Regarding this matter as well, he has provided contradictory statements (self-financed, support from his college, support from other universities that are interested in his book).

Since the Stasi had come to view my activities within the GDR as "subversive"and even begun to consider the possibility that I was a CIA operative, they recommended measures to be taken in the future. Had I not been an IREX scholar, I clearly would not have been able to obtain a visa for my next stay in East Berlin (May 15 – June 15, 1978). When I read the final section of this report, I was frankly astonished.

> It is recommended, for the further monitoring of Zipser as well as the clarification of his contacts and intentions, especially in the light of possible espionage activity, that the following measures be taken under the auspices of Main Department XX/7:
>
> - Zipser is to be put under investigation. When he enters the GDR on short notice, ways should be devised to allow Main Department VIII to keep tabs on him.
>
> - His known contacts in the GDR up to now have to be examined thoroughly and screened with regard to their operative usefulness. With Main Department XX/5 as well as with Main Department VIII, one needs to consider possible ways to illuminate his contacts in Westberlin.
>
> - It needs to be established whether Zipser can be so compromised by operative measures that he can be denied entry into the GDR in the future.

- One needs to ensure, through consultation with Main Department XX/2 and Department XV of the regional headquarters of the Ministry for State Security in Magdeburg, that the unofficial resources of this administrative unit will be utilized in a coordinated supervision of Zipser.

- By way of Main Department XX/3 one needs to ensure that Zipser, whenever he re-enters the GDR under the auspices of the UNESCO Organization IREX's scholar exchange through a predetermined program, will be so burdened by attending lectures at the Humboldt University, among other things, that it will no longer be possible for him to expand and maintain the connection to his GDR contacts, to a large extent unchecked until now. One needs to make certain that he is assigned a reliable minder, an unofficial collaborator with professional as well as political-operative qualifications.

- Through the assignment of appropriate living quarters it will be guaranteed that operative-technical measures can be carried out.

- One has to make certain that Zipser does not, by virtue of using his contacts, gain access to the Writers Congress that will take place in May 1978.

- It needs to be established whether Zipser's reputation can be so tarnished, by unofficial collaborators and within the Writers' Union through fitting well-directed remarks, that the negative forces [*i.e., voices of opposition*] will also avoid having further contact with him.

JUREK BECKER IN OBERLIN: FEBRUARY – MAY, 1978

I first met Jurek Becker in November 1975, when I visited his home in Berlin for the purpose of doing a tape recorded interview for *DDR-Literatur im Tauwetter* [*GDR Literature During the Thaw*]. In addition to being a very talented prose writer, Becker was a very likeable man; he had a marvelous sense of humor, a great deal of personal warmth and charm, and was one of the best storytellers I ever met. He was also candid, outspoken, and not afraid to express his views on controversial topics, such as problems in GDR society and his country's oppressive system of government. His criticism of the SED leadership and their violation of human rights brought him into conflict with the GDR authorities on many occasions.

International recognition came to Becker following the publication of his first and, in my view, most powerful novel, *Jakob der Lügner* (*Jacob the Liar*, 1969), which was translated into many languages and made into a motion picture of the same title. His books are serious in theme and, at the same time, highly entertaining reading. The Swiss writer, Max Frisch, said of himself: "I try on stories like clothes," an assertion that Becker could have made with equal force. Indeed, when it came to the not-so-simple art of telling a story, Becker was a master craftsman able to employ all the tools of his trade with uncommon skill.

During my visits to East Berlin in 1976 and 1977, I met with Becker on numerous occasions and over time we became friends. As I got to know him better, I became convinced that he was a perfect candidate for the German Writer-in-Residence program at Oberlin College. His outgoing personality, friendly and unassuming demeanor, and ability to relate to people—in addition to his talent and international reputation as a novelist—made him an ideal choice. And when he came to Oberlin for most of the spring 1978 semester, he dedicated himself to making his residency as successful as possible—and in every regard it was a memorable visit.

In December of 1977, Becker quietly moved from East to West Berlin. He was in possession of a unique two-year exit visa that enabled him to go back and forth from the West to the East, where his two teenage sons were living. At that time, he was the only East German writer to be permitted such freedom of movement. In November 1976, Becker had become embroiled in a human rights conflict with the government when he—along with eleven other GDR writers—publicly protested the forced exiling of dissident poet-singer, Wolf Biermann. In the ensuing months, he resigned from the GDR Writers' Union, was thrown out of the SED Party, and then barred from making public appearances and publishing his writing in the GDR.

Becker's decision to spend a semester as writer-in-residence at Oberlin College coincided with his decision to leave East Germany for a year or two. In June 1977, when Becker and many other writers were still preoccupied with the Biermann affair, I first discussed with him the possibility of coming to Oberlin. Following the expulsion of his good friend Biermann, a move Becker had protested more vociferously than most, his life had been a series of upheavals. "I've gotten out of everything," he jokingly told me, "out of the Writers' Union, out of the Party, and out of my marriage." Upon separating from his wife, Becker exchanged a comfortable home on the outskirts of Köpenick for a modest, rear-building apartment (no bathroom or telephone) in the working-class neighborhood of Friedrichshain [*Köpenick and Friedrichshain are districts of Berlin*]. This not only provided an interim solution to the problem of where to live, it also enabled him to withdraw and devote himself full time to writing the novel *Schlaflose Tage (Sleepless Days)*. Barred from reading in public, uncertain about his future, and in the midst of a midlife crisis of sorts, Becker sought and found refuge in his work.

Before the end of June 1977, *Schlaflose Tage* had been completed and submitted to the Hinstorff Verlag in the GDR and the Suhrkamp Verlag in the FRG. Initially Becker was assured by the editors at Hinstorff that the novel would be published. But later on, when he steadfastly refused to make certain recommended changes, it became clear that his novel would not appear in his own country. Becker, who maintained that he—unlike some of his colleagues—could not live and write in one Germany, only to be published and read in the other, was forced to begin contemplating possible solutions to his dilemma. In an interview printed the following month in the West German news magazine, *Der Spiegel* [*The Mirror*], he expressed a desire to remain in East Germany and the hope that his books would continue to be published there. "If it's a question of keeping my mouth shut," he remarked, "then I'd rather keep it shut in the Bahamas." However, the airplane carrying Becker to the New World landed not in the Bahamas but near Oberlin, Ohio.

Becker, our third writer-in-residence from the GDR, arrived in Oberlin on February 20, 1978, just a few weeks before *Schlaflose Tage* was published in the FRG by the Suhrkamp Verlag. For the next three months he lived in a dormitory on campus, where the Plenzdorfs had lived before him, and dined with students at the Max Kade German House most of the time. Jurek spent almost every morning in his apartment, writing short prose texts, then made himself available in his office every afternoon to those who wanted to stop by and talk with him. His office in Rice Hall was across the corridor from mine, so we saw each other and conversed almost every day, often about GDR-related topics. When he had finished a draft of a *Splittertext* [*splinter text*], as he called these short prose works, he would come to my office and read it to me, eager to hear my reaction. In Oberlin I was his one and only link, and he was also my only link, to East Germany.

Despite the publicity that had accompanied Jurek's departure from East Germany and his trip to the US, few people at Oberlin were aware of the tremendous upheaval that had occurred in his life during the previous fifteen months, and very few—if any—were in a position to appreciate the impact that these violent changes had had upon him. From the outset, Jurek found himself both isolated and insulated by his new, unfamiliar environment. He had been a celebrity in West Berlin, but in Oberlin he was for most people a nobody, and at first he had difficulty adjusting to his new status. He had been removed, suddenly and physically, from the problems that had consumed so much of his time and emotional energy in Berlin, from the problems that had led him to write a book like *Schlaflose Tage*, and now he was in Oberlin, a tranquil college town in northern Ohio with a population of 8,000.

Jurek, a gregarious man who liked and related well to young people, welcomed the daily contact with Oberlin students. He took an interest in their lives and concerns, suppressing for a time all thought of those difficulties and decisions awaiting him in Berlin. On Tuesday evenings he held a two-hour colloquium in the German House lounge. Sometimes, eager to get a response, he would read the latest of his prose texts, or he would simply talk about whatever happened to be on his mind (e.g., Jurek Becker, New York City, the so-called American way of life, similarities between the US and the GDR), or he would ask questions so that he could listen and learn. On Thursday evenings he always held an open house for anyone who cared to come, an opportunity to get to know the writer Jurek Becker as a flesh-and-blood human being and a chance for him to become better acquainted with persons who were interested in him.

While in Oberlin, Jurek learned to love Baskin-Robbins ice cream and, to my amazement, the game of baseball ("not at all boring, you just have to know the rules"). He was amused by his own appearance in an OBERLIN sweatshirt, unafraid of his second-hand Ford Pinto—despite our warnings—and fascinated by the AAA and all its services. He came to like the "apolitical" climate in Oberlin, and joined the rest of us in complaining about the nasty weather. Oberlin was good for Jurek, and he was good for us. He had time to write, to think, to take stock of the past, and to prepare for what the future had in store for him. After leaving Oberlin in late May of 1978, Jurek spent seven weeks touring the US—Miami Beach, New Orleans, Taos, and San Francisco—and visiting some of his new friends.

One of Jurek's friends at Oberlin was 18-year-old Hannah Zinn from Hayward, California, who was a first-year student when he met and began dating her. Hannah, a beautiful and highly intelligent young woman, was a student in my Elementary German class that spring. She lived in the Russian

House and dined at the Russian Table in the dining room of the German House, where Jurek frequently ate lunch and dinner. I introduced him to Hannah, and soon thereafter they began dating. It was the beginning of a romance that lasted for more than five years. In the summer of 1978, Jurek visited Hannah in California and met her parents. Infatuated with Hannah, he contemplated staying in the US, but eventually decided to return to Germany and invited her to join him. He flew back to West Berlin in July of that year, but without Hannah who wanted to complete her college education. However, at the end of the fall 1978 semester, she dropped out of Oberlin College, flew to West Berlin, and moved into Jurek's apartment. They lived together until the fall of 1983, when Jurek broke off the relationship.

After spring break, two journalists from Germany—Eva Windmöller and Dirk Sager—descended on Oberlin to do articles on Jurek. Windmöller's article, "Jurek Beckers Urlaub von der DDR" ("Jurek Becker's Vacation from the GDR"), appeared in a July 1978 issue of *Stern* [*Star*] magazine (No. 29, 116-120). It is illustrated with photos of Jurek interacting with students in the German House lounge and dining room, talking on the phone in his dormitory apartment, and chatting with a sheriff at the Midway Mall. Nice memories! Dirk Sager, whom I had met on several occasions in East Berlin, was a correspondent for the German TV channel ZDF. He interviewed Jurek for his weekly news program *Kennzeichen D* [literally: *License Plate G* (G for Germany)], and he kindly included a short conversation with me in the segment—my first and only appearance on television.

For me, Jurek Becker's visit as German writer-in-residence was the most enjoyable of any I experienced during my seventeen years at Oberlin College, probably because I knew him well and regarded him as a friend before he arrived. I know he regarded me as a friend as well, not only because he gave me a pre-publication copy of *Schlaflose Tage* with the following inscription: "Für Dick in Dicker Freundschaft" [*For Dick in close friendship*] Jurek Becker, Oberlin, Feb. 24, 1978." After leaving Oberlin and touring the US, he returned to West Berlin in late July, and when his special visa expired he decided to remain in the West. He remarried and lived in West Berlin until just before he died of cancer at age 59, much too young to depart this world, on March 14, 1997. [*In preparing the section above on Jurek Becker in Oberlin, I relied heavily on my essay, "Jurek Becker: A Writer with a Cause,"* DIMENSION, *Vol. 11, No. 3 (1978), 402-406.*]

RETURN TO EAST BERLIN AS AN IREX SCHOLAR: MAY, 1978

I returned to East Berlin in mid-May 1978, again with the support of an IREX fellowship. My housing was much nicer this time, a studio apartment located a short distance from the Alexanderplatz, right in the center of Berlin and within walking distance of the Plenzdorfs' apartment. Shortly after my arrival, I invited the Plenzdorfs (Helga and Ulrich) and our mutual "friends," IMV "Kurt" and IMV "Julia" for an evening visit. Since "Kurt" and "Julia" had two young children, they decided that "Kurt" would stay home and babysit. Below is "Julia's" report on our get-together in my apartment, exactly as it appears in my file.

FIRST REPORT FROM IMV "JULIA": MAY 25, 1978

Main Department XX/Operative Group
Berlin, 5/25/1978
Ta.

Transcript of tape recording
Source: IMV "Julia"
Received: Captain Paulitz on 5/25/1978

ZIPSER, Richard ("Dick"), American Germanist

On 5/24/1978, at around 8:00 p.m., I made my way together with Ulrich and Helga Plenzdorf to ZIPSER in his apartment, Berlin, Mollstr. 4, Apt. 0304 (3rd floor, 4th apt.), after receiving an invitation over the telephone. First of all, we handed over the objects we had brought along for the decoration of his apartment.

Family PLENZDORF brought him these items on loan:

> 1 large Baroque mirror
> 1 large earthenware bowl
> 1 picture

I gave him a bouquet of flowers in a Bürgel pottery jug. After ZIPSER had served us beverages (wine and sparkling wine), the conversation evolved and concentrated on the following topics:

1. ZIPSER asked me right away why I had rejected a short while ago his offer to visit me on 5/27-28/78 at our countryside premises near [*blacked out*]. After I had explained to him that I had arranged to have a party there with my former classmate friends from the County Party Academy, from which I had graduated recently, he showed greater interest in this topic.

He asked these questions, among others:

When was I enrolled at the party academy?

What did this sort of schooling entail (form of instruction)?

Which kinds of persons were studying there with me—viewed above all from the perspective of their functions?

Whether these types of instruction are only available in Berlin, etc.

I justified my dismissive response by indicating that I did not want to bring these comrades and friends as well as myself into disrepute by having an American citizen show up there.

ZIPSER found all of this to be rather astonishing (as regards the ban on contact with persons from the West and obligation to report such contacts, which were discussed in this context) and wondered if the GDR considers every foreigner to be a spy. He said that was not the case in his country.

2. Referring to this problem, ZIPSER pointed out, with much conviction and confidence, that he did not have to report on his stays in the GDR to his sponsoring organization or any other agencies.

ZIPSER said he is surprised anyhow that up to now neither the CIA nor any of the GDR's security agencies have approached him regarding a possible collaboration. [*Actually, at some point in the conversation, Julia asked if I was required to report to any agencies in the United States on my activities in East Germany, and that was my response to her question.*]

At that point Ulrich PLENZDORF said that he (ZIPSER) is a spy anyhow, even if he is not aware of it. Everything he has come to know about the GDR that he passes on in the form of reports or as part of his book or about the literary texts by GDR writers he has gathered as well, these pieces of information will be assembled at a central location so as to yield a picture of this country. ZIPSER vigorously resisted this kind of interpretation of his activity and asserted that he is not a spy.

3. Later in the conversation ZIPSER mentioned that he is going to pay special attention to the writers NEUTSCH, BŘEZAN, and SCHULZ during the Writers Congress. He plans to contact them then, but did not indicate how he would go about doing

that. ZIPSER put a list in front of H. Plenzdorf for her perusal; listed on it were the names of all the writers whom he had previously contacted and those he still plans to contact. The list was divided into three columns and filled with crosses. One column presented descriptions of the literary texts submitted by these writers. Anna SEGHERS and Ulrich PLENZDORF are the only writers who have not yet submitted texts. In the case of A. SEGHERS he does not know what will be selected, since some persons, including PLENZDORF among others, are of the opinion that SEGHERS has not written anything worthwhile in the 1970s.

At Ulrich PLENZDORF's initiative the conversation shifted to an article by Hermann KANT that appeared in <u>Neues Deutschland</u> [*New Germany*] on 5/24/1978. PLENZDORF went on to explain what the article is about. ZIPSER asked H. PLENZDORF to save this article for him, since he also wanted to read it. A short while later ZIPSER inadvertently revealed (so it seemed to me anyway) that he was actually already informed about the article. His remarks referred to the refusal of Christa WOLF and Stefan HEYM "to collaborate." Presumably, this had to do with collaboration in the Writers' Union. [*The newspaper Neues Deutschland was the official organ of the Socialist Unity Party in the GDR. It endorsed all policy decisions of the government and sought to elevate the prestige of each member of the leadership. It had a circulation of ca. one million in the 1970s and was the country's most important newspaper.*]

4. ZIPSER mentioned additionally that he had appealed to the cultural attaché of the USA assigned to the GDR concerning the installation of a telephone in his apartment. On 5/24/1978 he received notification that the technicians would be coming to install the telephone on 5/25/1978. [*The absence of a phone in my otherwise satisfactory studio apartment was surely not unintentional. It created a major problem for me during the first*

ten days of this one-month stay, since I had no other way to contact and set up meetings with writers. Fortunately, the Plenzdorfs' apartment was not far away and I could make all the phone calls I wanted from there. However, if I had not gotten the embassy involved, I doubt that a telephone would have been installed before my departure.]

On 5/27/1978 ZIPSER intends to visit the PLENZDORF family in [*blacked out*]. On the same day the married couple from Westberlin

> Hellfried and Brigitte KELLNER
> (further personal information known)

is intending to drive here and will also visit with the PLENZDORFs.

It was agreed that my husband and I would be picked up at our premises (about 4 kilometers outside of [*blacked out*]) and participate in the gathering of the aforementioned persons.

I have the impression that Ulrich PLENZDORF is extremely well informed about ZIPSER's initiatives. Among other things, he has precise knowledge about the circumstances related to the first apartment that was offered to ZIPSER, which ZIPSER said was unacceptable and rejected.

Also to be mentioned is that ZIPSER, during our conversation about contacts we have with persons from the West, asked if

Stefan SCHNITZLER

is likewise not permitted to have Western contacts. The PLENZDORFs commented that they did not know about that, but they did know that SCHNITZLER has contact with many persons from the West.

Around 11:30 p.m. we left the apartment, separated from the Plenzdorfs, and he walked me home. As we said goodnight at the front door to my apartment, ZIPSER asserted that the two of us would have to meet again alone in the near future.

He suggested a date during the week after next. At the same time, he stated that he had a lot to do during the week of 5/29 to 6/4/1978 on account of the Writers Congress and no time for a get-together then.

He will get in touch with me in any event by telephone.

It was obvious that ZIPSER was eager to have closer (intimate) relations with me.

On close observation one could perceive that ZIPSER was guiding the conversations on this evening. For example, he picked up on topics that sometimes were only foreshadowed and carried them forward very smoothly, so that without realizing it the others were inclined to be responsive.

Attachment
Sketch of the apartment, Mollstr. 4, Apt. 0304

[*"Julia's" report is a wonderful example of how a collaborator can misrepresent what was said or happened for self-serving reasons. I was not pursuing her or eager to have an intimate relationship with her, as she reports. In reality, "Julia" had been flirting with me for some time and toward the end of my 1977 stay in East Berlin had even expressed a desire to have an intimate relationship with me, asserting that her husband would not object. To pursue this objective, the purpose of which was obviously to gather information about me, my project, and my contacts in the GDR, she had her husband babysit and came to my apartment with the Plenzdorfs. When I walked her home that evening, she said she was tired of taking care of the children while her husband and I got together for beer and a bite to eat, and insisted that I take her out to dinner. I agreed, and soon thereafter we had dinner at the nearby Hotel Berolina. The fact that "Julia" had attended and recently graduated from the SED County Party Academy had made me wary and suspicious of her, since this was an institution dedicated to training communist party functionaries. For some time, I had been fairly certain that both she and her husband were collaborating with the Stasi. My association with them enabled me to channel misleading information to the Stasi, and I was not surprised when I discovered their reports in my file.]*

SECOND SURVEILLANCE REPORT: MAY 25, 1978

The second surveillance report in my file covers a three-day period, May 28 to June 1, 1978. The purpose of the 24-hour surveillance was twofold: to find out more about my contacts with writers and other persons and to see the places I was visiting frequently, the points of contact. The document has two parts, (A) the approved formal request to conduct the surveillance, which presents the rationale for it, then (B) the surveillance report itself.

(A)

Council of Ministers of the
German Democratic Republic
Ministry for State Security
Registry No. 1097/78W
Main Department VIII   Division VIII

Main Department XX/7

District Administration

County Object Authority

Person in Charge   Capt. Schiller
                                             Berlin, 5/25/1978

Assignment Request – Surveillance

Code name: "Eagle"

[*My real name appears beneath the code name, along with my date and place of birth, gender, marital status, home address, profession, etc.*]

Home address
102 Berlin, Mollstrasse 4, Apartment III/4

Owner/Operator of which vehicles?
VW Beetle, B – SR 949

Where are these vehicles parked?
on the street in the vicinity of his living quarters

Detailed physical description
ca. 1.75 meters tall, slim, blond hair, thick, parted on left side, neck-length, mustache, face full, estimated age: 28 years old

Use of which routes in transit/travelling through-GÜST
[*GÜST = Grenzübergangsstelle/border crossing point*]

GÜST Friedrich-Zimmer-Street [*Checkpoint Charlie*]

[*This is followed by a reference to the first surveillance that was carried out on December 13, 1977 by Main Department VIII/3/3, a note indicating that Main Department XX/7 will keep the record of this second surveillance, which is going to begin at my apartment: "commencement at living quarters," and then there is a reference to my contact with Klaus Schlesinger and Ulrich Plenzdorf.*]

Goal and Purpose of the Surveillance
The person is to be observed continuously from 05/28 until 01/06/78.

Where is the surveillance to take place?
Berlin, capital city of the GDR

Justification in concrete terms of the necessity and goal of the surveillance that is to be carried out. What specific information is going to be gathered through the surveillance?

contact persons and contact places of the person under surveillance

Entries only by Main Department VIII Division VIII

[*This is followed by two more references to my contacts with Klaus Schlesinger and Ulrich Plenzdorf, but the context is unclear on my blurred photocopy of the file.*]

Assignment request actualized by:
Main Department VIII/1 Major Saalfeld
When: 05/29-31/78

Contacts who have come into view:
Pitschmann, Siegfried [*blacked out*]. 1930, Rostock
[*blacked out*]

(B)

VIII/1   Berlin, June 1, 1978

                         sa-gü   1/398 /78

Saalfeld

75 372 64

XX/7

Director

Z i p s e r, Richard   born on: 01/23/1943
102 Shipherd Circle   Oberlin/Ohio (USA)
102 Berlin, Mollstr. 4

"Eagle"   1097/78 W

05/29/78   05/31/78

For 05/29/78 from 7:00 a.m. until 10:15 p.m.

At

7:00 a.m. the surveillance of "Eagle"was initiated at his living quarters

      located at Mollstr. 4.

9:15 a.m. "Adler" left his apartment house and walked to his automobile

      Make: VW Beetle
      Color: white
      License plate no.: B – SR 949

      and from Mollstr. drove in this vehicle through the auto-tunnel and via Leipziger Str. to Bebelplatz, where he parked his car. After that "Adler" walked directly to

      Hotel "Unter den Linden"

      which he entered at

9:25 a.m. Inside the hotel he proceeded to the reception desk and asked something. He received a negative reply and then tried without success to place a phone call within the hotel.

After exiting the telephone booth he briefly greeted a man who was in the middle of a group of persons. "Eagle" asked this person if they would be seeing each other later on upstairs. This male person quickly answered "yes" and they immediately parted company. This person was not observed any longer. "Eagle" subsequently sat down in the lobby and kept glancing at the elevators all the time.

9:35 a.m. a male person emerged from the elevator and looked around the foyer, searching for something. "Eagle" got up and quickly walked over to this person. They greeted each other eagerly with a handshake. The male person took a number of typewritten pages out of his jacket pocket and explained in words to this effect: "I cannot give you these pages here, not the way they are now written. Certain changes still have to be made. Unfortunately, I did not get to that earlier and also will not get to it in the near future, since I am leaving for the Soviet Union. The content will not be altered at all, but the form as well as some minor matters are in need of change." At that point "Eagle" stated that he would be leaving the GDR on the 15th, whereupon the male person replied that they would be returning from the Soviet Union on the evening of the 16th. In addition, it could also be overheard that "Eagle" arranged to meet with the writer Pitschmann in the evening hours. Afterward the male person put the typed pages back into the pocket of his jacket and declared: "He will correct and finalize what he has written while in the Soviet Union." The two of them then said goodbye and parted company.

[*This was prose writer Siegfried Pitschmann, who had come to Berlin to attend the 8th GDR Writers Congress. We had arranged to meet in the lobby of his hotel that morning, so he could give me the revised copy of the interview we had tape recorded in Rostock in June 1976.*]

9:40 a.m. "Eagle" left the hotel and headed in the direction of the Brandenburg Gate. The male person also left the hotel; he was not under observation any longer.

"Eagle" proceeded until he reached Café "Unter den Linden" at the corner of Schadowstr., then turned around and walked back in the direction of Hotel "Unter den Linden." Along the way he took a look at the places of interest to sightseers. He continued walking across Friedrichstr. / Französische Str. to the

Aufbau-Verlag [*Aufbau Publishing House*]

which he entered at

10:02 a.m. [*Aufbau-Verlag was founded in Berlin in 1945 and became the biggest publisher in the GDR. It specialized in publishing socialist and Russian literature.*]

10:30 a.m. he came back out of the building and walked to his automobile, which he then drove to the gas station on Holzmarktstr.

10:44 a.m. from here he drove via Alexanderstr. to his apartment house, where he parked his automobile in front of the building and entered it at

10:51 a.m.

12:12 p.m. "Eagle" emerged from the building again and climbed into his vehicle. He drove directly to

[*blacked out*]

where he entered an apartment house at

12:19 p.m. "Eagle" spent time on the 2nd floor, where

Endler [*Adolf, GDR writer*]
Erb [*Elke, GDR writer*]
G. Theuser
R. Freese

reside.

12:32 p.m. he came back out of the above-mentioned apartment house and drove directly to Spandauer St., where he parked his automobile and a short time later entered the bookstore

"Das Internationale Buch"

Here he visited the top floor and bought 8 books.

1:12 p.m. "Eagle" left "The International Book," climbed into his automobile and drove via Unter den Linden boulevard to the

American Embassy

which he visited at

1:21 p.m. After a short while he left the embassy, climbed into his automobile and drove directly to the well-known place of refuge

Wilhelm-Pieck-Str. [*blacked out*]

[*This was the Plenzdorfs' apartment, which I visited frequently. Helga Plenzdorf had kindly given me a standing invitation to join their family for the main meal of the day, which always began at 1:30 p.m. Their home was indeed a "place of refuge."*]

which he entered at

1:30 p.m.

2:04 p.m. "Eagle" came out of the building and drove from here to

Wolliner Str. [*blacked out*]

where he arrived at

2:10 p.m. Shortly thereafter he entered the house.

2:15 p.m. he came out of the building, went over to his automobile and from it retrieved his knapsack. After that, he visited the apartment house again.

2:26 p.m. "Eagle" emerged from the place of contact, climbed into his vehicle and drove directly to his apartment building. Here he parked the automobile and removed some books, a cassette tape recorder, and his knapsack from the vehicle. Shortly thereafter he entered the apartment house.

2:42 p.m. he appeared again in front of the apartment building, looked around briefly as if searching for something, and then re-entered it.

4:01 p.m. "Eagle" left his apartment building and walked along Hans-Beimler-Str. in the direction of Alexanderplatz. "Eagle" crossed Hans-Beimler-Str. at the Haus des Reisens [*House of Travel*] and made his way through the pedestrian tunnel to

Hotel "Stadt Berlin"

which he entered at

4:08 p.m. He was carrying a white envelope that measured 10 x 20 cm. "Eagle" walked to the front desk and told a female employee: "I would like to drop off a letter for Mr. Czernitzky [*Czechowski, Heinz, a prominent poet*]. This gentleman comes from Halle and is participating in the Writers Congress." Without hesitation the hotel staff person checked for that name on a list and put the letter in mailbox 27/23. After that "Eagle" left the hotel at

4:15 p.m. and went to the bookstore

> "Das Gute Buch"
> [*The Good Book*]

> on the Alexanderplatz. Here he spent time primarily at book shelves displaying contemporary authors and was interested in GDR literature. He bought around 6 books, among others a two-volume set of Friedrich Wolf's plays.

4:40 p.m. he came back out of the bookstore. "Eagle" then walked past the Haus des Lehrers [*The Teacher's House*], through the pedestrian tunnel to Hans-Beimler-Str. and entered his apartment building at

4:47 p.m.

5:49 p.m. he left the apartment house again. He was carrying a light brown shoulder bag. "Eagle" climbed into his automobile and at

5:51 p.m. drove off in the direction of Leninplatz. He turned and reversed direction on Mollstr., drove via Hans-Beimler-Str. and Mühlendamm to Behrenstr., where he parked his car at

5:57 p.m. near the parking lot on the corner of Charlottenstr. "Eagle" got out of the car and at

6:00 p.m. entered the restaurant

> "Lindencorso".

> A waitress in the restaurant seated him and gave him two menus. "Eagle" drank a beer and began reading a paperback book from the bb-Reihe [*bb-Series*]. He wrote something in a notebook with a green binding.

[Next is a report of my meeting in the restaurant Lindencorso with prose writer Fritz Rudolf Fries, who had come to Berlin to participate in the 8th GDR Writers Congress which was in session from May 29 – 31, 1978. At the time, I did not know that Fries was collaborating with the Stasi, but after having been warned by several writers I suspected that he might be. Following our meeting, he remained in the restaurant for 30 minutes, then he went outside to meet his Stasi-handler and drove off with him in a Wartburg.]

6:45 p.m. Fritz [*Rudolf*] Fries, a person known to the service unit that is intending to give him an assignment, entered the restaurant. For the remainder of the report he has been given the code name

"Falke" ["Falcon"]

"Eagle" motioned to him and greeted him with a handshake. Both of them sat down at the table, ate, drank, and conversed animatedly. It could be overheard that "Falcon" named some dates which "Eagle" noted down. The dates mentioned were 7/15—9/21 and 8/12. During the course of the conversation "Eagle" took a book with a gray cover and white border out of his knapsack and placed it in front of "Falcon," who wrote something in it. [*The book is Fries's 1974 novel, "Das Luft-Schiff" ("The Airship")]. Fries inscribed it as follows: "for Richard Zipser, from one continent to another—the flying author. Fritz Rudolf Fries, Berlin, May 78".*] After that "Eagle" returned the book to his knapsack. "Falcon" then handed "Eagle" a large manila envelope, from which "Eagle" removed a large portrait photo, a head-and-shoulders image of "Falcon." "Eagle" put the photo back in the envelope and thanked "Falcon."

7:58 p.m. "Eagle" said goodbye to "Falcon," took his knapsack and the envelope, left "Lindencorso" and walked over to Hotel

"Unter den Linden"

which he entered at

7:59 p.m.

"Falcon" remained in the restaurant for another 30 minutes, purchased a bouquet of flowers, and then made his way to the parking lot at the corner of Charlottenstr./Behrenstr., where he seated himself beside a male person in the familiar vehicle

Make:Wartburg 353
Color:blue
License plate no.:EO 51 – 97

They drove off in the direction of Unter den Linden. The owner of the vehicle is known to the service unit intending to make an assignment.

In the lobby of Hotel "Unter den Linden" "Eagle" greeted a male person who spoke English. They conversed for a short while. This person was not observed further.

"Eagle" went to the reception desk, inquired about something and then entered the telephone booth for making calls within the hotel. A short time later "Eagle" joined a male person seated at a table in the lobby area. For the remainder of the report this person has been given the code name

"Habicht" [*Hawk*]

With "Hawk" we are talking about (probably, since the name could not be understood precisely):

Pitschmann, Siegfried
born on: [*blacked out*] 1930
resident: Rostock
                  [*blacked out*]
                  writer

residing from 5/28 – 31/78

in Hotel "Unter den Linden"

"Eagle" and "Hawk" conversed in a spirited manner. "Eagle" handed "Hawk" the envelope that was mentioned previously. Several times during the conversation "Eagle" leafed through the book referred to earlier from the bb-Series, while they were discussing it. "Hawk" wrote several sentences on the title page inside the book.

8:34 p.m. they shook hands and bade farewell to one another.

"Eagle" said thank you to "Hawk" and left the hotel, walked to his automobile and at

8:37 p.m. drove via Friedrichstr., Leipziger Str., Karl-Marx-Allee to Schillingstr., and here he entered the apartment house located at

[*blacked out*]

He made his way to

Pohl/Plew

on the fourth floor.

9:08 p.m. "Eagle" left the apartment house, accompanied by a female person, and both of them climbed into his automobile. They drove via Alexanderstr. to his living quarters where he parked his vehicle and, together with the female person, entered his apartment building at

9:13 p.m. Since "Eagle" and the female person did not reappear until

10:15 p.m. the surveillance was interrupted. In "Eagle's" apartment only a dim light was visible.

For 5/30/78 from 7:00 a.m.– 1.00 a.m.

7.00 a.m.   the surveillance at "Eagle's" apartment house resumed.

2:38 p.m.   "Eagle" came out of his apartment building, walked to his automobile and drove off in the direction of Karl-Marx-Allee. He drove to Schillingstr. [*blacked out*], got out and made his way into the apartment house located at

Schillingstr. [*blacked out*]

2:42 p.m.   "Eagle" reappeared, walked to his automobile and drove directly to the

American Embassy

on Neustädtische Kirchstr. Here he parked his vehicle and entered the embassy at

2:50 p.m.

3:32 p.m.   "Eagle" emerged from the embassy and made his way to the bookstore on Unter den Linden boulevard

"Verlag für die Frau"
[*Publishing House for Women*]

which he entered at

3:34 p.m.   There he purchased several pamphlets and took a look at some works of contemporary literature.

3:51 p.m.   "Eagle" left the bookstore carrying a packet of books. He walked to his automobile, climbed in and—after making a U-turn—drove off at

3:54 p.m.   in the direction of Alexanderplatz. He drove via Unter den Linden boulevard and Karl-Liebknecht-Str. to Wilhelm-Pieck-Str., where he parked his vehicle near apartment house no. [*blacked out*]. "Eagle" then made his way to the apartment house located at

Wilhelm-Pieck-Str. [*blacked out*]

and entered it at

3:59 p.m.

4:19 p.m.   "Eagle" came out of the building conversing with a male person (U. Plenzdorf) known to the service unit seeking to make an assignment. The male person stayed behind at the apartment house while "Eagle" went over to his automobile and drove off. He drove via Strassburgstr., Schönhauser Allee, Luxemburgstr., Karl-Marx-Allee, Warschauer Str., Kopernikusstr. to Gubener Str., parked his vehicle here at

4:32 p.m., got out and made his way to the apartment house at

[*blacked out*]

which he entered shortly thereafter. (E. Panitz [*prose writer*] lives in this apartment house).

4:39 p.m.   "Eagle" came back out of the house and drove on in his automobile in the direction of Treptow, via Stralauer Allee as well as Kynaststr. Here "Eagle" made a U-turn and then drove via Hauptstr., Schlicht-Allee, Hans-Loch-Str. to Fr.-Matt-Str. He stopped here, got out, and focused his attention on the tenant name plates at apartment house no. [*blacked out*] on

[*blacked out*]

and at the same time glanced at a slip of paper. A male person who was entering the house let "Eagle" come in with him. Living in this apartment house (apartment 9/3) are [*prominent prose writer*]

Irmtraud Morgner

and [*blacked out*].

These names are not listed outside by the doorbell.

4:55 p.m. "Eagle" came out of the apartment house, still holding the slip of paper, climbed into his automobile and drove directly to the neighborhood of Schöneweide, via Sterndamm to Lindenhorstweg, parked his vehicle and made his way at

5:22 p.m. to apartment house

[*blacked out*]

Living in this house are:

[*six illegible surnames are listed*]

5:48 p.m. "Eagle" left the apartment house, walked to his automobile and at

5:51 p.m. drove back via Sterndamm to Schneller Str., from there via Oberspree to Köpenick, Bahnhofstr., Mahlsdorfer Str., Hultschiner Damm through Alt-Mahlsdorf to Alt-Kaulsdorf and from there directly to Adolfstr. Here he parked his vehicle in front of residential house no. [*blacked out*] at

6:31 p.m. and entered the house

[*blacked out*]

Residing here are

W. and M. Moese [*Willy and Maria*]

7:00 p.m. an automobile drove onto the property at Adolfstr. [*blacked out*]

Make:	Lada
Color:	green
License plate no.	EO 40 – 87

7:28 p.m. "Eagle" came out of the house and drove his automobile onto the property. Then he re-entered the house mentioned above.

12:25 a.m. "Eagle" came out of the house. It could be overheard that he was conversing with someone.

12:31 a.m. "Eagle" drove via Strasse der Befreiung in the direction of Marzahn. He made a U-turn in front of the Friedrichsfelde East Railway Station and again drove in the direction of Biesdorf. [*At that time, Biesdorf was a locality within the Berlin borough of Marzahn*]. After ca. 300 meters he made another U-turn and then drove via Karl-Marx-Allee directly to his living quarters, where he parked his vehicle and while carrying a packet of books entered the apartment house at

12:56 a.m. Shortly thereafter the light was on in his apartment.

1:00 a.m. the surveillance was interrupted.

For 05/31/78 from 7:00 a.m. until 11:45 p.m.

7:00 a.m. the surveillance at "Eagle's" apartment house resumed.

10:56 a.m. "Eagle" emerged from the building, walked over to his automobile, took a quick look inside and then returned to his apartment house.

2:01 p.m. "Eagle" did some shopping in his neighborhood (groceries, baked goods, and sweet goods) and again returned to his apartment house.

2:15 p.m. "Eagle" came out of the building, got into his automobile and drove directly to August-Bebel-Platz. Here he parked his vehicle in front of "St. Hedwig's Cathedral" and walked to the

"Aufbau Publishing House"

which he entered at

2:22 p.m. An inspection of "Eagle's" automobile revealed that there were items of clothing in it that "Eagle" had worn the previous day. In addition, there was an envelope on the passenger seat.

There was handwriting on it that was not very legible. Only the following could be deciphered:

Richard . . .
. . . 988
. 36830

2:50 p.m. "Adler" emerged from the publishing house and walked back to his automobile, climbed in and drove off in the direction of Friedrichstr. He came to a stop at the corner of Behrenstr./ Friedrichstr., got out and made his way to Hotel

"Unter den Linden"

"Eagle" was carrying a large envelope, ca. 10 x 20 cm in size, and his knapsack.

2:55 p.m.   "Eagle" entered the above-mentioned hotel and proceeded to the reception desk. Here he asked a hotel staff person for an envelope in format A4 that had been set aside for him, which he then received. "Eagle" left the hotel and walked directly via Mittelstr. to the

American Embassy

which he entered at

3:00 p.m.   He was carrying both envelopes and his knapsack with him. After about 5 minutes he came back out of the embassy building and made his way along Unter den Linden boulevard and Friedrichstr. to the automobile he had parked on Behrenstr. While on the way he removed some A4 sheets of paper from the A4 envelope and read them.

3:15 p.m.   "Eagle" climbed into his automobile and drove directly to Leipziger Str., where he parked his vehicle a short distance away from the Gertraudenbrücke [*Gertrude Bridge*]. Then "Eagle" went into the apartment house located at

Leipziger Str. [*blacked out*]

He was carrying with him an A5 slip of paper.

3:50 p.m.   "Eagle" came out of the apartment house, still carrying the slip of paper on his person, climbed into his automobile and drove via Mühlendamm, Stralauer Allee, Holzmarktstr., Lichtenberger Str., Rüdersdorfer Str. to Gubener Str. Here he made his way to a familiar apartment house located at

Gubener Str. [*blacked out*]

and entered it at

4:01 p.m.   "Eagle" left this place of contact at

5:19 p.m. proceeded to his automobile, climbed in and drove via Singerstr. directly to Beimler-Str. and then on to Mollstr. Here he parked the automobile in front of his apartment house and entered it at

5:30 p.m. "Eagle" was carrying his knapsack, the two envelopes, and the slip of paper with him.

5:53 p.m. "Eagle" came back out of the apartment building, got into his automobile and drove via Mollstr., Wilhelm-Pieck-Str. to Chausseestr. and parked his vehicle in the parking lot located there. While carrying his knapsack he walked directly to the apartment house at

[*blacked out*]

which he entered at

6:04 p.m. Residing in this building is

Erk [*probably Elke Erb, the poet*]

11:32 p.m. "Eagle" appeared with his knapsack at his automobile and drove via Invalidenstr., Brunnenstr., Wilhelm-Pieck-Str. to his living quarters. Here he got out and at

11:40 p.m. entered the apartment building located at Mollstr. 4.

11:45 p.m. the surveillance was terminated.

Head of the Department	Head of the Unit
On behalf of	
[*signature*]	[*signature*]
Schulze	Saalfeld
Major	Major

[The following description of "Eagle" is attached to the surveillance report, along with a photo which was not sent to me.]

Description of Person

subject:	"Eagle"
sex:	male
age:	ca. 27 – 32 years old
height:	165 – 170 cm
build:	slim
head shape:	oval
position of head:	erect
face/color:	yellowish
forehead:	medium-rise
back/axis:	back straight, axis horizontal
chin:	dimple in chin
hair:	light brown, thick hair, normal haircut, wavy
eyes/color:	light blue
eyebrows/form:	arched, separated, bushy
lips:	thin
gait/posture:	bent forward slightly, casual, shoe tips point outwards when walking
language:	speaks German
clothing:	light-colored velour pants and jacket, yellow turtleneck shirt, black shoes, striped sweater

accessory item: shoulder bag – light brown with dark leather trim

distinguishing features: eyeglass wearer, eyeglasses with gold frame, mustache, gold ring with dark-colored stone on little finger of right hand

SECOND REPORT FROM IMV "JULIA": JUNE 6, 1978

IMV "Julia's" next assignment was to arrange a private meeting with me, in order to gather information on my activities in connection with the 8th GDR Writers Congress (May 28-31, 1978) and my views on certain East German writers. The transcription of her tape-recorded report appears in its entirety below.

Main Department XX/Operative Group
Berlin, June 7, 1978
Pau/P

Tape-recorded report

Source: IMV "Julia"

Received: Captain Paulitz

On: 6/6/1978

Richard ZIPSER, American Germanist

In accordance with the assignment, the unofficial collaborator met with Zipser in the hotel-restaurant of Hotel "Berolina" on 6/5/1978 from 8:00 p.m. until 12:00 midnight. The unofficial collaborator had the following to report about how their encounter proceeded:

Zipser and I agreed over the telephone to meet at the hotel just mentioned and have dinner together. The rationale for that was the invitation he had previously issued along with his expressed desire to get together with me alone on some occasion (see report dated 5/25/1978). [*As I pointed out earlier, it was actually the other way around. Julia had been pressuring me to invite her to dinner so she could have an evening out and away from her children, but of course she had another motive.*]

Regarding the subject matter of our conversation, the following can be said: Zipser was very evasive when we talked about his activities during the Writers Congress.

When I asked him if Stefan Hermlin's address was actually presented in the form that was printed in ND [*"Neues Deutschland", the national daily newspaper in the GDR and official party newspaper of the SED Party*], he simply answered yes.

When I indicated abruptly that portions of Hermlin's contribution to the discussion, possibly taken out of context, had been reproduced in ND, Zipser reconsidered and stated that he was not too certain about that either. As yet, he said, he had been able to exchange only a few words with Plenzdorf on that subject. It was quite obvious that Zipser did not want to dive deeper into this problematic topic of conversation (Writers Congress), so I refrained from pursuing it intensively at that time. [*Stefan Hermlin, poet and prose writer, was an influential member of the GDR's literary establishment. He was a friend of the country's leader, Erich Honecker, and also a friend of the ideologue President of the Writers' Union, Hermann Kant.*]

In a different context, we talked about the quality of the GDR writers' works, also about how he had been received by these persons here in the GDR.

Zipser asserted upfront that all writers are very egotistical and to some extent egocentric, but said he had grown accustomed to that. He made very derogatory remarks about

Jurij Brězan.

His writings are, in Zipser's opinion, mundane. He says that Brězan regularly makes use of our national minority issues in a distasteful way to promote himself. From a telephone conversation I had with Zipser on 6/5/1978, it was apparent that he must have spent this day with Brězan, since he mentioned that he had just returned from Lusatia. [*Lusatia (German: Lausitz) is a region that is located between the German states of Saxony and Brandenburg. The region is the home of the ethnic population of Lusatian Sorbs, which was an officially recognized and protected minority group in the GDR. Brězan was a Sorbian writer whose works were available in two languages, German and Upper Sorbian. He lived in Lusatia and was a loyal member of the SED Party.*]

He considers Hermann Kant and Peter Hacks to be genuine writers, and to a lesser extent Erwin Strittmatter and Anna Seghers. In his opinion the best German-language women writers are Christa Wolf and Sarah Kirsch.

I have noticed that he raves about Christa Wolf in particular, just as he did earlier about Sarah Kirsch.

Zipser plans to get me a book by Christa Wolf which I am supposed to read quickly and then return it. He did not mention the title but said this book is outstanding.

Later in the conversation we talked about his personal connections to

Ulrich Plenzdorf
Martin Stade
Stefan und Dagmar Schnitzler

Zipser gets along well with Stade and Plenzdorf. When it comes to Plenzdorf, what Zipser admires most of all are his generosity and modesty as well as his ability to communicate with children. Zipser said that Plenzdorf does not just take, but also gives a lot of himself on the personal level. By that he meant his (Plenzdorf's) feelings, his private thoughts and desires that he shares with Zipser.

That is not the case with the Schnitzler family, he said. To a certain extent he has the impression that there is a wall separating them. Up to now, the Schnitzlers have never discussed any personal matters with him. Above all, it bothers him that they have never inquired about his work or asked for his impressions of anything. He thinks that this, especially, is abnormal behavior and has no explanation for it.

In connection with the non-admittance of Plenzdorf's son, Morten Plenzdorf, to a program combining vocational training with a high-school diploma, Zipser remarked that considering the current circumstances [*in the GDR*] the selection principles we have are good, however these principles are too often violated. He says he has gotten to know a group of German studies students, who come almost exclusively from families of Party functionaries. In particular, he talked about a married couple with one child (he: a fourth-year student, she: a second-year student) residing in Berlin-Weissensee, 3 bedroom apartment, very nicely furnished—with whom he apparently has become well acquainted. Some of these students asked him for an invitation to visit Oberlin. Due to their connections, they claimed, they would be able to organize a trip there.

Zipser thought this was very strange and made some inquiries; he discovered that all the students enrolled in this seminar had parents or other relatives who are working for the government in a ministry.

I was unable to find out how he acquired this information.

[*"Julia's" frustration over her inability to gather more valuable information that evening, as well as on other occasions, surfaces in this report.*]

During our time spent together, I noticed particularly that Zipser not only remains silent about things he does not want to discuss but generates intense defensive reactions that may at times take on aggressive forms.

Let me mention, for example, a telephone conversation he had in my presence on 6/5/1978 with a certain Klaus (presumably the person in question was Klaus Sterry from Westberlin, whom I also know). Zipser stated several times in a stern tone that he could not discuss a specific problem at this point in time, without mentioning that he had a visitor.

Since I first got to know Zipser about two years ago I have had the impression, and that has proven true increasingly up to the present day, that it is not easy to carry on a casual conversation with Zipser. One really has to make an effort, otherwise the conversation and the get-together will remain quite formal. I also have observed this demeanor on Zipser's part in his conversations with other persons.

In connection with my account of my relationship with the family of

Hellfried KELLNER
resident: Westberlin
close contact partner of Zipser
(personal information known)

he expressed regret that we are experiencing relatively strained relations at the present time.

He explained that, for the most part, he is very tolerant and open-minded vis-à-vis the shortcomings and deficiencies of the people he interacts with here. He also accepted my view that this is very easy for him to do, since he is only staying here as a visitor and can combine his profession and work with the private sphere. [*This passage is particularly interesting, inasmuch as it reveals more about "Julia's" conflicted perception of life in the GDR than it does about me.*]

Zipser did not offer to take any steps, in an effort to improve my relations with the Kellner family again.

Regarding his private problems, Zipser commented that he had put his divorce well behind him, that he did not want to remarry right away but also was not planning to remain single forever.

At present, he would consider a steady relationship to be a constraint on his personal freedoms.

Furthermore, he wants to enjoy this freedom fully in the near future.

Main Department XX/7 has been informed. [*This handwritten note concludes the report.*]

ASSERTIONS ABOUT RICHARD ZIPSER

Shortly before my departure from East Berlin on June 15, 1978, an undated and unsigned document containing assertions about the hostile nature of my work in the GDR and recommendations for the future was added to my file. The primary recommendation is that consideration be given to prohibiting me from re-entering the GDR. The document, which was probably composed in the second week of June, appears in its entirety below.

Assertions about Dr. Richard Zipser

Pursuant to existing references on hand to activities directed against the GDR by

> Dr. ZIPSER, Richard
> born on January 23, 1943 in Maryland/USA
> residence: Oberlin, Ohio/USA
> 102 Shipherd Circle
> profession: Germanist

consideration should be given to subjecting him to a travel ban, so that after the conclusion of his current contractually fixed period of residence in the GDR he will not receive any new opportunities to enter the GDR.

Since 1975 ZIPSER has maintained active contacts primarily to those writers and authors in the GDR that the Ministry for State Security considers to be politically hostile, contrary, or wavering. Upon the recommendation of Christa and Gerhard WOLF, who undertook a lecture tour in the USA in 1974 and became acquainted with ZIPSER there, he was granted permission—via an agreement between the Writers' Union of the GDR and the Central Committee's Department of Culture—to prepare a book in the GDR about contemporary GDR literature.

Since then he has travelled to the GDR a number of times and in 1977 obtained additional official clearances for re-entry as a scholar designated by the USA organization IREX (International Research and Exchange Board) within the discipline of German studies.

(The re-entry clearances mentioned above were possible due to a May 1977 agreement between the GDR Ministry of Higher Education and IREX—IREX is a private USA organization with legal authority to negotiate contracts with corresponding research institutes in socialist countries regarding the exchange of scholars between the USA and socialist countries.)

The purpose of ZIPSER's re-entry is specified in the contract: the carrying out of studies related to the preparation of an 800-page book on GDR literature, for which he requires contacts to ca. 35 GDR authors, the GDR Writers' Union, and the Humboldt University.

ZIPSER, who at present is again residing in the GDR from May 15 until June 15, 1978, did in point of fact establish contacts in this quantity, but predominantly to such writers as Christa and Gerhard WOLF, Ulrich PLENZDORF, Klaus SCHLESINGER, Martin STADE, and Jurek BECKER and now Erika Becker [*Jurek Becker's first wife, who was not a writer*]. In a large number of interviews that ZIPSER conducted within these circles, he prompts the interviewees to take positions on problems in the development of the GDR in the cultural, political, and ideological spheres. By proceeding in this way he was also able to obtain detailed information about "literary" projects, for example in 1975 on the anthology project "Berlin Stories," which was hostile to the SED Party. Proceeding in a focused manner he gathered extensive information from the cultural sphere following the events related to BIERMANN. ZIPSER is always aiming to screen additional GDR writers with respect to their basic political stance. For this activity he has had at his disposal triple the amount of time than normally would be the case, while the source of funding for his travels still remains unclear.

A few years later, the Stasi would conclude—wrongly, I might add—that I was in fact a CIA agent and recommend that I not be permitted to re-enter the GDR. Fortunately, by that time I had completed my work there and did not need to return for professional reasons.

ANTHOLOGY OF CONTEMPORARY EAST GERMAN POETRY: A NEW PROJECT

Before returning to the GDR in May 1978, I conferred with the editors of *FIELD*, a poetry journal published by Oberlin College, about the possibility of preparing a special bilingual issue devoted to East German poetry of the 1970s. The editors were enthusiastic about my idea, and we agreed that I would serve as guest editor of this publication. The main purpose of the bilingual volume was to make contemporary East German poetry available not only to students of German literature and the GDR, but to a much broader audience of readers as well.

As guest editor, my first tasks were to choose the poets for this anthology and gather from them a selection of poems which would be translated into English following my return to Oberlin. In choosing the fourteen poets who ultimately were included, I consulted with GDR poet Adolf Endler, Gerhard Wolf, and several other persons conversant with the GDR poetry scene, all of them knowledgeable insiders. Our goal was to make the chapbook representative of the very best that East Germany had to offer during the seventies, and a consensus on the most important GDR poets of that era emerged with surprising ease. The list included Erich Arendt, Thomas Brasch, Volker Braun, Heinz Czechowski, Adolf Endler, Elke Erb, Bernd Jentzsch, Rainer Kirsch, Sarah Kirsch, Wulf Kirsten, Günter Kunert, Reiner Kunze, Kito Lorenc, and Karl Mickel.

Fourteen different persons—poets, faculty members, and students—shared the task of translating the poems into English. I wrote an introduction to the chapbook, prepared a bio-bibliographical sketch for each poet, and also translated some of the poems, including Elke Erb's "Sommerzeit" ("Summertime," 1975), one of my favorites.

SOMMERZEIT

Durch dichtes hohes Gras, von lichten Rispen
so sanftes Schwanken seh ich, schritt mein Vater,
und dies ist wahr, dass er zu schweben schien
beinlos auf eine Eiche zu, so dick,
dass sie sechs ausgestreckter Arme Längen,
umarmten sie drei Männer, nicht umspannten.
Bis auf den Wipfel stand sie überwachsen
von dunklem Efeu, dunkle Pyramide,
ein hohler Efeuberg um einen Baum.
Und in den Rankenschaukeln seines Dauerns
hing Erde, angeweht vom Wind, darin
spross Farn und keimten Samen, Wespen
   bauten . . .

Das Licht, das durch die Blätter ging, durchgrünte
die unscheinbaren Blattläuse; es frassen
von ihren Rücken Honigtau, die Tröpfchen,
Ameisen, wandernde. Vor allem stand
mein lieber Vater damals und nahm Proben.

SUMMERTIME

I see my father stepping through thick, high grass,
the delicate panicles swaying ever so gently,
and this is true: he seemed to float legless
toward an oak tree, so thick that three men

could not stretch their six arms around it.
Up to the treetop it stood overgrown
by dark ivy, a dark pyramid,
a hollow ivy-mountain around a tree.
And in the rustling creepers of its permanence
hung dirt, blown there by the wind; in it
fern sprouted and seeds germinated; wasps were
   building
The light through the leaves made
the unassuming aphids glow green;
ants, wandering, ate tiny droplets of honeydew
from their backs. My dear father stood
before it all then and took samples.

Contemporary East German Poetry, A Special Issue of *FIELD*, was published in the fall of 1980. The initial printing of 1,500 copies sold out within a few years.

REPORT ON VISIT WITH KITO LORENC IN WUISCHKE AM CZORNEBOH: JUNE 3-4, 1978

The next document in my file is dated June 26, 1978; it is a report on my visit with the Sorbian poet, Kito Lorenc, and writer/translator Adolf Endler, in the tiny Lusatian village of Wuischke am Czorneboh, located in eastern Saxony. The report was prepared in the nearby city of Bautzen and is based on information provided by an unofficial source—i.e., an informant. The purpose of my visit was to gather materials from Lorenc for my book on GDR literature, *DDR-Literatur im Tauwetter*, as well as texts for the above-mentioned anthology of contemporary East German poetry.

Lorenc and his wife lived on what once had been a farm located in an idyllic, rural setting in the Lusatian countryside. The farmhouse and other buildings had been purchased by a group of poets who were friends—Adolf Endler and Elke Erb, who were married at the time, and the Halle poet Heinz

Czechowski. Lorenc resided there permanently; the others used their farmhouses as weekend and vacation retreats from their apartments in the city. Lorenc invited me to stay overnight in his house, which gave me an opportunity to have lengthy discussions with him and Endler about problems associated with the 8th GDR Writers Congress that had just concluded and the recent developments in the GDR literary scene.

The one-page report on my visit with Kito Lorenc, his wife, and Adolf Endler on June 3 and 4, 1978 was prepared in Bautzen and then sent to secret police headquarters in Dresden, and forwarded from there to the Ministry for State Security (MfSS) in Berlin. The date, June 27, 1978 is stamped onto the report, along with the following information: MfSS/DR 32, 3422, Main Department XX. It is particularly interesting to see that there is no reference to Lorenc's wife in the report, which appears in its entirety below.

Regional Headquarters for   Bautzen, 06/26/1978
State Security Dresden   Reh/Thr
County Authority Bautzen   Binder-No.: 2332/78
Ministry for State Security
Main Department XX
Comrade Generalmajor Kienberg

B e r l i n

via Regional Headquarters Dresden – Division XX

Visitation of the American Germanist Z i p s e r with the Sorbian lyric poet L o r e n c, Kito und the translator E n d l e r, Adolf

Unofficially, it became known that the American Germanist Zipser spent time visiting the Sorbian lyric poet Lorenc, Kito in 8601 Wuischke, Bautzen County. Zipser was seeking contributions from Lorenc for a GDR poetry anthology as well as for another book on the topic of GDR literature, which is supposed to be about 1,000 pages in length. For this purpose he plans to interview 40 prose writers and poets from the GDR;

he will present these interviews together with a short biography and a picture of each writer as well as some poems or short prose works by each.

Zipser stayed overnight at Lorenc's place and engaged in a longer conversation with the translator Endler, Adolf in his dwelling, also located in Wuischke. It was not possible to gather any information regarding the content of their conversation.

The discussions between Lorenc and Zipser focused on, among other things, problems associated with the Writers Congress as well as with the development of GDR literature. Zipser was very cautious during this process and noncommittal in his comments. His conduct was characterized by constant self-control and impartiality. Zipser confirmed that he would get back in touch with Lorenc and also with Endler in due course. A fixed date was not set. Nothing was learned about Zipser's further travel destinations.

Director of the County Authority

[*signature*]

On behalf of K u b e l

- Major -

REPORT ON MEETING WITH STUDENTS ON JUNE 15-16, 1978

During my first stay in Berlin as an IREX scholar, from mid-October to mid-December 1977, I had gotten to know a group of students from the Institute for German Studies at the Humboldt University. I would meet with them informally from time to time, and the file contains a report based on what one of these students told his professor, Anneliese Löffler (aka IM "Dölbl"), who was still my official minder. The report appears in its entirety below.

Main Department XX   Berlin, 6/23/1978

Information

Dr. Richard ZIPSER – USA Germanist

In a face-to-face meeting with unofficial collaborator "Dölbl,"

EDELMANN, Gregor,

a German studies student at the Humboldt University, stated that he together with another German studies student,

RESE, Tatjana,

had met on the night of 6/15 to 6/16/1978 with the USA citizen

Dr. ZIPSER, Richard.

Edelmann und Rese have been acquainted with Zipser since his last stay in the GDR toward the end of 1977.

According to Edelmann, Zipser had been under the influence of alcohol and expressed views on the situation among GDR writers.

While doing so Zipser stated his belief that the writer Rolf Schneider as well as Jurek Becker would soon be applying to leave the GDR for an extended period of time. Zipser apparently learned that in a conversation with Schneider.

In addition, Zipser related some impressions derived from his conversations with young GDR writers.

In his opinion, the functionaries in the GDR should not let themselves have any illusions about the young generation of GDR writers. The overwhelming majority, he claims, embraces positions that are aimed against the policies of the State, and the GDR is going to have "lots of trouble" with them.

TOP SECRET INFORMATIONAL REPORT: JULY 17, 1978

Following my departure from Berlin and return to Oberlin on June 16, 1978, the Stasi prepared a confidential report on my activities in the GDR that were related and unrelated to my book project. This "top secret" report, which appears in an abridged form below, begins with information on the purpose of my visit as an IREX scholar and the contractual basis for it. It concludes with the recommendation that the GDR Ministry of Higher Education not enter into another agreement with IREX that would permit me to return to the GDR.

Main Department XX

Top Secret

Berlin, 07/17/1978

prepared 7 copies

684 / 78

Information

about the residence in the GDR of USA Germanist Dr. Richard ZIPSER in May/June 1978

....

The USA Germanist known operatively

Dr. ZIPSER, Richard

Born on 01/23/1943 in Maryland

Residence: 102 Shipherd Circle/USA

Associate Professor at Oberlin College in Ohio/USA

was residing in the GDR from 05/15 – 06/16/1978.

[...]
[...]

During his residence in the GDR ZIPSER got together on numerous occasions with Ulrich PLENZDORF – his closest contact person during earlier stays in the GDR as well – and also spent a good amount of time at his weekend retreat in [*blacked out*].

In addition, ZIPSER had personal encounters (several times in some cases) with Fritz Rudolf FRIES, Klaus SCHLESINGER, Rolf SCHNEIDER, Helga SCHÜTZ, Adolf ENDLER, Kito LORENC, Erik NEUTSCH, Siegfried PITSCHMANN, Eberhard PANITZ, Willy and Maria MOESE, Max Walter SCHULZ, Martin STADE, and others. Beyond that he met and had discussions with, among others, Heiner MÜLLER, Volker BRAUN, and Günter GÖRLICH as well with some German studies students from the Humboldt University of Berlin.

During his stay ZIPSER sought above all to obtain from these writers their revised and authorized contributions for his forthcoming book. At times he issued emphatic warnings that this period of residence would be the final opportunity for him to take delivery of the texts.

ZIPSER stated a number of times that he plans to conclude all work on the book manuscript by the end of 1978/beginning of 1979, so it can be published in the USA in the fall of 1979 or thereabouts. He says provision has been made for the publication of a 1,500-volume edition in the German language, intended primarily for students of German studies in the USA.

In various conversations related to the 8th GDR Writers Congress, ZIPSER put on a display of naïveté as regards the importance and objective of a congress like this one, so he would be able to ask seemingly "innocent" questions, according to the assessments on hand.

On the other hand, ZIPSER displayed considerable interest in the female person who is Director of the Cultural Division of the Central Committee of the SED (Socialist Unity Party), in details of the events related to Biermann's expulsion from the GDR, in creative artists who are on so-called blacklists (e.g., DEFA documentary filmmaker Jürgen BÖTTCHER and feature film director Egon GÜNTHER), as well as in problems of artistic creativity from the perspective of given possibilities for veiled depiction of deplorable aspects of society. [*DEFA (Deutsche Film-Aktiengesellschaft) was the state-owned film studio of the GDR throughout the country's existence.*]

[...]

ZIPSER designated STADE and PLENZDORF as the persons with whom he got along especially well over the course of his stay in the GDR. In the case of PLENZDORF he admires above all the open and generous way he shares his feelings, his private thoughts and desires with him, ZIPSER.

In some conversations ZIPSER signaled his intention, following the completion of his current book manuscript, to undertake a new book project focusing specifically on lyric poetry of the GDR. This would give him a reason for additional stays in the GDR and for establishing connections to additional GDR writers. [*Actually, when I returned to the United States in mid-June 1978, I already had in my possession texts from each of the fourteen poets represented in the "Contemporary East German*

Poetry" anthology, as well as written permission from each writer to publish his/her poems. It was not necessary for me to return the GDR to complete this project.]

Considering ZIPSER's shadowy behavior, his deliberate attempts to lure away GDR creative artists during his stays in the GDR up to now, which have previously been reported a number of times, it is recommended that the GDR Ministry for Higher Education not enter into a new contract with IREX that would enable ZIPSER to have another period of residence.

Distribution List:

Deputy Minister
Director Main Department XX
Colonel Stange
Central Evaluation and Information Group
Main Department XX/7
Main Department XX/Evaluation and Information Group

TOP SECRET INFORMATIONAL REPORT: AUGUST 4, 1978

The next document in my file is a 16-page informational report, also labelled "top secret," which for the most part restates and updates the information contained in the 15-page report dated January 7, 1978. However, it also provides an assessment of my activities in the GDR, characterizes me as an enemy of the state in the cultural realm, and sets forth the measures that needed to be taken to curtail my subversive activities in the future. Those sections of the report appear below.

Main Department XX	Berlin, 08/04/1978
Top Secret	prepared 6 copies
	730 / 78

Information

Richard ZIPSER's harmful-hostile activities against the cultural sphere of the GDR.

[...]

Upon evaluating the results to date of the political-operative handling of Zipser, the following measures are being recommended:

1. Main Department XX will take the steps necessary to ensure that Zipser will no longer be considered for future IREX exchange programs.

2. Main Department XX will exert influence so as to ensure that Zipser will not receive invitations and support from the Writers' Union and other relevant bodies that need to approve Zipser's projects.

3. With the goal of establishing proof that Zipser has been engaging in intelligence activity

4. a comprehensive operative surveillance will be initiated whenever Zipser enters the country;

   an additional targeted monitoring of Zipser and his contacts will be carried out;

   a close collaboration with the service units that have got the unofficial resources for operative surveillance and processing will be assured.

The following memorandum is attached to the report:

Comrade Lieutenant Colonel Gessner

The information on ZIPSER should be kept ready for delivery on demand.

POSSIBLE DENIAL OF RE-ENTRY INTO THE GDR

The next document in the file, a single page, reveals that consideration was given to not permitting me to re-enter the GDR. The top section of the document is typewritten and dated June 11, 1979. Toward the bottom of the page there are handwritten notes, which were added on September 16, 1982. These notes indicate that a decision had been made in Main Department XX to permit me to re-enter the GDR ("no re-entry ban"). The document appears in its entirety below.

Main Department	Berlin	6/11/1979
Capt. Tischendorf	2642/2812	2633
	Re-entry ban	
	[*handwritten*]	

Dr. Z i p s e r

Richard
1/23/43
Maryland/USA
USA
Germanist
Oberlin, Ohio/USA
102 Shipherd Circle

<u>Block re-entry</u> – check back with service unit issuing this order to see if re-entry application may be approved

[*Below are the handwritten notes that were added in 1982.*]

Main Department XX/7

X

XII: 15672173   [*signature/initials only*]

9/16/82 No Re-Entry Ban [*as per*] Main Department XX

8TH GDR WRITERS CONGRESS: MAY 28-31, 1978

In 1977, in the wake of the infamous Biermann affair, a number of gifted GDR writers—Bernd Jentzsch, Thomas Brasch, Reiner Kunze, Sarah Kirsch, and Hans Joachim Schädlich—were permitted or forced to depart for the West. Government authorities, embarrassed by the exodus of these prominent authors, were anxious to stop the westward flow of literary talent. Hence, in a conciliatory move aimed at avoiding further adverse publicity, they granted Jurek Becker's request for a special two-year visa, enabling him to move to West Berlin and visit Oberlin. However, the cultural-political atmosphere continued to deteriorate in the GDR, especially in East Berlin, and the liberal tendencies that were present during the first five years of the Honecker era (1971-1976) disappeared altogether by the end of 1979. The "Berlin Spring" ended with the expatriation of Biermann, and the ensuing public protests by rebellious writers and artists convinced SED Party leaders that a crackdown was necessary in the cultural sphere. In the spring of 1978, seven preeminent GDR authors (Franz Fühmann, Stefan Heym, Günter Kunert, Ulrich Plenzdorf, Klaus Schlesinger, Rolf Schneider, and Christa Wolf) were barred from participating in the GDR Writers Congress, not only to prevent them from focusing attention in that forum on the Biermann crisis and its aftermath, but also to send a stern warning to other writers.

The 8th GDR Writers Congress, which took place during my second stay in Berlin as an IREX scholar, was orchestrated to reinforce in GDR authors' minds and have them reaffirm the close relationship between East German literature and socialism. SED Party loyalist Hermann Kant was elevated to the position of President of the Writers' Union, replacing the ailing and frail grande dame of GDR letters, Anna Seghers. The theme of the Congress, introduced by partisan prose writer Erwin Strittmatter in his opening address on May 28, set the tone: The responsibility of writers in the struggles of our time. He did not mention or allude in any way to Biermann's expulsion or incidents related to it, nor did SED leader Erich Honecker when he addressed the 300 assembled delegates later that day. Kant delivered the keynote address, and in it he acknowledged the taboo subject of expelled colleagues. But none of the other speakers mentioned by name any of their departed colleagues; they followed Honecker's lead. The Congress concluded with an official declaration of loyalty to the State, further stressing the role that writers were expected to play. In the end, the 1978 GDR Writers Congress simply reflected the cultural-political climate of the day, which did not tolerate open discussion and debate. The message was clear: GDR writers were expected to toe the Party line, be loyal to the State, and refrain from criticizing actions or policies of the SED leadership.

Siegfried Pitschmann, a prose writer from Rostock who had come to Berlin for the Writers Congress, certainly got the message. He and I had arranged to meet in the lobby of Hotel Unter den Linden on May 29, 1978, at 9:30 a.m., so he could give me the revised transcript of the interview we had tape recorded in Rostock back in June of 1976, for publication in *DDR-Literatur im Tauwetter*. Pitschmann was obviously intimidated by what he had heard Honecker, Kant, Strittmatter and others say on the first day of the Congress, so he decided not to give me the typewritten sheets he had brought to Berlin. The surveillance report in my file captured our brief meeting and conversation that morning:

9:35 a.m. a male person [*Pitschmann*] emerged from the elevator and looked around the lobby in a searching manner.

> "Eagle" stood up and quickly approached this male person. They greeted each other eagerly with a handshake. The male person pulled several typewritten sheets out of his coat pocket and said something very similar to this: "I can't give these to you, not the way they read now. Changes have to be made. Unfortunately, I didn't get to that earlier, and I

won't be able to do it in the near future either since I'm travelling to the USSR [*Union of Soviet Socialist Republics*]. The content won't be changed, but the form and some minor details are in need of revision." "Eagle" then indicated that he would be departing on the 15th, whereupon the male person replied that he would be returning from the USSR on the evening of the 16th. It could also be overheard that "Eagle" arranged to meet with the writer Pitschmann in the evening hours. After that the male person put the typewritten sheets back into his coat pocket and declared that he would finish correcting what he had written while in the USSR. They then said goodbye.

According to the surveillance report, Pitschmann and I met again that evening, at approximately 8:00 p.m. We sat at a table in the lobby of the Hotel Unter den Linden and had an animated conversation, presumably about his refusal to give me the interview he had revised before coming to Berlin and now claimed he needed to revise further. The report also mentions that Pitschmann gave me a book he had published in Aufbau Publishing House's *bb-Reihe* (a series of inexpensive paperbacks) in 1973. It is a volume of his short stories entitled *Männer mit Frauen* (*Men with Women*), and Pitschmann identified three texts that he wanted me to publish in *DDR-Literatur im Tauwetter*. He inscribed the book as follows:

"Für Richard Zipser mit besten Wünschen für seine Arbeit –"
["*For Richard Zipser with best wishes for his project –*"]
S. Pitschmann
Berlin / May 78

Pitschmann never sent me the revised transcript of our interview, which—given the way he had behaved during our two meetings in Hotel Unter den Linden—did not surprise me. I received a letter from him in the second half of August 1978, explaining why he had decided to withdraw the interview. The original text of that letter appears below, followed by my translation of its body into English.

Siegfried Pitschmann
DDR 252 Rostock 22
Stockholmer Strasse 4

Rostock, d. 10. August 1978

Herrn
Dr. Richard Zipser

102 Shipherd Circle
O b e r l i n, Ohio 44074
U S A

Sehr geehrter Herr Dr. Zipser,

nach langen und gründlichen Überlegungen, die auch mein – nicht aus Unhöflichkeit oder Nachlässigkeit geschehenes – Schweigen und offenkundiges Zögern erklären, möchte ich Sie so freundlich wie dringlich darum bitten, meinen Beitrag für Ihre geplante Arbeit nicht zu verwenden, das heisst ihn aus dem Buch zu streichen.

Zwar ist es richtig, dass ich vor nunmehr wohl drei Jahren ganz in Übereinstimmung, ja auf Anraten der Leitung des Schriftsteller-verbandes der DDR gerne bereit war, Ihre Unternehmung über unsere zeitgenössische Literatur zu unterstützen und Fragen – so gut es ging – zu beantworten – wie ich ja auch noch im Mai diesen Jahres grundsätzlich derselben Meinung schien, und doch sehe ich in der Tatsache, dass ich jetzt meine Auskünfte zurückziehe, keinen Bruch irgendeines Abkommens. Ich bitte Sie, die folgende kurze Begründung zu bedenken und zu akzeptieren.

1. Zwischen dem Erscheinen meiner letzten Arbeit und dem künftigen mutmasslichen Termin, an dem etwas neues in die Öffentlichkeit kommt, besteht ein allzu grosser Zeitabstand: es ist mir einfach peinlich, in der ganzen Zwischenzeit immer nur Theoretisches über Schreiberei abzuliefern.

2. Damit in Zusammenhang steht nach wiederholter Püfung die Feststellung, dass meine Antworten auf Ihre 14 angenehm konkreten Fragen überaus "wolkig", geschwätzig, also unkonkret wirken. Nicht, dass ich den inneren Kern mancher Aussagen – die ja lange zurückliegen – zurücknehmen möchte, agesehen davon, dass ich sie heute vermutlich differenzierter, überlegter oder modifizierter formulieren würde – aber ich halte sie nun einmal für völlig ungenügend und unnütz und damit auch irreparabel, zumal bei einer echten "Bearbeitung" am Schreibtisch die ursprünglich von Ihnen geplante Spontaneität zerstört würde. Und selbst das vorgegeben, käme doch wieder nur Gerede heraus, statt eines Literatur-Textes wieder einmal nur Reflexion über Literatur – und dagegen ist meine Abneigung inzwischen geradezu unüberwindlich.

Kurz: Ihnen sowie mir wäre mit einer – autorisierten oder nicht autorisierten – Publizierung kein guter Dienst erwiesen, und deshalb bitte ich Sie nochmals darum, davon abzusehen.

Ihrem übrigen Vorhaben wünsche ich trotzdem gutes oder nützliches Gelingen, indem ich mit freundlichen Grüssen verbleibe

Ihr
[*signed*]
Siegfried Pitschmann

Dear Mr. Zipser,

After prolonged and thorough deliberations, which will also explain my silence and patently obvious hesitancy that are not the result of impoliteness or negligence, I would like to ask you in a friendly yet urgent way not to use my contribution in the project you have in the works, in other words to delete it from your book.

It is indeed true that now more than three years ago I was completely in agreement and prepared, acting upon the advice of the GDR Writers' Union, to support your undertaking on our contemporary literature and to answer your questions—as well as possible—and in May of this year I also seemed basically to be of the same opinion, and yet I do not think the fact that I am now withdrawing my pieces of information amounts to a breach of any contract. I ask you to consider and to accept the following brief justification.

1. The time interval that exists between the publication of my last work and the probable date on which something new will appear in the public arena is much too long: it is simply embarrassing to me only to be providing theoretical thoughts on writing during the entire interim.

2. Related to that is the realization, after repeated examination, that my answers to your 14 agreeably specific questions come across as extremely "cloudy," loquacious, hence unspecific. Not that I would like to take back the inner core of certain statements which of course were made a long time ago, except for the fact that today I probably would formulate them in a more sophisticated, discreet, or modified way—but right now I consider them to be completely insufficient and useless and as such irreparable, particularly by substantial editing at my desk which would destroy the spontaneity you originally desired. And even by doing just that, the result would only

be idle talk again, instead of a literary text, once again only reflections on literature—and my aversion to that at this point is virtually insurmountable.

In short: Publishing this material—with authorization or without authorization—would do a disservice to you and to me, and I therefore ask you once again to refrain from doing so.

For the remainder of your project I nevertheless wish you a good or useful outcome, while remaining with kind regards

Yours,
[*signed*]
Siegfried Pitschmann

Since I had the original transcript of our tape-recorded interview, as well as the tape cassette, Pitschmann was clearly afraid that I might proceed to publish it without his authorization. I did not do that, but I did publish the above letter in the section of the book focusing on him, under the heading "Anstatt eines Interviews" (Instead of an Interview). Today, with objective distance and the much greater knowledge I have about what took place at the 8th GDR Writers Congress, I can understand Pitschmann's fearful reaction. I also realize how very fortunate I was that he was the only one of the 45 writers represented in *DDR-Literatur im Tauwetter* who decided to withdraw the interview.

FRITZ RUDOLF FRIES: IMS "PEDRO HAGEN"

The first reference in my file to prose writer/informant Fritz Rudolf Fries, aka IMS "Pedro Hagen," occurs in the surveillance report that covers the three-day period May 29 to May 31, 1978, while the 8th GDR Writers Congress was underway. Fries does not resurface in my file until March 1985, but—as I would discover—he was busy gathering information on me and reporting it to his Stasi-handler from 1978 on.

In November 2002, almost four years after I had received my Stasi-file, I found another package from the Stasi Records Agency in my mailbox. Its contents came as a real surprise. A cover letter dated November 5 enlightened me:

Dear Dr. Zipser,

With a letter dated 01.15.99 you received copies of the documents from the Stasi-files that had been assembled on your person.

For the purpose of historical and political reappraisal of the activities of the State Security Service, according to §§ 32 ff. of the Stasi Records Act, researchers and representatives of the media may also have access to the documents. Personal information about personages of recent history, holders of political positions, or public officials carrying out their duties will—when they are related to the public actions of these individuals—also be made available without their explicit consent.

As the result of such requests from researchers and the media new documents were discovered in the files of an unofficial collaborator, from the circle of writers in the GDR, that contain information about you as a third party.

[...]

In compliance with §32 a of the Stasi Records Act, I hereby am notifying you of their planned release for the purposes of research and media projects, and I am also now sending you copies of these documents, so that you will have the opportunity to raise objections to allowing access to information that is related to your person.

[...]

[...]

Attachments

44 Pages

The cover page of the enclosed document reveals that I had been sent a portion of IMS "Pedro Hagen's" Stasi-file. When I looked up the meaning of IMS, an acronym not used in my own file, I found that it stands for "Inoffizieller Mitarbeiter zur politisch-operativen Durchdringung und Sicherung des Verantwortungsbereichs" (literally: unofficial collaborator for political-operative penetration and safeguarding of the area of responsibility). Evidently, Fries was a highly trusted Stasi collaborator who was given special assignments related to state security. One of those assignments was to gather information and report on the activities of Richard Zipser. (For the record, I did not object to allowing access to any of the information Fries had gathered on me.)

What disturbed and still disturbs me most about the reports on me from Fries's file, which are longer and more detailed than those of any IM in my own file, is the fact that there is no cross-reference or mention of "Pedro Hagen" in my file. In the May 1978 surveillance report in which Fries is mentioned, he is given a different alias, "Falke" (Falcon), presumably to protect his "Pedro Hagen" cover. Now I had a new question to ponder: How many other IM reports on me exist in the files of GDR writers and acquaintances, reports that were placed only in their files and not in mine? In September 1999, about nine months after the arrival of my Stasi-file, I sent the names of eight persons I thought might be collaborators to my case worker at the Stasi Records Agency, in an effort to obtain additional information. However, I never received a response to my inquiry. In the end, I decided not to pursue the matter further, which is probably what the officials overseeing the Stasi-files desired.

FIRST REPORT IN THE FILE LABELLED "PEDRO HAGEN"

The first document in what I am calling the Fries/Zipser file is dated May 23, 1978, and reports on a May 22, 1978 meeting between Fries and his Stasi-handler, First Lieutenant Gerhard Hoffmann. There are three pages, a two-page form labelled "Treffbericht" (Report on Meeting) with four sections, into which Hoffmann entered information, and an attachment. In the first section one finds the names of the informant and his handler, the date, time and place of the meeting; the second section is titled "Treffvorbereitung" (Preparation for Meeting) and makes reference to the attachment; the third section, on page two, is for an evaluation of the meeting ("Treffauswertung"); and the fourth section, also on page two, is for information related to the informant's new assignment ("Neuer Auftrag und Verhaltenslinie"). The third page is an attachment with Fries's notes on preparation for the meeting ("Treffvorberei-tung") he would be having with me on May 23, 1978, and some other matters he was planning to look into. All the information on the form and attachment, most of which I have reproduced below, is handwritten.

Service Unit: Regional Headquarters Frankfurt (Oder), Dept. XX/7
Date: 05/23/78

Approvals

[*signed*]

Diepold

Report on Meeting

Category/Code Name IMS "Pedro Hagen", V/MOG/72

Date/Time	Meeting Place	Staff Member
05/22/78	Petershagen	Hoffmann

15:30-17:00

Next Meeting	Time	Meeting Place
on 05/24/78	09:00-10:00	Petershagen
Reports 2 oral		

Preparation for meeting:

(e.g., meeting planned / scheduled on short notice, brief summary of the agenda for the planned meeting, focal points of the assigned mission, instructions, preparation and qualification)

- planned meeting

- preparation for meeting (see attachment)

Evaluation of meeting:

(e.g., reference to content of the reporting, conforms to assigned direction of the mission, behavior of the unofficial collaborator, signs of dishonesty / unreliability / deconspiration, operative value and objectivity of the reporting, utilization of the gathered information, ideological problems, disciplinary measures, benefits)

In follow-up to our last meeting the IM [*informant*] once again raised questions about further collaboration. It was made clear to the IM again that the main goal is to guide those GDR writers who recently addressed problematic issues publicly to realistic positions, in the sense that they accept the existing circumstances and not seek refuge in illusory viewpoints.

The IM accepted the statements concerning this matter and agreed to continue collaborating on that basis with the MfSS.

The IM communicated an operatively valuable piece of information related to the behavior of the American professor of literature, Dr. Zipser.

In addition, he provided an assessment of problems that are connected to the 8th Writers Congress.

It may be presumed that the conversations held during the last two meetings have contributed significantly to improving the relationship between the IM and the MfSS and to further reducing the reservations that existed previously.

The IM seemed more relaxed and more open-minded with respect to the operative problems.

Regarding the information and assessment communicated by the IM, it must be emphasized that on the part of the IM there is evidence of an understanding of the set of issues and a higher degree of trust in the MfSS than before.

Also, the IM was active and constructive in the setting up of another meeting.

The IM did not receive an invitation to a meeting of and with other authors at Klaus Schlesinger's residence in Berlin or at the home of another writer, in advance preparation for the Congress! [*Many GDR writers were wary of Fries, suspecting—although not knowing—that he was collaborating with the Stasi. Hence, they avoided his company and did not invite him to participate in informal private gatherings like the ones mentioned above. Fries's Stasi-handler clearly wishes the informant had received invitations, but the exclamation point is the only indication of his displeasure.*]

New assignment and guidelines

For the meeting with Prof. Zipser on 5/23/78

1. Find out and clarify what has become of Zipser's project, the reason why he was doing research in the GDR about two years ago.

2. Clarify who else is participating in the project, in whose company the IM is going to find himself.

3. Whom does Zipser still intend to call on, for what period of time will he be in the GDR, where is he staying during the Writers Congress?

4. Which GDR writers is Prof. Zipser considering for a period of residency at USA universities?

Preparation for meeting "P. Hagen", 05/22/78

- Birthday
- Delegation for the Congress

- Executive Committee?
- Smooth sequence of events at the Delegates Conference
- What played out in the background?

Many of those who were expected to be delegates are not, how was that received?

- How did circle of friends react to selected delegates?
- Is there a desire to speak at the Congress?

- Are there plans for authors who are not delegates and want to meet before or during the Congress?

- Have Zipser, Gross, publishers made appointments for visits even before the Congress?
>Specifics

>Concrete travel plans   W[est] B[erlin] Sarah [Kirsch]
>Expectation of apartment in Berlin
>Meeting in Rüdersdorf

- Meeting during the Congress > readiness

going to be driven home each day?

REPORT ON MAY 24, 1978 MEETING: IMS "PEDRO HAGEN" AND HIS STASI-HANDLER

As planned, Fries met with Stasi officer Hoffmann on May 24, 1978, to report on his meeting with me the previous day. According to the handwritten "Report on Meeting," which Hoffmann completed on June 12, 1978, the meeting took place in Petershagen, where Fries was living, from 9:00 – 9:30 a.m. The form indicates that they would be meeting again during the GDR Writers Congress, May 29 – 31, 1978. The information in the report appears below.

Preparation for meeting:

- planned meeting
- reporting on meeting with Prof. Zipser on 05/23/78

Evaluation of meeting:

The IM reported that the meeting with Zipser has taken place.

Z. will be in the GDR until 6/16/78. He refers to himself as a GDR scholarship holder and indicates that he is able to continue working in the GDR due to an agreement between the governments of the GDR and the USA. His project has been sanctioned by the GDR Ministry for Culture.

He has an apartment in the capital city, Berlin [*blacked out*].

His project involves, first and foremost, paying visits to the authors with whom he already spoke during his last residency.

Z. expresses reservations with regard to the provision of lecture invitations at USA universities, asserting that his "benefactor" dislikes the GDR and for that reason it would be difficult for him to set up lecture bookings for GDR authors in the USA.

With respect to the IM, Z. declined to take action on his behalf in relation to planned lectures at USA universities.

As a result of the first exploratory talk, the IM and Z. agreed to meet again on 5/29/78, at 7:00 p.m., in "Lindencorso."

The IM consented to another meeting after Z.'s meeting with him.

New assignment and guidelines:

Identify Z.'s work plans, what is he intending to do?

When is the book that Z. intends to publish going to appear in print, in what form?

What stance is Z. taking on the 8th Writers Congress?

Fries was very eager to visit the United States and tried several times to persuade me either to invite him to be German writer-in-residence at Oberlin College or help arrange a lecture tour at US universities. Many GDR writers expressed interest in coming to Oberlin, as Christa Wolf and Ulrich Plenzdorf had done, but none of them were as pushy as Fries. In 1981, Fries was rewarded for his excellent work as a Stasi collaborator and permitted to visit the US, albeit with a special assignment related to me.

REPORT ON MAY 29-30, 1978 MEETINGS: IMS "PEDRO HAGEN" AND HIS STASI-HANDLER

The next "Report on Meeting," dated June 12, 1978, focuses on the meetings Stasi officer Hoffmann had with Fries while the GDR Writers Congress was underway, May 29-31, 1978. According to the handwritten report, which Hoffmann completed on the basis of information Fries provided orally, they had three meetings in Berlin at the Hotel Stadt Berlin and the Palace of the Republic, the seat of the parliament of the GDR. The substance of the report appears below.

Preparation for meeting:

meetings, arranged on short notice, were held in connection with the security demands of the 8th Writers Congress;

meetings took place on:

5/29/78, 1:00 – 1:30 p.m.
5/29/78, 8:00 – 9:00 p.m.
5/30/78, 2:00 – 2:30 p.m.

Evaluation of meetings:

Reports/Information on meetings were submitted to Main Department XX/7 for evaluation, since a colleague from Main Department XX/7 was assigned to active duty at the Congress.

The IM provided verified information and a report on the plans and intentions of the American literary scholar, Dr. Zipser.

Reports will be evaluated by Main Department XX/7 and processed into day-by-day information.

REPORT DATED JUNE 27, 1978

There is one more document in the 1978 section of the Fries/Zipser file, a two-page typewritten report prepared by Stasi officer Hoffmann, using information Fries had provided orally on May 22, 1978. It appears in its entirety below.

Department XX/7	Frankfurt (O), 06/27/ 1978
source: IMS "Pedro Hagen"	Pe [*Petershagen*]
received:	First Lieutenant Hoffmann
on:	05/22/1978

- <u>oral</u> -

<u>Prof. Z i p s e r</u> , American literary scholar

In relation to Prof. Zipser the IM provided the following new details, adding to the information he obtained on 04/14/1978:

On 05/18/1978 Prof. Zipser made contact via telephone and said that he was able to follow through on his plan and is staying in the GDR. He indicated that he was very interested in having a conversation and wanted to set up a meeting. He said he would be spending a longer period of time in the GDR, which would enable him to continue his work. After that an agreement was reached to hold a meeting on 05/23/1978.

<u>Comment:</u>

On 04/14/1978 the IM reported that Prof. Zipser gave advance notice of another working visit in the spring of 1978. After Prof. Zipser made contact recently, an agreement was reached to have a meeting in the IM's apartment. The IM stated that— without being prompted to do so—he was very interested in speaking with Zipser because he is eager to know if Zipser has completed the manuscript with interviews he conducted some years ago with GDR authors and where things stand with regard to its publication. In addition to that the IM is interested in learning in whose company he would find himself in the event of a publication, whether for example the authors who have left the GDR will still be published as GDR authors. Furthermore, the IM wants to discuss with Prof. Zipser opportunities to conduct seminars and give readings at USA universities in 1979. The IM is in possession of an invitation from a small university in Minnesota; but it makes no sense to accept this invitation without having the opportunity to read and/or offer seminars at other universities. That is why the IM intends ultimately to reach an agreement with Zipser that involves readings at more universities.

On the basis of the IM's plans with regard to the conversation with Zipser, the IM was given the following assignment:

a.) Find out and clarify what has become of Zipser's project, the reason why he previously spent time in the GDR;

b.) Clarify who else is participating in this project;

c.) Whom does Zipser still intend to call on, for what period of time will he be in the GDR, where is he staying during the Writers Congress, arrange a meeting during the Congress, if possible;

d.) Which GDR authors is Prof. Zipser considering for a period of residency at USA universities?

The IM showed interest in this assignment and agreed to make an effort to clarify these questions.

It seems significant that the IM accepted the assignment as such, because previously there were reservations in this regard.

Measures:

Consolidation of the information on hand and then forward to Main Department XX/7.

Distribution List: 1 x Main Department XX/7
                        1 x IM File

[*signature*]
Hoffmann
First Lieutenant

As one reads the first set of reports from the Fries/Zipser file, it is especially interesting to see how Fries becomes increasingly willing to cooperate as a Stasi collaborator, no longer expressing reservations about his assignments. Hoffmann, who worked with Fries for many years, patiently molded him into an exemplary informant. But Fries, eager for privileges such as permission to travel to the US and the assignment of an apartment in Berlin, was more than willing to let himself be molded by Hoffmann. In retrospect, one could say that this was the perfect marriage between a GDR writer and his Stasi-handler. Both parties benefitted from it, albeit in very different ways.

NEXT TWO YEARS AT OBERLIN COLLEGE: 1978 TO 1980

I returned to Oberlin in mid-June 1978, not knowing that it would be almost six years before I would again visit East Berlin. Over the next two years, while teaching full-time at Oberlin College, I worked on four projects related to the GDR.

The first project involved the preparation of a four-part publication on Jurek Becker, who—as I discussed earlier—had spent the spring 1978 semester at Oberlin College. The four-part package, which was published in the literary journal *DIMENSION* (Volume 11, Number 3, 1978, pp. 402-423), consisted of the following pieces: *New Yorker Woche / A Week in New York*, seven short prose texts Becker wrote during his first week in the US, which were translated into English by A. Leslie Willson; *Jurek Becker: A Writer with a Cause*, my short essay on Becker designed to introduce him to an English-speaking audience; *Interview with Jurek Becker*, an interview I conducted in May 1978, covering three major phases of Becker's life and career (1945-1960: Life and Experiences in the Years Following World War II, 1960-1977: The Launching of a Literary Career, 1978- : Jurek Becker Living on Foreign Soil); and *My Way of Being a Jew*, an essay Becker had written before coming to Oberlin and presented as a public lecture in April 1978. The interview and the essay were translated into English by Claudia Johnson, a student at Oberlin at that time, and me.

The essay caused quite a stir because of Becker's assertion that he did not consider himself to be Jewish, even though his parents were Jews. He explained his position, which later in life he modified, as follows:

> I maintain that belonging to a group of people called "the Jews" can be perceived only as a voluntary act; it is a choice that can be made in one way or another, in the last analysis an intellectual decision. I have encountered considerable opposition to this view, and at times I have wanted to defend it as fiercely as possible. I do not want to develop this idea beyond saying: The opponents of such a view come from all over—from the ranks of the believers, such as the Zionists, but also from the ranks of the most embittered anti-Semites, the authors of the race laws, for instance, who during the Third Reich did not want to leave the individual any freedom of choice whatsoever, whether he was Jewish or not. (p. 419)

Another controversial statement in this essay would prompt a major scholarly journal in the US to censor Becker. In an effort to explain his lack of identification with the Jewish religion or people, Becker asserted:

> Being a Jew does not arouse a feeling of good fortune because I, willingly or not, belong to an extended group of people who, like other groups of comparable size, accomplish things, both admirable and miserable. I do not feel a surge of pride because Kafka was a Jew, although I suspect that his writings were very significant for me. I do not feel upset because Max Frisch is not a Jew, although he is of similar importance to me. I do not feel ashamed that the Jews in the Near East have established themselves as a master race (*Herrenmenschen*) and are practicing a type of politics that I can only describe as predatory. I just feel angry that people deal with people in such a way.

This last assertion was unacceptable to the editors of the scholarly journal that had eagerly committed in advance to publishing the four-text package Becker and I agreed to prepare for this periodical—without reviewing or revising it. Despite their commitment, which had been put in writing, they demanded that Becker remove the reference to a "master race" and the word "predatory" from his essay, otherwise they would not publish it. I refused to ask Becker to do this and was incensed. After all, Becker had left East Germany at the end of 1977 to escape censorship, only to find himself now being subjected to censorship in this country. How ironic—and how sad!

Since I had negotiated with one of the principal editors of this journal (a prominent Germanist who shall remain anonymous, since he many years later apologized for engaging in editorial censorship) to publish the four texts as a package, I was infuriated when the journal refused to proceed unless Becker would remove the references they considered offensive to their readership. Becker, who was accustomed to being censored from his years as a writer in the GDR, shrugged it off with his typical good humor. In a letter to me dated September 22, 1979, he wrote:

Lieber Dick,

Danke für Deinen Brief, es steht ja viel drin. Die Geschichte mit der New German Critique regt Dich offenbar mehr auf, als sie mich aufregen kann. Wahrscheinlich liegt es daran, dass Du schon so lange der Überzeugung bist, Amerika ist ein demokratisches Land, ich nicht. Das ist aber ganz in Ordnung so—ich habe umgekehrt ja auch viele Jahre fest geglaubt, die DDR ist ein demokratisches Land, und Du nicht. Es ist nicht schön, dass wir uns beide geirrt haben, aber wir sind alt genug, damit fertig zu werden.

Dear Dick,

Thanks for your letter; it provides lots of information. The episode with the New German Critique apparently upsets you more than it can upset me. That's probably because you've been convinced for so long that America is a democratic country; I haven't. But it's entirely okay like this—I also believed firmly for many years, in reverse, that the GDR is a democratic country, and you didn't. It's not nice that we both were mistaken, but we are old enough to deal with that.

I proceeded to place the four-text package with *DIMENSION*, a journal devoted to contemporary German arts and letters, and today I am actually glad that I—like Becker and so many GDR writers—have directly experienced the sting of editorial censorship. While this was my first censorial experience, there would be other such experiences in the years that followed due to my point of view on the repressive GDR state, its rigid cultural politics, and its harsh treatment of writers and artists who dared to voice opposition.

The second project was my three-volume book, *DDR-Literatur im Tauwetter* (*GDR Literature During the Thaw*), which I continued working on as time permitted while teaching at Oberlin College. The voluminous amount of material I had gathered needed to be organized, edited, and assembled in a format suitable for publication. In the spring of 1978, I decided to ask my friend and colleague Karl-Heinz Schoeps, professor of German literature at the University of Illinois at Urbana-Champaign, to collaborate with me on this undertaking. Karl-Heinz, a specialist in twentieth-century German literature with a scholarly interest in GDR literature, agreed to team up with me. In the summer of 1978, we met and decided how to divide the tasks that remained to be done—e.g., writing an introduction, a task we shared equally, preparing bio-bibliographical sketches on the 45 writers, arranging the inter-view materials, and so on. Karl-Heinz translated the foreword I had written in English into German, also my half of the introduction, and anything else that needed to be translated. To this day, I remain immensely grateful to him for his able assistance, without which I never could have completed the project.

The third project involved preparation of a bilingual special issue of the journal *FIELD* on contemporary East German poetry in the 1970s. I had collected poems from the fourteen GDR writers who would be represented, but those works had to be translated into English, a job that fourteen profes-sors, students, and poets would carry out. Also, I needed to write an intro-duction to the anthology as well as a bio-bibliographical sketch for each of the poets. All work on this project was completed in the summer of 1980, and the special issue was published in the fall of that year. It received excel-lent reviews, including one by distinguished Germanist Peter Demetz (Yale University) in the *Washington Post*.

The fourth project was to apply for a National Fellowship at the Hoover Institution in Stanford, California. By the fall of 1979, a little over a year after my return to Oberlin, I realized that I needed a concentrated period of time to bring these various GDR-related projects—especially *DDR-Literatur im Tauwetter*—to their conclusion. At that time, the National Fellows Program allowed established scholars holding a doctoral degree, who were under the age of forty, to devote a full year to research and writing at the Hoover Institution. There was a preference for candidates whose proposals embodied empirical studies of significant public policy issues, which is difficult to design in the humanities. Nevertheless, I managed to give my proposal a public policy slant and was fortunate to be awarded a fellowship for a full year at full pay, from mid-August 1980 to mid-August 1981.

PROPOSAL FOR ANOTHER PROJECT: ANTHOLOGY OF LITERATURE BY YOUNG GDR WRITERS

In an attachment to my file from the central archive, labelled MfS HA XX 2MA, Nr. 976, Z i p s e r, Dr. Richard, 2. Karte (Ministry for State Security, Main Department XX 2 staff members, No. 976, Z i p s e r, Dr. Richard, 2nd card), there is a note that reminds me of yet another project I had planned to carry out—this time in collaboration with dissident prose writer Martin Stade. The note, which is dated July 5, 1979, refers to an anthology of literature by twenty to twenty-five young GDR writers that Stade and I had tentatively decided to prepare together. The focus would be on writers who were born in the GDR—i.e., not before October 7, 1949, the day the constitution of the GDR went into effect. Writers in this age group had spent their entire lives in the GDR; and unlike the older generations of writers in the GDR, they had no recollection of the Third Reich or postwar Germany. All of these writers, none of whom was older than thirty at that time, had grown up in the GDR and therefore did not compare their Germany to Germanys of the past. They tended to be highly critical of the SED regime, its oppression of GDR citizens in all walks of life, and the "really existing socialism" that prevailed in their state-controlled society. Stade was mentoring some of these writers, which explains why he was familiar with their unpublished works.

Regional Headquarters Frankfurt/O., bulletin 6/79, on 5/7/1979:
In anticipation of criminal prosecution due to the signing of
a letter to Comrade Honecker, the writer Martin STADE has
relocated materials that incriminate him to the residence of
Pastor Ralph RITSCHEL [*blacked out*].

The materials under discussion are notes and research
information that STADE prepared for FRG [*West German*]
newspapers as well as approximately 20 manuscripts from GDR
writers with cover letters that go with them. Presumably, these
materials are the result of efforts STADE made on Z.'s behalf. Z.
is planning to compile an anthology with ca. 40 GDR authors.
Originally, a German-language edition of this was supposed to
be published in spring 1979 in the USA.

I reach into the depths of my memory and recall that Stade had not only
discussed this project with me in the summer of 1978, but drafted and given
me a proposal outlining his concept. The anthology was his idea, not mine,
and he viewed it as a logical sequel to *DDR-Literatur im Tauwetter* (*GDR
Literature During the Thaw*). It, too, was not going to be a book that could
have been published in the GDR. Fortunately, after a little searching I was
able to locate Stade's two-page proposal, which is cited in its entirety below.

Proposal for an Anthology with Young GDR Authors

After having presented the literature of this country with
more than 40 GDR authors and their views in the first book
[*DDR-Literatur im Tauwetter*], there have been developments
in literary events and cultural policy in general which make an
additional project in this area necessary and interesting.

The events related to the expatriation of Wolf Biermann, along
with the departure of important authors from the GDR, have
led to a deep divide between those who have conformed and

the others who want to make their very personal conceptions of literature become a reality and in so doing find themselves for the most part in opposition to the official cultural policy.

I would just like to add that, in the meantime, the SED functionary for economics Rudolf Bahro has published a book in the West that contains a comprehensive, fundamental critique of "socialism as it exists in reality," especially in the GDR. Legal proceedings against Bahro are to be expected later in the year. This whole process will have a strong influence on the authors. [*The title of Bahro's controversial book, published in September 1977, is "Die Alternative: Zur Kritik des real existierenden Sozialismus" (English title: "The Alternative in Eastern Europe"). In June 1978 Bahro was sentenced to eight years of imprisonment for 'treason.'*].

From the interviews with the authors in the first book, as well as from their contributions, one already learns in certain respects into which group each would be placed.

What is needed now, in my opinion, is a book similar in form to the first one, wherein other, young authors express themselves, those who have just come forward with their first book or are working on it, and from whom one can expect important books in the 1980s. A large number of these authors are much more forceful and rigorous, much more realistic and eager to experiment when it comes to their writing. The extent to which they master their subject matter artistically will be evident from the selection of stories and poems that will have to be made.

We are talking about some twenty to twenty-five authors, and it is likely that about half of them—due to their topics and the way they write—will one day come into sharp conflict with the Writers' Union and cultural policy. To some extent that is already the case or it is on the horizon. Of course, this development will also depend on the degree to which they remain resolute personally and how substantial their talent is.

It will certainly be interesting to find out how the Biermann incidents and the legal proceedings against Bahro have influenced and are influencing the young authors. What insights have they produced? Have they led writers to impose restrictions on themselves or have they generated courage and brought about the opposite.

It will be important to trace the process of disillusionment, which is taking place not only among the authors and within the intelligentsia but actually in the entire population. Where do the origins of this lie for each of the individual authors? How is the disillusion reflected in their works? Are they prepared, over and beyond their literary work, to become engaged politically and how will that happen?

Since the contributions of the authors will be on hand when the interviews begin, these conversations should go into the literary works to a great extent, in order to illustrate the intentions of the authors from them.

An additional point would be the social situation of the authors, their material and mental condition and the problem of solidarity with other authors.

Regrettably, Martin Stade and I did not follow through on this project, which would have resulted in an anthology offering unique perspectives on an important period in GDR literary history. After returning to Oberlin in the summer of 1978, I realized that I could not possibly take on more work and dropped this item from my list of things to do. And Stade, who was busy writing short stories and doing research for his historical novel on young Johann Sebastian Bach, did not pursue it further.

YEAR AT THE HOOVER INSTITUTION: AUGUST, 1980 – AUGUST, 1981

My year as a National Fellow at the Hoover Institution was without question the most enjoyable of my academic career, which began in September 1969 when I joined the Oberlin College faculty. In the intellectually stimulating environment of this prominent think tank on the Stanford University campus, where I was able to interact daily with eminent senior scholars as well as with accomplished younger research fellows, I was able to focus totally on my work. Indeed, I devoted myself almost exclusively to completing the *DDR-Literatur im Tauwetter* project, which at this stage involved writing, editing, putting the components of the book into publishable form, corresponding with East German writers and publishers about various matters, and interacting with my editor at the Nordland Publishing Company, Dr. Eva Hirsh. Dr. Hirsh, whom I never met but talked to frequently on the phone, conducted business from her office in New York City. During my year at the Hoover Institution, she asked me to revise many sections of my manuscript, an exercise that consumed a great amount of my time.

TWO NEWSPAPER ARTICLES OF INTEREST

While I was at the Hoover Institution, two articles appeared in California newspapers that should be of interest to readers of this memoir. The first resulted from an interview I had with Bob Lyhne, a columnist for *The Peninsula Times Tribune* in Palo Alto. Lyhne's article, titled "**When novelists take on journalistic responsibility**," was published on January 23, 1981. I have reproduced it verbatim below.

> **IF YOU LIVED** in East Germany, you'd read novels—not the daily paper—to keep up with the world.

That's the way I get it from Richard A. Zipser. East Germany is a long way from here, but Zipser's startling perception of fiction as the mainstream of social criticism is something to know about—and perhaps a reason for living here.

Zipser, who teaches German language and literature at Oberlin College, Ohio, has spent months in East Germany off and on, knows 60 writers and has interviewed 45 of them. That is how he formulated his ideas. Now he is working on his material on a year's fellowship at the Hoover Institution.

In a closed society, literature plays a role unfamiliar to us, Zipser observed. There is no free press. There is state censorship. Literature therefore leads into politics.

"There is almost no such thing as apolitical literature in East Germany."

FICTION ASSUMES MANY of the roles normally taken by journalism in an open society. "East Germany has no magazines which criticize society. There are no good news magazines, or magazines that point out social problems."

This puts a burden on writers to deal with problems that concern people. "Generally, the problems have to be cloaked. There are taboos—the wall, for one—and writers have to find a way to deal with them through symbolism."

"The people can't travel to the West, but literature can allow a person to dream about it. Literature can express that grand desire, and each reader can feel it—the sense of wanting to do it with the realization that it's not possible."

"Writers write about what they see, and the readers identify with it.

Take housing. People get divorced, yet they still have to share the same apartment. It's simple to get a divorce, since there's no private property as we have it. Women work; there's no alimony. The only problems are child support and getting an apartment.

So a writer describes the problems. Living together, they try to ignore each other. Remarry? Not much help, since housing is based on need."

"NO JOURNALIST could write about these problems. When a novelist does, people identify with it. When a child leaves the parents' house and enters the work force, he can get a studio apartment. The state wants workers, wants children. Therefore, getting pregnant is a short circuit way from the studio to a two-bedroom apartment."

These problems might not be discussed in the newspapers, "but it's hard to censor a description of such an everyday situation in fiction.

The writer has serious problems—how to say what he wants, yet get it into print. It starts with the first censor, who seems to be his friend, his publisher's reader, or editor. Why shouldn't the writer cooperate? Why shouldn't they be palsy? Why make trouble? The writer may avoid it through conscious or unconscious self-censorship."

Some writers, Zipser said, put "red herring" passages in their work. The strong stuff is there to be censored, with the expectation that the rest of the book will then be passed. The closed state cannot flatly deny publication to popular novelists.

THE EAST GERMAN state has its way with dramatists out of favor. "With some plays, they contrive to put on short runs, five days, say. Then the house is packed with party functionaries, for whom the tickets are a reward." They're immune to influence by the inflammatory ideas on stage, and the authorities cannot be criticized for suppression.

The West Germans read three times what we do in the United States, and the East Germans read more than the West Germans. There's not much else to do. "East Germany is a boring country," Zipser said. "The TV is boring. There's no night life. Yet you can't leave this dumpy country except to go to a few other countries that are backward. There are many restrictions on where they can go—never to the West.

"Yet the East Germans are westerners—they're Germans. And they all watch West German television—that's condoned now— which is spectacular. They know what life COULD be."

Zipser's analysis hardly favors the communist government of East Germany. Curiously, none of his interview subjects asked for anonymity. In fact, he said, "They're very eager to talk. They want to be sure they're recognized abroad."

The second article I co-authored with Lewis H. Gann, a prominent historian and political scientist who was a Senior Fellow at the Hoover Institution. The original title was "Anniversary of the Berlin Blockade: What If It Happens Again?" *The Sacramento Union* gave it a catchy title, "**Cuba offers U.S. a handy lever in a Berlin Crisis**" and published it on their op-ed page on June 14, 1981. In the article we propose that the U.S. adopt a new strategy for dealing with various types of hostile acts by the Soviet Union and its puppet state, East Germany, towards the city of West Berlin and its citizens. The new foreign policy would be based on the principle of linkage, as set forth in the op-ed piece I have reproduced verbatim below.

The 24th of June 1948 was a grim day in the history of the West. For on that date, the Soviet authorities in East Germany stopped all communications to West Berlin, hoping thereby to drive the Western occupation powers out of their bridgehead in the capital of the former German Reich. This move marked the first Soviet attempt to change the precarious four-power settlement between East and West. By this openly hostile act, the Soviets helped to start the Cold War.

THE SOVIETS did not attain their immediate objective; but their attempt to seize control of the entire city turned West Berlin into a bastion of democracy in Eastern Europe. Contrary to expectation, a Western airlift managed to keep more than 2 million West Berliners supplied with food and fuel, an achievement hitherto unparalleled in the history of air transport. In May 1949, the Soviets ended their Berlin blockade, yet West Berlin remained in a precarious position. In 1961, the East Germans built the Berlin Wall to stop the massive emigration to the West. Since then, Moscow has increased or diminished tension over Berlin in accordance with Soviet policy goals. The threat of interference with railway and highway traffic to and from West Berlin has become a recognized weapon in the political armory of the Soviet Union and its puppet state, East Germany. Over the last 30 years, the threat of a second Berlin blockade has unfortunately grown due to several developments: First, the size and strength of Soviet and East German military forces around Berlin have increased dramatically; second, West Berlin's dependence on East Germany for food, water, and sewage disposal has risen; and third, the growth of a militantly anti-Western student movement at the Free University of Berlin has created, for the first time, a strong anti-Western lobby within the confines of that traditionally pro-Western city.

THE BERLIN problem gave impetus to West Germany's Ostpolitik. West German policy-makers assumed that by cultivating economic relationships between East Germany and the West, by making West German funds available for investment and trade credits, the other German state could somehow be coaxed into charting a friendlier course. While Ostpolitik brought economic rewards to East Germany, it also brought millions of Western visitors to that country each year. And the influx of Westerners had a negative influence, as East German citizens—eager for more personal freedom and a higher standard of living—applied in large numbers for emigration to West Germany.

In order to reduce contact with the West without losing valuable hard currency and trade benefits, the East Germans in October 1980 raised the foreign exchange fees for visitors from the West and put new restrictions on West Berliners' family visits to the East. The East German regime thereby broke the 1972 four-power Berlin Agreement on East-West communications. The East German authorities also violated various provisions of the 1975 Helsinki pact. The many concessions made by West Germany since 1972 suddenly no longer mattered; the inter-German version of détente was in danger of collapse.

HOW SHOULD the Western alliance—and especially the United States as its leader—respond when West Berliners are victimized by such acts? According to the appeasers, we should do nothing more than protest through diplomatic channels. But if the West refuses to take action in a time of crisis, we can certainly expect more trouble around Berlin. If we continue the supply of loans and trade credits to Eastern Europe after East Germany and the Soviet Union have unilaterally abrogated their part of agreements, we shall only invite further exploitation of Western weakness—or what is perceived as such.

The United States has a powerful weapon that it has never attempted to wield in past disputes over Berlin: Cuba. If West Berlin is vulnerable, so is Cuba. Castro's island is an isolated bastion of communism within the American sphere of influence, militarily indefensible, and vulnerable to a naval blockade. Before the next crisis occurs, American leadership should make it clear to the Soviet Union and East Germany that all future sanctions against West Berlin will promptly be answered by similar sanctions against Cuba.

In the future, we must base our relations with the Soviet Union and its allies on the principle of linkage. This is the only policy that the communist leadership in Moscow understands. It is also the only policy that—in the long run—will preserve peace without surrender.

REVIEW OF STEFAN HEYM'S *DIE SCHMÄHSCHRIFT ODER KÖNIGIN GEGEN DEFOE*

Early in 1980, the editor of the *GDR BULLETIN: Newsletter for Literature and Culture in the German Democratic Republic* (published by the Department of Germanic Languages and Literatures at Washington University, St. Louis) contacted me and asked if I would write a review of Stefan Heym's novella, *Die Schmähschrift oder Königin gegen Defoe* (*The Lampoon or Queen Against Defoe*). Heym had initially published this delightful satirical tale in English, back in 1970, and in 1978 the German version was finally published in the GDR by Buchverlag Der Morgen. When I agreed to take on this assignment, I could not have anticipated that my harmless review would be the victim of editorial censorship—and without any consultation! The review appears in it entirety below, minus the final sentences which the editor—

Dr. Patricia Herminghouse—took the liberty of deleting:

Published first in English under the title The Queen Against Defoe (1970), Stefan Heym's short prose work did not appear in the GDR until 1978. Still, given the restrictive cultural-political climate that prevailed after the "expatriation" of dissident author Wolf Biermann in November 1976, it is remarkable that Heym's satirical story was ever approved for publication in his own country.

Die Schmähschrift recounts Daniel Defoe's clash with nobility and clergy during the reign of Queen Anne following the anonymous publication of his pamphlet, The Shortest Way with the Dissenters (1702). Appearing to support the English Establishment in the most exaggerated terms, Defoe satirized the extremist position of many high churchmen and Tories on the question of how to deal with religious dissent. Unfortunately, the trenchant humor in his treatment of this ecclesiastical/political problem was lost on most readers, and the anonymous author was denounced as an enemy of Church and State. When Defoe's identity was discovered, a reward was offered for information leading to his capture, and after several months he was apprehended. At the Old Bailey trial Defoe's defense was poorly managed, and he was persuaded to plead guilty. Consequently, he was fined 200 marks, condemned to be pilloried three times, and sentenced to indefinite imprisonment. His exposure in the pillory, however, was more a triumph than a physical punishment or public humiliation, for the people (aroused in Heym's account by Defoe's recitation of passages from his Hymn to the Pillory) took his side and protected him from bodily harm. Heym's historical novella is concerned chiefly with the role of literature and the problems facing writers in states which attempt to restrict artistic freedom. Not only is Defoe portrayed as a pillar of strength in the battle against his oppressors, but he is also shown to achieve that elusive socialist goal—the solidarity of proletariat and intellectuals—through his courageous defiance of the Establishment. Told in a manner reminiscent of the early 18th century, and based on the notes of the fictitious police agent Josiah Creech, Heym's tale has the ring of authenticity. In fact, it sounds so convincing that a professor of English at a well-known American university once asked Heym to help him locate the original Creech manuscript, as he had been unable to find any reference to it through libraries.

Like Defoe some three centuries ago, Heym has not shied away from political conflict and controversy, and he, too, has preferred to suffer the consequences rather than compromise himself as a writer. His first confrontation with the authorities came in 1931 because of an anti-imperialistic poem he wrote while a high school student in Chemnitz. This poem, an attack on General von Seeckt who was sending German officers to China to instruct Chiang Kai-shek's army, led to a public denunciation of Heym and his expulsion from school. More recently, following the publication in the West of his novel Collin (1979), which loyalist GDR writers described as "anti-communist rubbish," Heym found himself in trouble with the ruling Socialist Unity Party. Facing prosecution for alleged currency offences, he wrote to me in late April of 1979: "If you've been following the news, you may have noticed that there's trouble brewing in this place — I am going to be prosecuted on a trumped-up charge of violation of foreign currency rules, in reality, because I refused to ask the GDR authorities for permission to have my books printed abroad if they're forbidden here. I refer you to Schmähschrift — it's all told there." (Fall 1980, Vol. VI, No. 3, pp. 15-16)

The conclusion of the book review I had submitted read as follows:

. . . I refer you to Schmähschrift — it's all told there." (A few months later, Heym was tried and fined 9,000 West German marks, but he was not made to stand upon the pillory.)

As Heym said, read the Schmähschrift, it is all there!

When I asked why the final two sentences of my review had been omitted, Dr. Herminghouse told me that my contribution was too long. But a perusal of other issues of this bulletin revealed that book reviews longer than mine had been published. I had the strong sense that she was afraid the GDR authorities might find my concluding remarks offensive and was reluctant to offend them. I asserted that this was a blatant case of censorship and threatened to inform a number of influential US Germanists of the incident. In the end, the editor relented and agreed to reprint the entire final paragraph of my review in the next issue of the *GDR BULLETIN*. It appeared at the beginning of the book review section, prefaced by the following comment:

> We reprint the following conclusion of Richard Zipser's review of Stefan Heym's Die Schmähschrift at the author's insistence, including two final sentences that were cut because of its length. We regret any impression of censorship this may have caused, although we do not share the author's perception that their omission changes the overall tone and thrust of his comments. (Winter 1981, Vol. VII, No. 1, p. 5)

Needless to say, this book review was my first and final publication in the pages of the *GDR BULLETIN*.

NINE WRITERS EXPELLED FROM GDR WRITERS' UNION: JUNE, 1979

The *Collin* controversy mentioned briefly in the previous section, with rebellious Stefan Heym at its center, intensified in the spring of 1979. The SED leadership could not ignore his defiant transgressions and moved to punish him in a way that would discourage other writers from following his example. In May 1979, Heym was fined 9,000 West German marks for having published his novel in the West without securing authorization from GDR officials and for neglecting to report the income he had received in foreign currency. But this punitive move on the part of GDR authorities, meant to serve as a warning to all writers in East Germany, would only widen the divide that already existed between many GDR authors and the state. Eight writers—Kurt Bartsch, Jurek Becker, Adolf Endler, Erich Loest, Klaus Poche, Klaus Schlesinger, Dieter Schubert, and Martin Stade—sent SED Party chief Erich Honecker a letter protesting the persecution of Heym and other engaged, critical writers. In this letter, which was published in the West German press, they asserted: "Increasingly, attempts are being made to defame or muzzle politically involved, critical writers or, as with our colleague Stefan Heym, to prosecute. The linking of censorship and criminal laws is intended to impede the publication of critical works." (*Protokoll eines Tribunals*, ed. Joachim Walther, et al, Hamburg: Rowohlt, 1991, p. 11) SED leaders viewed this letter as a provocation and breach of protocol, of course, and decided to crack down on the oppositional writers in an unprecedented way, to teach them a lesson that no one would forget.

On June 7, 1979, there was a special meeting of the executive committee of the Berlin Writers' Union in the famous Red City Hall. The purpose of the meeting, which took the form of a tribunal, was to lend some legitimacy to the expulsion from the GDR Writers' Union of Heym and eight other renegade writers—Karl-Heinz Jakobs, Rolf Schneider, Joachim Seyppel, and five of the eight who had signed the open letter of protest to Honecker (Bartsch, Endler, Poche, Schlesinger, Schubert). These writers were accused of illegal actions that violated the laws of the socialist GDR state, undermined the cultural policies of the SED Party, and damaged the public image of the GDR and its government. This "show trial," at which Writers' Union President Hermann Kant had the pleasure of accusing and denouncing his colleagues, constituted one of the most shameful events in the cultural-political history of the GDR. In an unforeseen outcome, it firmly established Heym as East Germany's leading dissident writer; he became even more resolved in his crusade for more rights and greater personal freedom in the GDR, and he had no desire to move back to the West. For more than a decade, until the collapse of the Berlin Wall and the GDR, he would remain a persistent and consistent critic of the SED Party and its policies.

What occurred at the infamous tribunal has been carefully documented in *Protokoll eines Tribunals* (*Record of a Tribunal*), which Joachim Walther and several of the GDR's most famous authors (Wolf Biermann, Günter de Bruyn, Jürgen Fuchs, Christoph Hein, Günter Kunert, Erich Loest, Hans-Joachim Schädlich, Christa Wolf) co-edited in 1991. This slender volume contains documents that were discovered in the GDR Writers' Union archive after the "Wende" ("Turn" or "Turnaround") in 1989 and 1990; there are speeches and letters of some GDR writers accused of wrongdoing and GDR authors who came to their defense, as well as speeches and letters of some loyalist writers like Hermann Kant and some functionaries. Following are a few excerpts from Hermann Kant's keynote address, "Wir lassen uns von unserem Kurs nicht abbringen" ("We will not allow ourselves to be thrown off course"), an angry rebuttal of the assertions made in the protest letter to Honecker which unveils Kant's despicable character:

> "With growing concern," so the eight write – they are Kurt Bartsch, Jurek Becker, Adolf Endler, Erich Loest, Klaus Poche, Klaus Schlesinger, Dieter Schubert und Martin Stade – they followed the development of our cultural policy with growing concern. One is allowed to doubt the sincerity of even this first sentence, if one assumes that these authors would know how we react to letters that are made public via foreign satellites. Whoever uses Western press agencies to deliver his mail cannot expect that the addressee will read it without any suspicion— the suspicion for example that the letter writers are not at all concerned about the discussion with him, but concerned instead about bringing themselves up for discussion once again.

[…]

"Increasingly," it is said there, "attempts are being made to defame or muzzle politically involved, critical writers, or as with our colleague Stefan Heym, to prosecute."

One will have to give somewhat more attention to this sentence. Ultimately, it describes the direction of that "development of our cultural policy," which the letter writers "are following with growing concern." It goes in the direction of defamation, muzzling, and criminal prosecution, and increasingly at that. I find that defamation, in any case, is done by those who attribute this tendency to our cultural policy. And "muzzled" is certainly not the most accurate label for authors whose book publication numbers in the GDR land them on bestseller lists in the West. "Muzzled" is certainly not really true, if one can voice the most divergent opinions in front of hundreds of writers and if one finds discussion partners from Berlin to Oberlin in Ohio. Given the "travels" of this literature, the expression "muzzled" misses the mark. It is defamatory.

[I was astonished to find Kant's reference to Oberlin, Ohio, in the above paragraph of his speech. Obviously, he expected everyone present to know what he meant—and I take it as a compliment that Oberlin had become so well known among writers in East Berlin and throughout the GDR, from the visits of Christa and Gerhard Wolf, Ulrich Plenzdorf, and Jurek Becker, and from my extensive contact with authors in the GDR.]

[…]

We also immediately see in the following sentence from the eight letter writers several defamatory assertions: "The linking of censorship and criminal laws is intended to impede the publication of critical works."

The expression "censorship" is taken, ladies and gentlemen; it is not necessary to explain that to educated people. Whoever calls the governmental steering and planning of the publishing sector censorship is not worrying about our cultural policy, he does not want it.

[...]

Dear colleagues, I do not at all enjoy making angry speeches here, but one has to take on certain challenges.

Joachim Walther, in his preface to *Protokoll eines Tribunals*, comments on the purpose and Stalinistic nature of this tribunal:

It had the sole purpose of giving the verdict reached previously a pseudo-democratic appearance. The Party members of the [*Writers'*] Union were already brought into line beforehand, the majorities in the hall secured via the time-tested methods of communist exercise of power. However, the entire perfidiousness of the post-Stalinist cultural policy first becomes apparent when the accusers rise to speak—and with demagogy, hatefulness, and meticulously compiled insinuations the majority throws the nine ostracized writers to the wolves. (p.2)

IMB "PEDRO HAGEN" PLANS TO VISIT RICHARD ZIPSER IN CALIFORNIA

In early March 1981, while I was at the Hoover Institution, Fritz Rudolf Fries requested and received permission from the GDR authorities to travel to the United States from March 17 to May 4, 1981. While there is no mention of his trip in my Stasi-file, a large section of the Fries/Zipser file is devoted to it. His status as an informant had been upgraded from IMS to IMB, which signals a higher level of trust, reliability, and responsibility. IMB "Pedro Hagen" would not just collaborate with the Stasi and inform on persons of interest to them, he would actively help protect the GDR state against those persons who were considered threats to its security. The first report related to his trip to the US, a fascinating document, sets forth the informant's multifaceted assignment. One very important mission was to recruit German studies professors, especially those who were "sympathetic" to the GDR socialist state and its cultural policies, to actively help portray that country in positive terms. The report is presented below in its entirety.

Department XX/7   Frankfurt (O), 3/3/1981
                                                     ho-hi

Travel assignment
for the IMB "Pedro Hagen".
Register no. V/1106/72

The IM will travel to the USA for the time period of 3/17/1981 until 5/4/1981.

I. For his journey the IM was assigned the following tasks by Comrade Flehr, Regional Headquarters Frankfurt (O), Dept. XV

-- Clarification of the governance system

  - arrival and departure in New York
  - registration formalities at hotels, university camps [*sic*]...
  - contacts to official government agencies
  - travel arrangements for domestic trips

-- Clarification of contacts

  - at universities
  - in the state sector
  - in the private sector

When reviewing the contacts be sure to differentiate among established scholars, assistants, students.

-- Preparation of references to FRG citizens [*West Germans*] who are living in the USA (purpose, length of time, objective of the stay). In the case of FRG citizens consideration can be given to the possibility of inviting them to visit the GDR.

-- In the case of contact persons who are interested in further contact and exhibit a special interest in GDR literature and for the GDR in general, such invitations can be issued orally (universities, libraries, seminars can be offered).

-- Clarification and breakdown of the system of supervision (where, how, what, at which level)

-- Preparation of references to centers of research on the GDR, particularly in the area of German studies

At the meeting on 3/2/81 the IM was briefed on the set of issues cited. With regard to his behavior, it was determined that he is hesitant to initiate activities on his own, but focuses his attention fixedly on all activities dealing with America. In connection with the briefing it was made clear that the intelligence apparatus is active at universities in the USA and that for this reason the highest level of vigilance overall is essential. The IM accepted these points and agreed to keep the problem areas mentioned in mind during his trip.

II. The IM is being assigned the following additional tasks:

-- Based on the political situation at the present time, on the arms-buildup-oriented direction of the Reagan administration and on the peace program of the 26th Congress of the CPSU [*Communist Party of the Soviet Union*], there is a need to gather information about the political climate, particularly at the universities the IM will be visiting. In doing so, the important thing is to identify centers of power.

-- It must be assumed that trips to the USA by citizens of the GDR are not commonplace and that there is interest in the GDR's creative artists. Therefore

> * Information on the reasons for the invitation to the USA needs to be gathered. In doing so, one must keep in mind that the USA Germanist Dr. Zipser last visited the GDR in 1978, on the occasion of the 8th Writers Congress, and had contact with many GDR authors including the IM, so that a political assessment of the IM can take place.

> * Information needs to be compiled on GDR research, particularly in the area of German studies. In this connection an effort should be made to gather detailed information about Dr. Zipser and the book project he announced in 1978. Of particular interest would be a meeting with Dr. Zipser, during which the discussion would have to focus on his book project and his plans and intentions.

> * Information needs to be gathered on Germanists, particularly those who come from German-speaking countries, while taking into account that scholars and mid-level research personnel from the FRG would have to be given a special standing. Ongoing contacts with the designated individuals can be pursued.

-- It is to be expected that students in the USA know little about the development of society in the GDR and, as a result, are also unable to contextualize phenomena in its cultural development. In disputes, discussions, conversations, etc., the basic position has to be that in the GDR a new, peace-loving, humanistic, anti-fascist, socialist state was created, which differentiates itself fundamentally from the FRG. The desire for peace, humanism, and anti-fascism are to be emphasized. These concepts can be defined. Everything possible must be done to establish the boundaries of the argument for a unified German nation and culture.

-- It is to be expected that there will be questions on connections to GDR authors who have left the GDR, because some of them were also in the USA (Kunert, Becker, Kirsch).

REPORT ON MARCH 12, 1981 MEETING: IMB "PEDRO HAGEN" AND HIS STASI-HANDLER

In preparation for his trip to the United States, Fries met with Stasi officer Hoffmann on March 12, 1981. According to the handwritten report that Hoffman completed on March 13, 1981, the meeting took place in the town of Neuhaus. The report appears in its entirety below.

Service Unit Department XX/7

Date 3/13/81

Approvals

[signed] Diepold

17. 3. 81

Report on Meeting

Category/Code Name IMB "Pedro Hagen" V/MOG/72

Date/Time
3/12/81

Meeting Place
Neuhaus

Staff Member
Hoffmann

Participation by Supervisor
Major Heydal

Next Meeting
not arranged

Preparation for meeting:

Planned meeting to prepare the IM for his trip to the USA; see the attached preparation for meeting. In the discussion meeting the IM will be made aware of special problems that are related to the trip. The IM will be provided with a cover address and money in an EG-container.

Evaluation of meeting:

The meeting proceeded according to plan; the individual problems of the assignment were explained in detail to the IM during the meeting.

In this connection it was ascertained that the IM was himself working actively on preparations for the trip. He had worked out a good line of argumentation for possible questions relating to GDR authors who have left the GDR. He was informed in particular about investigating Dr. Zipser, since according to the information now on hand he will also travel to Oberlin. According to Dr. Zipser's own account, he works at this university. He does not know the person issuing the invitation, Dr. [*Otmar*] Drekonja. [*At that time, Dr. Drekonja was a professor of German at the College of Saint Benedict and Saint John's University in central Minnesota. He invited Fries to visit CSB/SJU, Catholic liberal arts colleges for women and men respectively, and make a presentation. This invitation was very important to Fries, as it provided an official rationale for his trip to the US. Fries had hoped to visit Oberlin College, which would have*]

*put him in the company of Christa Wolf, Ulrich Plenzdorf, Jurek
Becker, and Stefan Heym, who gave a public lecture at Oberlin in
November 1979.*]

The IM related that a woman [*blacked out*] from the International
Friendship League visited him and presented a list of addresses
in the USA that the IM can call upon. [*The mission of the
International Friendship League of the GDR, founded in 1961,
was to build and cultivate friendly relationships with countries
and individuals sympathetic to the communist GDR state.*] The
IM wrote down some of the addresses; it supposedly has to do
with persons who view the GDR favorably. Over and above that
the person mentioned asked him to generate interest among
Americans for the magazine "Panorama," which is going to be
published by the GDR in the future. The IM will not be engaging
in this activity because no copies of this magazine are available.

At 7:30 a.m. on 3/17/81, the IM will fly from Schönefeld [*Berlin
Schönefeld Airport*] to Copenhagen and from there to New York.
He will take along copies of literature published in the GDR.

He will be returning on 5/4/81.

The IM was handed 500 West German marks in an EG-container;
he was given instructions on how to go about opening and
destroying the container. [*Presumably, the special container with
the 500 West German marks would be recognized by the East
German border guards and not taken away from Fries. After
arriving in the West, he would be able to open the container,
exchange the marks for US dollars, and then destroy the container.
This sort of container could be a toiletry kit or a stuffed animal,
something small that would not look like it contains money.*] The
IM acknowledged receipt of the 500 West German marks.

In addition, he was provided with the cover address "Käthe Martin" and instructed to send a postcard from every place he stays, if at all possible.

The IM was given a copy of E. Honecker's book, "Aus meinem Leben" [*"From My Life"*], as a present. [*As I read this, I had to laugh and wonder what Fries did with this book after arriving in the West; he probably threw it away.*]

REPORT ON MAY 13, 1981 MEETING: IMB "PEDRO HAGEN" AND HIS STASI-HANDLER

On May 13, 1981, nine days after his return from the United States, IMB "Pedro Hagen" met with his Stasi-handler for seven hours and reported orally on his trip to the US. The handwritten report on their meeting, prepared by Stasi officer Hoffmann, appears in its entirety below and is followed by the detailed report Fries gave on what he experienced in the US. Note the level of satisfaction Hoffmann expresses about the way Fries carried out his assignment abroad and the loyalty he exhibited in various ways during their meeting.

Service Unit Department XX/7   Date 5/19/81

                                                      Approvals

                                                      [signed] Diepold

Report on Meeting

Category/Code Name IMB "Pedro Hagen" Reg.-No. V/MOG/72

Date/Time   Meeting Place
5/13/81   "Rense"
11:00-18:00

Staff Member	Participation by Supervisor
Hoffmann	Heydal

Next Meeting	On
after agreement by telephone	after 5/24/81

Reports   oral 8

Conditions/circumstances favoring the enemy 1

Preparation for meeting:

Planned meeting for reporting on the USA trip the IM undertook;

Comrade Heydal, Deputy Director of Department XX, will participate in the meeting; the IM will be led to the conspirative place "Rense."

Evaluation of meeting:

The meeting proceeded without incidents; the IM arrived on time, was prepared to deliver the report, and—contrary to his other reservations—had no objections with regard to the meeting being conducted in the IMK [*Inoffizieller Mitarbeiter Kammer, a chamber the Stasi used for debriefing informants*]. He gave a comprehensive report and began by relating his impressions; he proceeded concretely, naming names and drawing attention to connections. His overall behavior during the meeting was characterized by having faith in his collaborators. He emphasized several times that this was only intended to be an initial debriefing, because the set of issues is very complex.

In his political attitude the IM appeared steadfast and hardened by the wealth of experiences in the USA. He expressed his loyalty vis-à-vis the GDR and related, for example, that he obtained the official report on the 10th Party Congress of the SED from the GDR embassy, which put him in a position to provide up-to-date commentary and explain the policies of the GDR.

He initiated activities in the USA that enabled him to proceed as instructed and demonstrated perseverance, e.g., in the efforts he made to contact Dr. Zipser.

It may be presumed that the IM acted prudently and adhered to the assignment.

Using the cover address he maintained postal contact with the collaborator during the trip. He selected postcards in such a way that they facilitated an operative evaluation of the trip.

The report is considered to be valuable operatively, for defense as well as for reconnaissance purposes.

New assignment and guidelines

It is adjudged that the trip made a significant contribution towards the strengthening of the mutual bond of trust and the IM justified fully the trust that was placed in him.

The IM explained that he personally burned the EG-container that was given to him and it is completely destroyed.

In subsequent meetings an effort needs to be made to substantiate the basic information that has already been gathered.

IMB "PEDRO HAGEN" REPORTS ON HIS VISIT WITH RICHARD ZIPSER IN CALIFORNIA

Below is a three-page file report on Fries's trip to the San Francisco Bay area and Stanford University, where he visited with me as he had hoped and planned to do. The report was prepared by his Stasi-handler Hoffmann, based on information Fries communicated to him orally in their May 13 meeting. It is interesting to see how Fries was able to gain Hoffmann's trust following his return from the US. Clearly, Fries enjoyed his first trip to America and understood what he needed to say and how he should behave in order to be granted further travel privileges and perhaps other privileges in the future. He had learned how to play the system and decided to use it to his advantage. Of course, Fries—like everyone else—did not foresee the day when the Berlin Wall and the GDR state would collapse, leading eventually to the discovery of his Stasi-file and his outing as a trusted informant.

Department XX/7   Frankfurt (O), 5/15/1981
Source: IMB "Pedro Hagen"   ho-hi
received: Capt. Hoffmann
on: 5/13/1981
Travel report USA II

Meeting with Dr. Richard Zipser in San Francisco

As instructed the IM contacted the Germanist Dr. Richard Zipser during his stay in the USA and reported on that orally, as follows:

During his stay in Washington the IM made an effort to make contact with Dr. Zipser. It turned out that he was not as well established as expected in circles of American Germanists: first of all, people did not know him and, secondly, he was not to be found initially. An attempt was made to locate him at Oberlin College in San Francisco [*sic: in Ohio, not San Francisco*]. After a prolonged effort the IM managed to find out that he was not in Oberlin, but engaged as a research fellow in Stanford, California. Eventually, he was located and a telephone conversation ensued. He immediately recalled the person with whom he was speaking, but declared that he was under a great deal of stress and did not have time for a get-together. Then two invitations materialized, one of which apparently was meant to be for a reading. Both invitations were suddenly cancelled, one because the date could not be held open, and the second time [*remainder of sentence blacked out*]. In the telephone conversations Dr. Zipser made it clear that it would make no sense to come to San Francisco, that would be a waste of time, etc. It became obvious that he had little interest in getting together. Finally, an agreement was reached. On 4/19/1981 the flight took place from Washington to San Francisco, where Dr. Zipser was waiting in the airport. After a less than effusive greeting the trip was made to Stanford, which is about a one-hour drive from San Francisco. Stanford University is prominent and one of the best in the USA. Five Nobel Prize Laureates, among others, have positions there.

The Hoover Institution is affiliated with Stanford University. It is for all intents and purposes the center of the university. It is financed by the Hoover Foundation (the brother of the donor was the FBI director, Hoover). [*This is a case of mistaken identity. The reference should be to Herbert Hoover, 31st President of the US, not to J. Edgar Hoover, the first Director of the FBI. The Hoover Tower, one of three buildings that comprise the Hoover Institution, houses a library founded in 1919 by Herbert Hoover.*] Scholars in the USA consider the Hoover Institution to be extremely conservative.

Dr. Zipser is currently working at this Hoover Institution, which has awarded him a research fellowship. The purpose of the fellowship is to enable Dr. Zipser to complete work on his book about GDR literature. He intends to return to Oberlin

College in August 1981. Dr. Zipser's project is therefore being finished with financial support from the Hoover Institution. He is working on the three volumes that comprise the book and has no other responsibilities. The publication of the three volumes is also being financed for the most part by the Hoover Institution. [*Untrue. The Hoover Institution did not subsidize the publication of "DDR-Literatur im Tauwetter".*]

The title of the edition is "Wandel, Wunsch, Wirklichkeit – DDR-Literatur 1971 bis 1978" [*"Desire, Change, Reality – GDR Literature 1971 to 1978"*]. The interviews with GDR authors will be published in the first volume, the authors' literary texts in the second volume, and the biographies in the third. Dr. Zipser is going to write a foreword. The book will be published in the English language by Nordland Publishing, USA.

Only prose writers of the GDR will be published here. [*Incorrect: In addition to prose writers, there are poets, playwrights, essayists, etc.*] Priorities are not being established; all GDR authors are to be represented. The book Dr. Zipser is preparing should be the most comprehensive work on GDR literature to date; there is nothing comparable up to now. This work is supposed to satisfy the needs of American Germanists primarily.

A certain Schoeps, who works as instructor of German studies at Oberlin College, is co-editor of the book. [*Dr. Karl-Heinz Schoeps was Professor of German at the University of Illinois at Urbana-Champaign.*]

At the Hoover Institution Dr. Zipser is regarded as the foremost expert in the area of GDR literature, since he has in-depth knowledge of GDR literature and its development, and in addition to that he knows a large number of GDR writers from personal experience.

Apparently, he is also very aware of his status. He made an affable and approachable impression.

In conversations he wanted to know what is going on in the GDR literary scene, what Schlesinger, Plenzdorf, Stade, Hermlin, and Hacks are doing. He knows Schlesinger, Stade and Plenzdorf as the initiators of the proposed Berlin-Anthology (former "self-publishing" project).

Dr. Zipser has published a volume of poetry by GDR lyric poets in the USA. The book appeared in two languages and supposedly contains a representative cross section.

The impression came into being that in the USA Dr. Zipser occupies a central position among the Germanists and would like to control those Germanists who are dealing with GDR literature. For example, he was very upset to learn that an American Germanist had given a talk on [*Jurij*] Brězan at a conference in Boca Raton, Florida ("2nd International Conference on the Fantastic in Literature and Film," 3/18—3/21/1981, [*Florida*] Atlantic-University Boca Raton), because Brězan is not an important figure in GDR literature. On the other hand, this Germanist warned [*IM "Pedro Hagen"*] about the Hoover-people.

Dr. Zipser's vanity was also wounded when he learned that his review of Stefan Heym's book "Seven Days in June" [*sic: the title is "Five Days in June"*] had been reproduced in a mutilated form in the American publication "GDR-Revue", a journal devoted to GDR literature. Exactly who publishes this journal is not known. [*Fries is referring to the "GDR Bulletin", which was published by the Department of Germanic Languages and Literatures at Washington University, St. Louis, from 1975 to 1999. The review Fries mentions was of Heym's novella, "The Queen Against Defoe", not of his novel "Five Days in June".*]

In the near future he is planning to prepare and publish a book on contemporary German-speaking writers living in [*self-imposed*] exile. According to his statements, he will restrict himself to authors who are living in the FRG [*West Germany*]. He did not provide further details on that.

[*The next paragraph, which has just three lines, is blacked out.*]

All in all, the impression that emerged was that the visit was not particularly enjoyable for him. He did behave in a friendly, jovial manner, but was not as pleasant-natured and outgoing as during his visits in the GDR.

There was no mention of visiting the GDR in the foreseeable future. He did not rule out a residency in the FRG in connection with the preparation of the book on German-speaking writers living in exile, and of course also a possible stay in the GDR related to that.

Comment

The IM reported as per instructions; there is no reason to doubt the truthfulness of the information provided.

Measures to be taken

1. Excerpts of report to Director of Main Department XX

2. Evaluation strictly guaranteeing protection of [*confidential*] source when reporting

3. Evaluation using operative process "Narr" [*"Fool"*]

[*signed*]
Hoffmann
Hauptmann

FRITZ RUDOLF FRIES'S IMAGINATIVE ESSAY ON HIS VISIT TO SAN FRANCISCO

The day after his reading at Stanford University, which I helped organize and the University's German Department generously supported with an honorarium, I drove Fries to San Francisco where he spent two days before flying to his next destination. He was fascinated by San Francisco and wrote an impressionistic short prose piece entitled *Mit der Strassenbahn übers Meer* (*Crossing the Ocean by Streetcar*), which was published in the September/October 1982 issue of *SINN UND FORM* (*MEANING AND FORM*), the leading literary and cultural journal in the GDR. While sitting on a park bench in Union Square, in front of the stately St. Francis Hotel, Fries daydreams; he lets his mind roam all over the city, sharing his thoughts and impressions with the reader. Caught up in the multifaceted experience of San Francisco, he imagines with the help of a fortune cookie that he has arrived at a crossroads in his life. "In der Empress of China, einem Restaurant mit Blick auf die Stadt, ziehe ich die auf einen Papierstreifen gedruckte Wahrsagung aus dem Teegebäck: *Jetzt kommt es darauf an, dein Leben zu ändern.*" (1054-1055) / "In the Empress of China, a restaurant with a panoramic view of the city, I pull a strip of paper with a printed prediction of the future out of a tea cookie: *Now the time has come to change your life.*" As I read this, knowing now what I did not know back then about Fries, I wonder for a second why he did not follow through and make a profound change in direction. But I know the answer: Fries did not really want to change the nefarious aspects of his life, he only wanted to contemplate doing it.

The essay concludes with a somewhat sarcastic tribute to a "friend" of Fries, a Germanist who pulls him out of his reverie and back to earth with questions about the GDR. Fries writes:

Ich schliesse die Augen und hoffe, mich in einen alten Chinesen zu verwandeln, so dass ich noch im Jahre 5679 hier auf diesem Platz sitzen würde, eine kleine Zigarre zwischen den gelben Fingern. Aber das Wunder bleibt aus, vor dem Erdbeben oder der Zukunft hat Gott auch in San Francisco die Kritiker und Freunde und Schriftgelehrten gesät. Von der anderen Seite des Parks seh ich Freund Dick [*Zipser*], Professor für Germanistik, mit schnellen kurzen Schritten heraneilen. Dick holt mich aufs gemeinsame euro-amerikanische Festland zurück mit der Frage: Du hast mir überhaupt noch nichts von (XY) erzählt. (1055)

I close my eyes, hoping to transform myself into an old Chinese man, so that I would still be sitting in this square in the year 5679 with a small cigar between my yellow fingers. But that miracle fails to occur, for God also sowed the critics and friends and literary scholars in San Francisco before the earthquake or the future. From the other side of the park I see my friend Dick [*Zipser*], Professor of German, approaching swiftly with rapid short steps. Dick brings me back to our common Euro-American mainland with his inquiry: You still have not told me anything about (XY).

CREATING A NETWORK OF GDR SYMPATHIZERS AT US UNIVERSITIES

In the mid-1970s, after joining the United Nations and gaining the international recognition it had long sought, the GDR began to systematically develop a network of sympathizers comprised of academicians from universities throughout the US. The object was to identify persons, professors and doctoral candidates working in the general area of German studies, who were interested in the GDR and sympathetic to its system of government. In the effort to create a fifth column, two groups were targeted: first, intellectuals from the far left who viewed the GDR with its communistic brand of socialism as a model society; and second, professors who could be cultivated in various ways and transformed into advocates for all that the GDR represented. The GDR Embassy in Washington, DC played an important role in this nationwide propaganda effort, by organizing lecture/reading tours for East German authors loyal to the SED Party and by disseminating pro-GDR materials in a remarkably effective way. The GDR needed to ensure that US universities and colleges would not just invite oppositional East German writers to visit their campuses, but also a significant number of writers who had a positive view of the GDR state, political system, and society—writers like Hermann Kant. These writers would be rewarded for their loyal support and, while visiting the US, they would be able to help expand the network of GDR sympathizers that had already been established at some institutions of higher learning. This eventually led to the formulation and implementation of what became known as the "Delegierungsprinzip" (delegation principle), which I will discuss later on.

IMB "PEDRO HAGEN" FINDS A GDR SYMPATHIZER IN MINNESOTA

From the next report in the Fries/Zipser file, which is based on information IMB "Pedro Hagen" communicated to his Stasi-handler Gerhard Hoffmann on June 12, 1981, we gain insight into the GDR's strategy for recruiting and developing a cadre of GDR sympathizers at major US universities. The report focuses primarily on what the informant experienced while visiting the University of Minnesota. It appears in its entirety below.

Department XX/7	Frankfurt (O), 6/15/1981
	ho-brä

source:	IMB "Pedro Hagen"
received:	Capt. Hoffmann
on:	6/12/1981

Regarding possible visits to the GDR by Americans

During his stay in the USA the IM got together with persons who were thinking seriously about visiting the GDR. In this connection the IM provided the following comments orally, as an addendum to the information reported previously:

It is certain that Dr. Zipser will travel to the GDR before the end of 1981. His fellowship at the Hoover Institution of Stanford University expires at the end of August 1981. After this, he intends to travel to Europe—and also to the GDR. Until August 1981 Dr. Zipser can be reached at the following address:

> Stanford University
> Stanford CA 94305

Nothing came to light regarding Dr. Zipser's objectives and plans for such a trip.

The actual central focus of those persons who want to travel to the GDR, which was discovered during the USA trip, is

> Prof. Dr. [*blacked out*]

of the University of Minneapolis [*University of Minnesota*]. By his own account, Prof. [*blacked out*] has ties to the International Friendship League of the GDR and was also in the GDR on a number of occasions. Among other things he took part in the Weimarer Hochschultage. [*This was an annual summer conference in Weimar for college and university professors from other countries. It featured a program of events organized around a specific topic or related topics, with lectures, seminars, podium discussions, readings and talks by GDR writers, film screenings, exhibitions, and excursions.*] Prof. [*name blacked out*] must be known in the Writers' Union of the GDR and among Germanists at universities in the GDR. Hermann Kant visited this university during his stay in the USA and also gave a reading there. [*Hermann Kant, a prose writer known for staunchly supporting the Honecker regime and representing the socialist point of view in his works, became president of the GDR Writers' Union in 1978. In that capacity, he made a lecture tour to the US and visited (along with other colleges and universities) the University of Minnesota. There he made the acquaintance of GDR literature specialist Prof. Frank Hirschbach and other professors and students in the German program, some of whom were interested in visiting the GDR.]*

[Note: Hermann Kant was not invited to visit Oberlin College, which he was very eager to do and would have done at his own expense—that is, with financial support from the GDR Embassy. Their cultural attaché, a woman named Tischbein, called me from Washington, DC and requested formally that our German Department invite Kant to give a talk and reading. When I told her we did not have the funds for his honorarium, travel and other expenses, Ms. Tischbein indicated that the embassy would cover all expenses related to this trip. When I then told her that we still could not invite Kant to visit and speak at Oberlin College, she of course asked why. I told her to ask Kant that question because he will know why.]

Grouped around Prof. [*blacked out*] are several students—their names are not known—who also have already spent time visiting the GDR and are intending to travel to the GDR again. On the one hand these students are interested in getting to know the GDR somewhat and, on the other hand in learning how our vocational training operates at the university level. During his stay in the USA he [*Kant*] was asked on various occasions if it is possible for Americans to study in the GDR.

Thus, interest in the GDR definitely exists and Prof. [*blacked out*]

In Minneapolis can be viewed as the focal point for persons who are interested in the GDR. The International Friendship League is present in Minneapolis, at the university. According to his own account, Prof. [*blacked out*] is also involved editorially with the publication of the "GDR Bulletin" Newsletter for Literature and Culture in the German Democratic Republic (attachment).

Comment

The IM supplemented his report on the USA trip. The information presented by him cannot be clarified further.

Measures to be taken

- review of report [*blacked out*]

- send report for operative evaluation to Main Directorate for reconnaissance via Department XV

[*signed*]
Hoffmann
Hauptmann

IMB "PEDRO HAGEN" REPORTS ON NORDLAND PUBLISHING

In January 1977 I had entered into an agreement with a small academic press, Nordland Publishing Company, for the publication of *DDR-Literatur im Tauwetter* (*GDR Literature During the Thaw*). The GDR authorities were understandably eager for information about this publisher, and Fries provided what he could in the June 1981 report that appears below.

Department XX/7   Frankfurt (O), 6/15/1981
                                   ho-brä

source: IMB "Pedro Hagen"
received: Capt. Hoffmann
on: 6/12/1981

Activities of the Nordland Publishing Company, Houston USA

On 6/9/81 the IM received a letter from Nordland Publishing
International, Houston USA. With reference to that he provided
the following information orally:

The letter, dated May 14 and signed by one [*name blacked
out*], is apparently directed towards all of the GDR authors
interviewed by the American literary scholar, Dr. Richard
Zipser. It announces that the Nordland Publishing Company is
about to publish Dr. Zipser's book, "DDR-Literatur 1971–1978"
[*"GDR Literature 1971 – 1978"*]. It supposedly is going to be a
three-volume work, the third volume of which will be reserved
exclusively for Dr. Zipser's interviews with the GDR authors.

This announcement coincides completely with the statements
Dr. Zipser made during the IM's visit to the USA.

The publishing company indicates that it has also received offers
to publish the interview section abroad and that a possible
preprinting of excerpts in a scholarly journal is under discussion.

Due to this situation the publisher is now seeking a broadening
of the copyright.

Accompanying the letter is an attachment which lists all of
the questions that Dr. Zipser asked (the questions are indeed
identical to the ones Dr. Zipser asked) and the declaration of

consent for a worldwide publication in book format both in the German language and in translation. This copyright declaration is supposed to be sent back to the Nordland Publishing Company.

It seems reasonable to assume that this letter was sent to all of the authors Dr. Zipser interviewed, because only the interviews taken as a whole would be of interest and because the letter itself is one of multiple copies made.

Comment

The IM took it upon himself to report on this matter. The details are verified through the presentation of the letter by the IM as well as through information from Department V. In addition, this information is consistent with the information the IM gathered in the USA.

The IM raised the question of how he should proceed with respect to the copyright declaration. [. . .]

Agreement was reached with the IM to hold off on this decision and possibly consult with other colleagues.

Measures to be taken

- Preparation of a report for Main Department XX/7.

- Evaluation in reports by Main Department XX/AI.

Hoffmann
Captain

PROBLEMS WITH NORDLAND PUBLISHING: 1980-1982

By the end of 1980, Karl-Heinz Schoeps and I had completed all work on the manuscript of *DDR Literatur im Tauwetter* (*GDR Literature During the Thaw*), including many revisions recommended in 1980 by the Nordland editor assigned to this project, Dr. Eva M. Hirsch. From Dr. Hirsch, I learned to my dismay that Nordland Publishing Company was experiencing severe financial difficulties, which meant that there would in all likelihood be a considerable delay in the publication schedule. On January 25, 1981, I wrote to Dr. Richard S. Haugh, Executive Vice President of Nordland, urging him to move quickly with the publication of my book. The concluding paragraphs from this lengthy letter appear below:

> Several of the 45 East German writers I interviewed have written and asked about the state of the book, why they haven't received a complimentary copy yet, etc. At first I took all the blame for the delays myself, explaining that I had other publishing/professional commitments and a full-time teaching position as well, that a serious illness and an upsetting divorce had interrupted my work schedule. More recently, however, I have indicated that the manuscript has been in the publisher's hands since last August and that I expect it to appear in print soon ("demnächst"). If we continue to delay, we run the risk of alienating and losing credibility with the many East German writers who have been extremely patient, understanding, and cooperative to date. Since I plan to continue working in this field, my reputation is on the line, and that frankly worries me these days. But Nordland will also emerge a big winner or a loser—depending on 1) how soon this book appears in print and 2) how good a job we have done. If all goes well, as it still can and should, we will have proven ourselves to the writers and will be able to count on their support for future projects. Such contacts are particularly important, in my opinion, in light of the Nordland German Series we are contemplating.

In sum, Richard, it is in my interest as a specialist on East German literature, in Eva Hirsch's interest as editor of this book, and in your interest as a publisher, that we get moving on this project now. All of us stand to benefit if we do, all of us stand to lose something if we don't. I have entrusted you with much more than my manuscript, and I can only hope you will take whatever action is necessary to get this valuable material into print soon.

I had indeed entrusted Nordland with far more than the manuscript; my reputation was also at stake and I was at the mercy of this publisher. For Nordland had possession not only of the manuscript, but of all materials related to the book—black-and-white photos of the 45 East German writers represented, permissions to publish literary texts from the writers and their publishers, transcriptions of the interviews, everything!

Following my return to Oberlin in August 1981, I received a letter from Eva Hirsch informing me that circumstances had forced her to terminate her employment with Nordland Publishing. Then, in a letter dated September 28, 1981, Richard Haugh updated me on the status of Nordland Publishing Company:

Dear Dick,

We are in the process of relocating everything in Boston. Hence, the New York office [*where my editor, Eva Hirsch, had been working*] has been closed and the Houston office only handles circulation.

We have received about 15 boxes from the New York office. It will take time to go through each to sort and file. I would assume the work Dr. Hirsch has done on your book will be there.

Please, just give me some time to reorganize. If I am in when the phone rings, I am not in that part of the house. I play back the tapes late at night about twice a week.

Give me some breathing space and we will get this published.

Best wishes,/
[*signed*]
Richard S. Haugh

In October 1981, I received a personal letter from Eva Hirsch, who had returned home to Vienna, Austria. Although she was no longer with Nordland, she had decided to write and advise me regarding the "actual procedure of getting hold of both [... *my*] manuscript and the other things." I have not had any contact with Dr. Hirsch since that time, but I will always be grateful for the guidance she gave me at this critical stage of my project.

After coming to grips with what had happened, I realized that I would have to move swiftly and decisively, in order to retrieve from Nordland all the materials related to my book, and I also would need to engage the services of a lawyer. It was a very frustrating and upsetting situation, to say the least, especially since I had remarried in late July 1981 and was again working full-time at Oberlin College. I did not have much time to devote to this matter, but I nevertheless had to pursue it energetically.

In the first half of 1982, I wrote several letters and made many telephone calls to Richard Haugh, who had relocated from Houston to Belmont, Massachusetts, and was now acting as an agent for Nordland Publishing. In a letter dated May 13, 1982, Haugh warned me not to take legal action: "If you litigate, then there will be no chance of publishing the book quickly. It would take 3-5 years to get a court decision and Nordland has a very good chance to win the case." Haugh suggested that I offer to pay Nordland a buy-back fee, which is what I ultimately decided to do. In July 1982, we finally reached agreement, and in the first week of August Haugh and I signed a legal document that terminated my contract with Nordland and led to the return of my book materials. I was now free to negotiate and contract with another publisher for the publication of *DDR-Literatur im Tauwetter*.

STASI CORRESPONDENCE ON RICHARD ZIPSER: MAY/JUNE, 1981

My visits and correspondence with the Halle poet, Rainer Kirsch, in connection with *DDR-Literatur im Tauwetter* and *Contemporary East German Poetry*, led the secret police in that district to seek information on me from Stasi headquarters in Berlin. The exchange of letters between Lieutenant Colonel Joachim Gröger, the head of Department XX in the Halle district, and Generalmajor Willi Damm, the head of Department X in Berlin, appears below. It is clear from Damm's response to his colleague's inquiry that Richard Zipser, operating within the cultural sphere, was considered to be an enemy of the GDR state.

County Authority   Halle, May 18, 1981
for State Security   7/ste-schr 4417/81
Department XX

Ministry for State Security
Department XX

<u>B e r l i n</u>

<u>Dr. Zipser, Richard, born 1/23/1943 in Maryland/USA</u>

In accordance with the F 10 screening conducted on 5/5/81 by our service unit, the above-named person is registered as No. F 27 69 13 for your service unit.

Since the USA citizen maintains ties to the [*several words blacked out*] freelance writer

Kirsch, Rainer
[*born*] 7/17/34 in Döbeln
4020 Halle, [*blacked out*],

we would like to know the reason for the acquisition of information [*on him*], and whether your service unit has on hand references to the connection between these two persons.

Director of the Department
[*signed*]
G r ö g e r
Lieutenant Colonel

. . . .

June 12, 1981
X/ 3898 /81 Es.

Department X
Director

PERSONAL

County Authority for State Security
Department XX
Director

H a l l e

Dr. ZIPSER, Richard, born 1/23/43 – USA citizen
Letter of 5/18/81, Binder-No.: 7/ste-schr/4417/81

Recorded information on Dr. ZIPSER is in the archive material of Department X.

It contains correspondence with the security agencies of the CSSR [*Czecho-Slovak Socialist Republic*] as well as Main Department XX in relation to the operative handling of persons engaged in hostile activity in the cultural sphere.

In accordance with the information from Main Department XX, in 1976 Z. was working as a literary scholar at Oberlin College in Oberlin/Ohio/USA, however living temporarily in Vienna, Hörlgasse 11/6. He is said to have travelled to the GDR a number of times, in order to have conversations with writers in preparation for his planned publication on GDR literature.

Vis-à-vis official organizations he is said to have presented himself as a progressive. However, it was determined that he was exclusively oriented toward those writers who had reservations regarding the development of socialism in the GDR and who in the past had behaved in a hostile/negative manner.

Further information on Z. is not available.

It should be noted that archived material on ZIPSER exists in the Main Directorate Reconnaissance/IV/Reckling—AP 15612/73.

[*signed*]
D a m m
Generalmajor

IMB "PEDRO HAGEN" RECEIVES A PRESENT FROM RICHARD ZIPSER

The next document in the Fries/Zipser file is a handwritten report dated November 24, 1981 on a meeting between IMB "Pedro Hagen" and his Stasi-handler Gerhard Hoffmann that took place on November 20, 1981 in Neuhaus. There is an amusing reference to me in the final paragraph: "The IM handed over for usage a publication he had received from Dr. Zipser: *Contemporary East German Poetry. A Special Issue of Field*. Published by

Oberlin College. Oberlin, Ohio, 1980. This is an anthology of GDR poetry with a foreword by the editor, Zipser. The book contains a personal dedication that is going to be saved photographically, so it can be evaluated operatively."

IMB "PEDRO HAGEN" PLANS A SECOND TRIP TO THE UNITED STATES

Attached to the report discussed above are two handwritten pages, prepared and signed by Stasi officer Gerhard Hoffmann, which focus on Fries's upcoming travel plans. These notes, which are based on information Hoffmann gathered in his November 20 meeting with IMB "Pedro Hagen," are cited below.

Department XX/7   Frankfurt (O), 11/24/81

Comment on travel plans of IMB "Pedro Hagen"

At the meeting on 11/20/81 the IM related that he is thinking about travelling to the USA again, perhaps in the second half of 1982.

In order to look into the feasibility of such an undertaking, he is going to take the following steps:

--There is an invitation from [*blacked out*], to give lectures again at

Saint John's University, Minnesota. [*Blacked out*] would have to make this invitation more specific and guarantee that the cost of the flight and expenses related to the stay will again be covered. If this commitment is made the IM would

--Contact Dr. Richard Zipser and take him up on his offer to arrange for the IM to give readings at Oberlin College. Dr. Zipser would have to be made to feel responsible for the remainder of the stay in the USA.

--In order to persuade Dr. Zipser to organize this stay, the IM plans to

write him immediately and inquire if he is still intending to come to the GDR in the spring of 1982—in case he has planned this trip, the IM would issue an invitation to him.

--The length of trip should amount to approximately 12 weeks, according to the IM.

--If commitments from the American side are in place, then the Writers' Union, the PEN Center, and the publisher would be called upon to sanction the trip properly. [*PEN Center: a branch of PEN International, the world's leading international literary organization.*]

Issues were raised during the meeting. It was pointed out to the IM that it seems appropriate, before starting to make arrangements in the USA, to check with the GDR Writers' Union and see the extent to which it is interested in such a trip, in order possibly to be able to proceed from the outset with the approval of the Union. If the approval is forthcoming, one should move forward as proposed. Importance should be attached, in particular, on coming into contact with Dr. Zipser. The IM agreed to proceed in the approved manner and to provide information on all goals that are achieved.

[*signed*]

Hoffmann

BERND JENTZSCH IN OBERLIN: FEBRUARY – MAY, 1982

When he met with his Stasi-handler Gerhard Hoffmann in late November, 1981, IMB "Pedro Hagen" did not know that the German faculty at Oberlin College, acting on my recommendation, already had invited former GDR writer Bernd Jentzsch to be the 15th Max Kade German Writer-in-Residence during the spring semester of 1982. Jentzsch, a well-known poet, prose writer, editor and translator, who also worked as a publisher's reader, accepted our invitation and arrived in Oberlin in February 1982.

When I met Jentzsch in November 1975, he and his family—which included his mother—were living in Wilhelmshagen, a town situated on the outskirts of East Berlin. Jentzsch led a quiet life until the fall of 1976, when his fortunes took a dramatic and unexpected turn. That fall, when he was in Switzerland doing spadework for an anthology of Swiss poetry, he learned about the expatriation of prominent poet-singer Wolf Biermann and the expulsion of fellow writer Reiner Kunze from the GDR Writers' Union on the order of the GDR government. Stunned and angered by the harshness of these actions, he spontaneously demanded that the regime reverse its decision; he wrote a scathing and detailed open letter to head-of-state Erich Honecker, submitting it for publication to several newspapers in the GDR, in the Federal Republic of Germany, and in Switzerland, without considering possible negative consequences. The reprisals against Jentzsch, his family, his long-since widowed mother, and his friends were not long in coming. His open letter was not published by any GDR newspapers but turned over to the Stasi, which promptly indicted him for "hostile agitation against the State." Faced with the prospect of a mock trial and two to ten years of imprisonment, he decided to stay in Switzerland. His wife, her brother, his son, and even his pensioned, staunchly and actively socialist mother were harassed, humiliated, and ostracized by the GDR authorities.

In the spring of 1977 Jentzsch's wife, Birgit, and their son, Stefan, were finally permitted to leave the country with a passport for stateless persons and joined him in Switzerland. His mother, however, was repeatedly denied permission to visit him and his family; their correspondence was scrutinized, their occasional telephone conversations were monitored and disrupted; she was driven to despair and, ultimately, to suicide in the fall of 1979. Jentzsch himself was officially branded as a criminal fugitive from the GDR; his publications were banned, his name was removed from reference books, and his contributions were deleted from subsequent editions of anthologies. From 1977 on, the Jentzsch family lived in Küsnacht near Zurich; Jentzsch was able to find work as a publisher's reader, and his wife became director of a home for deaf-blind children.

Our decision to invite Jentzsch to spend three months at Oberlin College as German writer-in-residence infuriated government and Writers' Union officials in the GDR, especially since the previous GDR writer to visit Oberlin had been outspoken regime critic Jurek Becker in 1978. GDR authorities would soon formulate and seek to implement the "Delegierungsprinzip" (delegation principle), a procedure that would enable them to pre-select writers from the GDR for Oberlin College and other institutions with guest writer programs in the US.

During my seventeen years as an Oberlin College faculty member, I had the pleasure of co-hosting and interacting with twelve Max Kade German writers-in-residence, always during the spring semester. Typically, the visiting writer would arrive in mid-February and depart in mid-May, which is precisely what Bernd Jentzsch did. Of all the writers I experienced in Oberlin, Bernd was probably the most even-keeled and modest, also one of the least self-absorbed. He was an unusually good listener, genuinely interested in what others had to say and eager to hear their comments on his literary texts and various issues. His responses to these comments were always measured and thoughtful. He was less emotional and more cerebral than most of the writers we hosted, an intellectual in every respect, and both the small college setting and academic environment seemed to suit him well. My wife Ulrike and I spent many hours in his company each week. We enjoyed his presence at our dinner table on numerous occasions as well as our conversations on a wide range of topics.

A nice memory: That spring, as newlyweds, Ulrike and I were in the process of completing the construction of a new house on a quiet cul-de-sac close to the college campus. On a daily basis, we would check on the progress of work being done inside the house. Bernd would often join us and help us make decisions regarding aspects of the interior design. He also went to home furnishing stores with Ulrike and helped her select such items as floor tiles, wallpaper, lighting fixtures, etc. He marveled at the number of options available to us in every category, as he recalled how few choices he'd had in the GDR when renovating his family's dwelling in the mid-1970s. We recognized that his artistic creativity extended to the areas of design and decor, so we welcomed his input. Bernd, who had not had an easy life since resettling in Switzerland, benefited greatly from his stay in Oberlin which I think was in many ways therapeutic.

IMB "PEDRO HAGEN" CULTIVATES A GDR SYMPATHIZER: JULY, 1982

The GDR made a practice of inviting US Germanists it considered to be sympathetic to its communistic form of government to attend summer seminars and workshops, where they would interact with carefully selected writers and scholars from around the GDR. The goal was not only to create a bond between intellectuals from the GDR and the US, but also to showcase the GDR in the most positive way, in the hope that the US scholars would project that image to their students in their colleges and universities. Special summer seminars were held in East Berlin, Weimar, and Leipzig, and the GDR would typically cover the cost of registration, room, board, and excursions for the participants it had invited. In his September 15, 1982 report to Stasi officer Gerhard Hoffmann, Fries refers to one such gathering, a conference in Leipzig held in July, 1982. It is interesting to note that the informant had not abandoned the idea of making another visit to the US, but to do that he needed an institution in the US to invite and sponsor him—i.e., to cover the expenses of his trip.

Department XX/7   Frankfurt (O), 9/15/1982

                                   ho-hi

source: IMB "Pedro Hagen"

received: Capt. Hoffmann

on: 9/15/1982

[Name blacked out] / Zipser, Richard (USA)

The IM provided the following information orally on [*name blacked out*]: In July of this year [*blacked out*] was in the GDR along with other Germanists from the USA. He was participating in an international conference for Germanists that was held in Leipzig. As far as is known [*blacked out*] stayed in private housing while in Leipzig.

The conference in Leipzig focused on problems in applied German studies. The Deputy Cultural Minister [*Klaus*] Höpcke was one of the speakers at the conference. According to [*blacked out*], Höpcke was well received by the Germanists from foreign countries because he spoke convincingly.

After the conference in Leipzig [*blacked out*] made his way to Berlin, so he said, at the invitation of the International Friendship League of the GDR. Interrupting the trip to Berlin, he made a stopover and that led to a three-day visit.

During the course of this visit the past stay in the USA was a topic, and there was discussion of a personal nature about what had been successful and less successful.

In our conversations the project that involves taking another trip to the USA was also discussed. [*Blacked out*] thinks this project is feasible. He will investigate the preconditions for a stay in Florida in spring 1983. An idea that emerged was the possibility of bringing along to the USA a copy of the just completed feature film which deserves to be exported and shown at festivals. [*The film is "Das Luftschiff ", based on Fries's novel with the same title, directed by Rainer Simon.*] One would need to check and see just what the possibilities, preconditions are in relation to this.

The conversations with [*blacked out*] did not lead to any commitments.

Our conversations also focused on the Germanist Zipser, who during the last stay in the USA showed [*the IM*] the galley proofs of a book he authored on GDR literature. [*Blacked out*] had no information whatever on Zipser and his whereabouts. He knew that Zipser had completed his work at the Hoover Institution of San Francisco University [*Stanford University, actually*], but did not know where he is now living and working. [*Blacked out*] was also unable to provide any information about the publication of Zipser's book; he had not yet seen a copy of it in the USA.

From Berlin [*blacked out*] was planning to travel on to Austria, in order to take a vacation there.

Comments

The IM took it upon himself to report on this matter; the encounter with [*blacked out*] was unplanned. The IM asserted that—apart from the information presented—the conversations had no particular significance; the subject matter was the creative work of the IM, personal things, and general topics.

Measures to be taken

- Review [*blacked out*] in archive files of Main Department VI

- Evaluation of the information on Zipser using operative process "Narr" [*"Fool"*] and materials on hand

- Initiation of further measures after results of the review have been received.

Hoffmann

Captain

REQUEST FOR SURVEILLANCE OF RICHARD ZIPSER: JANUARY 26, 1983

On January 26, 1983, the GDR Ministry for State Security instructed border personnel to closely monitor and report on my travel to and from the GDR, also to prevent me from bringing into or taking out of the country any illegal manuscripts or printed materials. The surveillance request, valid initially until January 31, 1984, would be extended later on until March 30, 1987. This one-page document, which provides the justification for and objectives of the surveillance, has been reproduced in its entirety below.

Secret!

COUNCIL OF MINISTERS
OF THE GERMAN DEMOCRATIC REPUBLIC
Ministry for State Security

Berlin, 1/26/83

Service units codes:
Main Directorate/Main Department/In-house: Dept.
BV/V XX
Dept. XII
Staff member   Pönig [*initialed*]

Surveillance Request

1. Name Last name	Zipser
2. First name	Richard
3. Date of birth	1/23/43
4. Place of birth	Maryland
5. Citizenship	USA
6. Profession	Professor of German Studies
7. Place of residence Street	Oberlin/ OhioUSA 102 Shipherd Circle

Person is registered in Dept. XII.   **10: 276532**

Justification of the operative necessity of the surveillance request, taking into account the information on the other side of this page:

Zipser seeks contacts with hostile-negative creative artists in the GDR, in order to misuse them in non-socialist regions through their literary publications that are directed against the GDR.

Goal

1. Immediately notify the service unit that gave the order when the surveillance target enters and leaves the country, including license plate number and type of automobile being used, documentation of travel documents.

2. Transmission of the personal data and documentation of travel documents of the persons accompanying the surveillance target, including license plate number and type of automobile being used.

3. Customs inspection for the purpose of detecting and preventing the illegal import and export of manuscripts and other written documents.

The surveillance target last entered the GDR from Westberlin on 01/19/1982.

The surveillance is in effect [*until*] 1/31/84.

NO SIGN OF RICHARD ZIPSER OR HIS BOOK

Returning to the Fries/Zipser file, the next document of interest is the informant's two-page report to Stasi officer Gerhard Hoffmann on controversial activities related to the forthcoming 9th GDR Writers Congress in East Berlin, May 31 – June 2, 1983, which had world peace as its principal theme and focused on the contribution of GDR writers in the struggle for international peace. The final paragraph of the report, which is cited below, focuses on another topic—the whereabouts of Richard Zipser and his book.

Also of apparent interest is the fact that the American Germanist, Dr. Richard Zipser, who up to now has shown keen interest in individual GDR authors and GDR Writers Congresses, has not yet expressed interest once again. He has not signaled in any way that he intends to come to Berlin for the Congress. One factor, possibly, is that the books on GDR literature he announced with fanfare have not yet been published. As far as is known, the publisher that originally was interested in the publication has withdrawn its interest. Hence, the publication did not occur. Evidently, there is also not yet a new publisher interested in

Zipser's works. It could be said speculatively that Zipser did not intend to prepare a book, but rather to gather information about the problems in the GDR literary scene. But this thought is a matter of subjective speculation, based solely on the knowledge that Zipser for one carried out his work in part with a fellowship from the HOOVER Institution of San Francisco University [*Stanford University, actually*] and now the non-publication of the book is being explained by the fact that there is no publisher.

The next document in the Fries/Zipser file, dated October 1, 1984, also focuses on the whereabouts of Richard Zipser and his book as well as on Fries's desire to return to the US. The informant reports via tape recording to Stasi officer Hoffmann on a meeting/conversation he had on September 25, 1984, with a professor from a small university in the US who is identified only with the initial D. This might well be the same Germanist who in July 1982 attended the conference in Leipzig and then had three days of meetings with Fries, as reported earlier in the document dated September 15, 1982. The heading of the report and the text on the second page appear below; the text on the first page has been completely blacked out, probably to protect D.

Department XX/7   Frankfurt (O), 10/1/1984
                                    ho-hä

source: IM
on: 9/25/1984

- Transcript of tape recording -

Dr. Zipser, Richard, was also a topic of conversation. It turned out that D., in spite of his efforts, had received no information about whether the book Zipser announced on GDR literature in the 1970s has been published. According to information from D., the book announced by Zipser is not to be found in the USA. D. surmises that Zipser's research results were either so unimportant that no publisher wanted to have anything to do with it or that the research results are of such an inflammatory nature that one steers away from their publication. However, as D. explained, what speaks against that possibility are the publication practices in the USA where publishing is unscrupulous. So, there is no information about Zipser.

Also discussed was the issue of another educational trip to the USA. D. made it clear that, as far as he is concerned, there are no possibilities because his small university cannot provide the financial resources for such an undertaking. It would be advisable to use a conference as an opportunity [*for a trip to the USA*] or a residency at a large university. He agreed to be on the lookout and to intently investigate ways to make a residency in America possible for me. We did not make commitments of any kind.

Likewise, he was not able to say if he would be returning to Europe.

In sum, one can say that D. is making himself small, small at his university, not producing anything of significance and probably also not interested in doing so.

With regard to politics he seems to be indifferent and colorless, which however is not unusual in the American context.

Speaker IM

Comments

The IM took it upon himself to report; the information has been checked partially through data in Dept. VI.

<u>Measures to be taken</u>

Addition to D.'s index card and evaluation within existing material on D.

[*signed*]
Hoffmann
Captain

A PUBLISHER FOR *DDR-LITERATUR IM TAUWETTER*

Although I was able to retrieve all materials related to *DDR-Literatur im Tauwetter* (*GDR Literature During the Thaw*] from Nordland Publishing Company by the fall of 1982, I was unable to search actively for a new publisher that year. I had undergone a major operation in June 1982, just before my wife and I moved into a new house we had built that year, and on September 1, 1982, I became chair of Oberlin College's Department of German and Russian. My plate was full, as the saying goes, and the stress was difficult to cope with. In February 1983, I came down with pneumonia, which interfered with my teaching and administrative duties. Not until the summer of 1983 was I able to begin searching for a suitable publisher for my three-volume book on GDR literature, which was going to be published entirely in German. For political reasons, I could not approach West German publishing houses, but publishers in politically neutral Austria and Switzerland were possibilities. My first choice was Peter Lang Publishing in Bern, Switzerland, which in 1974 had published my scholarly monograph on *Edward Bulwer-Lytton and Germany* (Vol. XVI of *German Studies in America*, ed. Heinrich Meyer).

In the fall of 1983, I contacted the Bern headquarters of Peter Lang Publishing and sent them a prospectus with information on my book. By coincidence, my wife and I were planning to spend Christmas vacation in a ski resort near Interlaken, about an hour away from Bern. Fortunately, I was able to get an appointment with Peter Lang himself and we had a very positive meeting and discussion of my project. Peter Lang had never published anything on East German literature and viewed this as a possible new direction for his company. Most of the books published by Peter Lang are in a series of one sort or another, but Peter Lang decided to do *DDR-Literatur im Tauwetter* as a free-standing book not connected to a series. I was delighted to have landed safely after the long delay.

In the spring semester of 1984, while Peter Lang Publishing was preparing my book manuscript for publication, I was directing an Oberlin College study abroad program in Germany and Austria. Before departing for Europe, I had applied for a full-year sabbatical leave in 1984-1985. It was fortunate that my application was approved, for this leave gave me the time I needed to work uninterruptedly on the book manuscript during the various production stages. I was extremely pleased with the appearance and layout of the book Peter Lang ultimately produced, and it was apparent that they had not tried to save money on this publication. *DDR-Literatur im Tauwetter* finally appeared in print in the fall of 1985, and complimentary copies were sent to all the East German writers represented and their publishing houses. The response from the writers was uniformly positive, which was very gratifying, especially in light of the prolonged delay we had experienced. One eminent author who had left the GDR in 1979 wrote and congratulated me on the book and its portrayal of GDR writers, offering this flattering comment: "Es ist das letzte Gruppenbild" ("It is the last group portrait."). Indeed, it was and still is.

PROMOTION TO FULL PROFESSOR AND NEW POSITION: 1985 – 1986

The publication of *DDR-Literatur im Tauwetter* (*GDR Literature During the Thaw*) benefitted me and my career in two ways: first of all, it led to my promotion in the fall of 1985 to the rank of full professor at Oberlin College; and secondly, it helped me secure a position at the University of Delaware, where I was employed until I retired on August 31, 2013. While I was on sabbatical leave during the 1984-1985 academic year, I decided to apply for some department chair positions at other colleges and universities. I submitted seven applications and was invited for campus interviews in February 1986 at the following institutions: Monterey Institute of International Studies (deanship), University of Arizona (department chair), and Texas A & M University (department chair). While I was not the top candidate for any of these positions, I was runnerup at Arizona and Texas A & M, where the jobs went to the persons who were serving as acting chair that year, an encouraging outcome. In November 1985, I saw that the University of Delaware was searching for a person to chair its Department of Foreign Languages and Literatures. After learning that there were no internal candidates for the position, I decided to apply. This time I emerged as the top candidate, received an attractive offer that I could not refuse, and in August 1986 moved to Newark, Delaware. I served as department chair at UD for twenty-seven years and have had a wonderful career and life here in Delaware. Without the publication of *DDR-Literatur im Tauwetter*, this major career move and life change would not have been possible.

INVITATION TO HELGA SCHÜTZ

Acting on my recommendation in the fall of 1984, the German faculty at Oberlin College decided to invite GDR prose writer Helga Schütz to be the 18th Max Kade German Writer-in-Residence during the spring semester of 1985. I had visited her a few times at her beautiful villa overlooking Gross Glienicke Lake, toured the DEFA (Deutsche Film-Aktiengesellschaft, the first film production company in post-War Germany) studios in Potsdam-Babelsberg with her, and was certain that she would interact well with our undergraduate students and Oberlin's German-speaking community. Since I was on sabbatical leave that fall, the acting chair of the department—Dr. Peter Spycher—issued the official invitation to her. Helga Schütz was not a controversial or oppositional writer, so I did not expect her to have any difficulty securing permission and a visa for the trip to the US, but the unexpected happened. In mid-January 1985, just a few weeks before the beginning of the spring semester, Peter Spycher received the following heart-wrenching letter from her, which he later passed along to me. The letter, which bears testimony to the cruel and inhumane nature of the GDR Writers' Union functionaries and higher authorities, is cited below. The original text appears in its entirety, followed by my translation of it into English.

Helga Schütz, DDR-136 Berlin,
Franz-Mett-Strasse 12
Berlin, den 31. 12. 84

Sehr geehrter Peter Spycher,

heute geht ein Jahr zu Ende, ein erlebnisreiches Jahr, ein Jahr voller Hoffnungen und Pläne, so dass ich – in diesen Zeiten beinahe anrüchig zufrieden und fröhlich gelebt und gearbeitet habe. Pläne hatte ich vor allem für Oberlin, für die Monate bei Ihnen am College. Alles schien mir vorwärts zu gehen und gut zu sein – bis zu dem Tage vor Weihnachten. Ich fand ein Telegramm im Briefkasten, dass ich beim Schriftsteller-Verband vorsprechen sollte. Auch da ahnte ich noch nichts böses. Ich glaubte, es fehlte vielleicht eine Unterschrift oder ein genaues Reisedatum. Ich hatte Ihre Einladungen ja immer gleich nach dem Eintreffen vorgelegt und mein grosses Interesse erklärt. Es kam anders – mir wurde beschieden, dass man an meinem Aufenthalt in Oberlin nicht interessiert sei und das Ausreisevisum nicht erteilen würde. Die Begründung verlor sich in einem nebelhaften Wortwechsel, dem grade noch zu entnehmen war, dass Sie sich für Oberlin immer die falschen Schriftsteller aussuchen würden (Wolfs, Plenzdorf und Jurek Becker, Bernd Jentzsch) und dass sich der Schriftsteller-Verband mit der Entsendung meiner Person nach Oberlin keinen Gewinn für die DDR verspräche. Ich war fassungslos, bedauerte bald, mich in einen Wortwechsel eingelassen zu haben, wollte grade gehen, da erteilte mir der Herr vom Verband den Rat, die Absage meines Aufenthalts bei Ihnen mit Krankheit zu begründen. Ich kann Ihnen meine Gefühle in diesem Augenblick nicht beschreiben. Wie ein armes Insekt bin ich anschliessend durch die Strassen geschlichen und habe mit dem Rest meiner in den letzten Monaten gesammelten Laune das Weihnachtsfest für die Familie vorbereitet. Hab mich dann zu den Feiertagen hingesetzt und einen Brief an den Kulturminister geschrieben, in dem ich ihm versucht habe zu erklären, um wieviel wichige Erfahrungen ich gebracht werde und dass ich mich geistig monatelang auf Oberlin vorbereitet habe. Zudem wollte ich in der Fremde, mit fremder Sprache ringsherum und neuen Bildern und gewiss auch Einsamkeit an meinem Romanmanuskript arbeiten. Ich wollte einige Kapitel – mich an zu Hause erinnernd – frisch und von ferne bedenken. Ich dachte, die Studenten daran teilhaben zu lassen. Es wäre ein Versuch, ein Wagnis, aber vielleicht doch, in einer nicht vorher zu beschreibenden Weise, möglich gewesen. Ich war sehr neugierig auf diese Situation.

Unter den neuen schäbigen Bedingungen weiss ich nicht, wie ich das Manuskript nun anpacken soll. Für die von mir herbeigewünschte und ausgedachte Konstellation gibt es eigentlich keinen Ersatz.

Beim Briefschreiben an den Minister wurde mir klar, dass ich im besten Falle auf Verständnis stossen könnte, aber dadurch ja nichts mehr zu retten sein würde. Sollten die grauen Mächte ihre Entscheidung revidieren, wären gewiss wieder Wochen nötig, ja Monate und das Semester in Oberlin hätte angefangen – der Start hier würde nervös, ohne die notwendige Gelassenheit und schöpferische Vorfreude. Ich weiss nun nicht einmal, was ich mit meinen Beschwerden erreichen will. Für einen bedauernden Händedruck wären mir meine Kräfte fast zu schade.

Ich möchte Sie nun in meiner Lage rundheraus fragen, ob Sie – <u>falls</u> es eine Korrektur und ein Einsehen gibt – die Möglichkeit haben, dass ich später – im Herbstsemester oder im nächsten Jahr – zu Ihnen kommen kann. Denn nur dann hätten meine Revolten einen praktischen Sinn.

Lieber Peter Spycher, ich meine, ich hätte Ihr Verständnis für meine Situation am Telefon herausgehört, dennoch möchte ich Ihnen noch einmal sagen dass ich mich für das Verhalten des Schriftsteller-Verbandes schäme. Es ist schäbig, in dieser Art und so kurz vor Beginn eines Ihrerseits mit so viel Aufwand und mit so viel Liebe vorbereiteten schönen Unternehmens kalt und ohne Vernunft "nein" zu sagen.

Bitte nehmen Sie meine besten Wünsche zum Neuen Jahr

Ihre
Helga Schütz

....

Berlin, 12/31/84

Dear Peter Spycher,

Today this year is coming to its end, a year rich with experiences, a year full of hope and plans, so that I have lived and worked during this time contentedly and happily—almost offensively so. I had plans for Oberlin, first and foremost, for the months with you at the College. It seemed to me that everything was moving forward and going well—until the day before Christmas. I found a telegram in my mailbox, telling me to visit the Writers's Union. There, too, I still did not sense that anything was wrong. I thought that perhaps a signature was missing or a precise travel date. I had always presented your invitations right after their arrival and expressed my strong interest. Things turned out differently—I was informed that there was no interest in my residency in Oberlin and that the exit visa would not be issued. The justification got lost in a nebulous exchange of words from which it was just possible to glean that you were always selecting the wrong writers for Oberlin (Wolfs, Plenzdorf and Jurek Becker, Bernd Jentzsch) and that the Writers' Union does not expect sending me to Oberlin would benefit the GDR in any way. I was stunned, regretted right away that I had let myself engage in a verbal exchange, wanted to leave just then, as the man from the Union advised me to use illness as the reason for cancelling my residency with you. I cannot tell you how I felt at that moment. Afterwards I crept through the streets like a lowly insect and, with what remained of the positive mood I had stored up over the last months, I prepared the Christmas celebration for our family. I then sat down over the holidays and wrote a letter to the Minister of Culture, wherein I tried to explain to him that I was being deprived of many important experiences and that I had for months been preparing myself mentally for Oberlin. In addition, I wanted to work on the manuscript of my novel in a foreign setting, with a foreign language all around and new images and, of course, solitude as well. I wanted to think about some chapters, fresh and from afar, while reminiscing about home. I planned to let the students participate in that. It would have been an attempt, a venture, but perhaps possible after all in a way not to be described in advance. I was very curious about this situation.

Under the new, shabby circumstances I now do not know how I ought to approach the manuscript. There is actually no substitute for the plan I devised and was longing to carry out.

While writing the letter to the Minister I realized that in the best case scenario I might be able to encounter understanding, but through that nothing more would be salvageable. Should the gray powers revise their decision, it would surely again take weeks, even months, and the semester in Oberlin would have begun; the departure here would be nervous, without the necessary calmness and creative anticipation. I do not even know now what I want to achieve with my complaining. I would almost not want to waste my strength on a commiserative handshake.

In my situation I would now like to ask you point-blank whether there is the possibility—in the event of a revision and an understanding—that I can come to you later on, in the fall semester or in the following year. For only then would my revolting make practical sense.

Dear Peter Spycher, I think I could detect your sympathy for my situation on the telephone; nevertheless I would like to tell you once again that I am ashamed of the behavior of the Writers' Union. It is outrageous to say "no" in this cold and unreasonable manner, and just before the start of a wonderful undertaking prepared on your part with so much time and effort and with so much love.

Please accept my best wishes for the New Year.

Yours,

Helga Schütz

Eventually, the Helga Schütz story had a happy ending. The German faculty at Oberlin, appalled by the way she had been mistreated by the GDR authorities, resolved to keep inviting her and not to invite any other writers from the GDR until she had visited Oberlin. In the fall of 1985, we invited her to be writer-in-residence for the spring 1986 semester, but her visa application was again denied and she was unable to accept the invitation. We then invited Karl-Heinz Jakobs, a GDR writer who—following his vigorous public protest of Wolf Biermann's expatriation—had been forced to move to West

Germany in 1977. Two years later the GDR authorities finally relented, and in the spring of 1988 Helga Schütz became the 21st Max Kade German Writer-in-Residence at Oberlin College.

Why did the GDR Writers' Union and, presumably, higher authorities treat Helga Schütz so harshly? In retrospect, I think they were very angry about our earlier selection of two outspoken dissident writers, Jurek Becker in 1978 and Bernd Jentzsch in 1982, who in their view did not in any way represent the GDR. They clearly decided to use Helga Schütz to punish us for selecting oppositional writers as representatives of the GDR, and that also would explain why they waited so long to deny her visa application. They knew we would have difficulty finding a replacement for her on such short notice, but fortunately we were able to do so. As I would learn in March 1985, the GDR Writers' Union was determined not only to participate in the selection process but to select appropriate writers for residency in Oberlin. They wanted us to contact them when we were ready to have a writer from the GDR; they then would either make the selection for us or propose two writers for our consideration. This would enable them to reward loyalist writers and at the same time ensure that the GDR would be represented by authors who were supportive of the SED Party's decisions and actions in the cultural domain.

RETURN TO EAST GERMANY: MARCH, 1985

Early in 1985, I received a telephone call from Cynthia Miller, USIA Public Affairs Officer at the US Embassy in East Berlin, who was serving as cultural attaché. (USIA is the acronym for the United States Information Agency, which existed from 1953 to 1999. It was an independent foreign affairs agency devoted to public diplomacy, much of which was carried out through US embassies.) Ms. Miller invited me to come to the renowned Leipzig Book Fair in March and preside over a special exhibit the embassy was putting together on "The Best Books in America: 1983-1984." This was the first time our embassy had participated in the Leipzig Book Fair and it wanted to make the exhibit as impressive as possible. Prizewinning books in every category—fiction of all kinds, poetry, biography and autobiography, children's books, documentaries of various sorts, photo essays, etc.—would be on display. Ms. Miller explained that my job would be to preside over the exhibit, which simply meant that I was to be present most of the time and prepared to converse with the attendees from the GDR in a friendly way. The embassy wanted the presider to be someone who was knowledgeable about the GDR and its society, fluent in German, and not affiliated with the US embassy or the US government. The expense of my roundtrip flight, hotel rooms, meals, and incidental expenses related to this assignment would be covered by the embassy. It sounded like it would be a great experience and—best of all—it would reconnect me with the GDR and many East German writers. I accepted the invitation with great pleasure and anticipation.

I flew to West Berlin on March 5, 1985 and—according to the stamps in my passport—entered East Berlin on March 6 via Checkpoint Charlie, in a US Embassy automobile which picked me up at West Berlin's Tegel Airport. The embassy chauffeur, a GDR citizen, took me to the Hotel Metropol where I stayed for three nights before heading for Leipzig. I remember that day very well because I had a terrible bout of food poisoning that started not long after my lunch in the hotel restaurant, where I had foolishly ordered beef tartare. However, I recovered within 24 hours and was able to meet with Cynthia Miller on March 7, as planned.

CYNTHIA MILLER'S INVITATION TO A RECEPTION IN HONOR OF RICHARD ZIPSER

Shortly before my departure for Berlin, Ms. Miller asked me to provide her with the names of some GDR writers I would like to see again before heading to Leipzig. She was planning to have a cocktail party and buffet dinner in my honor at her residence in Berlin Niederschönhausen, an upscale neighborhood where many diplomats lived. According to the formal invitation still in my possession, the social gathering was scheduled for 7:00 p.m., on Thursday,

March 7, 1985. The party not only gave me an opportunity to reconnect with some writers I knew well, it also gave Ms. Miller an opportunity to expand her contacts with writers in an informal way. Invitations to events held at the US Embassy were viewed with suspicion in those Cold War days, so East German writers and artists were hesitant to attend. I imagine that all the writers were surprised to receive the invitation, which I have reproduced below.

Botschaftsrat für Presse und Kultur
der Vereinigten Staaten von Amerika
Cynthia Miller
und Herr Miller
laden

[Name of guest handwritten]

zu einem Cocktail—Buffet
am Donnerstag, dem 7. März 1985
um 18.00 Uhr ein.
Platanenstrasse 98, 1110 Berlin
Antwort erbeten
Telefon 220 2741. App. 246

According to the files, the following persons attended the reception: Ulrich Plenzdorf, his wife Helga, and their son Morten; Fritz Rudolf Fries and his wife; Martin Stade and his wife; and Eberhard Scheibner from the GDR Writers' Union. Because the invitations were sent out only a short time before the event, some invitees—including Stefan Heym, Christa and Gerhard Wolf, and an editor from the Henschel Publishing House by the name of Schuch—were unable to attend.

IMB "PEDRO HAGEN" REPORTS ON THE RECEPTION AT
CYNTHIA MILLER'S RESIDENCE

On March 6, 1985, when he received the invitation to the March 7 reception, IMB "Pedro Hagen" contacted Stasi officer Gerhard Hoffmann and they arranged to meet on March 8. There is a report on this meeting, with a three-page attachment, in the Fries/Zipser file. It appears in its entirety below.

Service Unit Department XX/7   Date 3/8/85
                                                Approvals

Report on Meeting

Category/Code Name IMB "P. Hagen"

Date/Time	Meeting Place	Staff Member
3/8/85	"Neuhaus"	Hoffmann
4:00 p.m.		

Next Meeting	on	Time	Meeting Place
as scheduled	3/15/85	4:00 p.m.	"Neuhaus"

Reports 1 oral

Number of pieces of information on adversarial offensive from the area of operations 1

Preparation for meeting:

Meeting was set up operatively as planned on 3/6/85 and held on 3/8/85, since the IM received an invitation on short notice to a USA Embassy reception which the person of operative interest attended.

Evaluation to be carried out at Main Department XX.

See attachments.

. . . .

Department XX/7   Frankfurt (O), 3/8/1985

                                          Ho-Scha

source: IM

received: 3/8/85

USA Embassy Reception in Berlin on 3/7/1985

On 3/6/1985 an invitation arrived by mail to a USA Embassy reception in honor of

Prof.   ZIPSER, Richard
           USA
           Oberlin

on 3/7/1985, starting at 6:00 p.m., in the quarters of the USA Embassy in Berlin Niederschönhausen, Platanenstrasse. [*The reception was at Cynthia Miller's private residence, which was located in a compound where many diplomats from capitalist countries lived—under constant Stasi surveillance, of course.*]

The invitation came from a Ms. [*blacked out*], who is apparently the cultural attaché at the USA Embassy.

The invitation was accepted, the house on Platanenstrasse visited. It is evidently a reception facility, lacking warmth, functional, without special features. Hosting were Ms. [*blacked out*] and her husband as well as another female employee of the Embassy whose name did not become known.

Prof. Richard ZIPSER was present when I arrived with my wife. The initial greeting was normal, without especial warmth, but conveying astonishment at meeting him here in Berlin, and on top of that in the Embassy.

Also present were Ulrich PLENZDORF with his wife and son, Mr. SCHEIBNER from the GDR Writers' Union, International Relations Department, and several employees. They were expecting Martin STADE as well.

Thus, at 6:00 p.m. there were 6 GDR citizens present.

STADE and his wife arrived around 7:30 p.m. By this time, PLENZDORF and his family members had already left because he wanted to go to the theater. I left the reception around 8:00 p.m.

A very generous cold buffet was provided and beverages, mainly whiskey, were served by the butlers.

Regarding the conversation with ZIPSER

He indicated that he entered the GDR on 3/5/1985. His destination is Leipzig; he is planning to participate in the book fair and is of the impression that the fair is a meeting place for writers. An attempt was made to dispel him of that notion because it is not the case.

He will be in Leipzig for the opening of the fair on 3/10/1985 and, after the fair concludes, he will fly back to the USA on 3/17/1985.

He did not mention plans to make visits with authors he knows. He did not accept invitations to organize a personal meeting in Berlin during or after the fair, making reference to his return flight on 3/17/1985.

He commented on his book as follows:

The work, a three-volume edition, is existent. It is entitled "GDR Literature During the Thaw."

He had offered it to a USA publisher, the project was accepted, then the publisher allegedly went bankrupt.

Now a Swiss publisher is attending to the three-volume edition.

ZIPSER explained that he had to buy back the contract from the bankrupt publisher, so that the book publication could actually come about, since it was already completed 4 years ago. The Swiss edition will be published in German. There are no plans for translations.

In our conversation I questioned its value, because it describes the literary scene from 1976. He said the book is now a contemporary document.

He did not respond to questions about the Swiss publisher.

His problem is how to go about delivering the complimentary copies to the GDR authors. His original plan to continue work on this project is apparently no longer in effect. He was not responsive to questions on this topic.

He is angry about the fact that GDR author Helga SCHÜTZ was not permitted to go to the USA last year; he had invited her to come to Oberlin.

Together with PLENZDORF we discussed possibilities for travel to the USA. One such idea ZIPSER expressed was always to invite two GDR authors. We explained to him that it would be better not to put two names forward, but rather one name and to let the Writers' Union designate an additional one.

ZIPSER did not comment authoritatively on that, but finally said that one would have to turn to the GDR authors living in the West if the authors from the GDR would not be allowed to come.

He evidently also discussed this problem with SCHEIBNER, since they were having an animated conversation. PLENZDORF and I were of the opinion that ZIPSER would even be able to negotiate with the Union about that.

It was surprising that ZIPSER did not inquire at all about the literary scene in Leipzig.

I had casual conversations with Ms. [*blacked out*] and her husband. She speaks very good German, he does not. Before coming to Berlin, both were at the USA Embassy in Vienna. Both seemed not to know anything about GDR literature. One indication of that is the fact that the conversation was only about the weather, Berlin and the surrounding area, and about him [*blacked out*] speaking to the police in front of the Embassy. Questions about cultural policy and politics did not enter into the discussion at all.

Also the question for SCHEIBNER, whether he too is a writer, provided evidence of ignorance.

STADE and his wife showed up at around 7:30 p.m., [*blacked out*]. He brought along his book-novel which, as far as I was able to learn, is going to be published first in the FRG. STADE did not clarify the circumstances. [*It was highly unusual for a literary work by an East German writer to appear in print in West Germany prior to its publication in East Germany. Fries was surely eager to learn more about this development.*]

PLENZDORF and I were in agreement and surprised by the invitation on short notice. It did not make sense, and [*the reception*] went off in the typical Anglo-Saxon short-winded way.

I found out that Christa and Gerhard WOLF and the editor SCHUCH from Henschel Publishing House had been invited. The reasons why they did not attend are not known. With these persons, the invitees would have been GDR citizens who have spent time in the USA in recent years.

ZIPSER's purpose for being in the GDR is unclear.

Presumably he is not here of his own accord, otherwise he would have visited Berlin and not the fair in Leipzig.

The literary scene in Berlin has more to offer than Leipzig's.

It was surprising that he turned down invitations to Berlin and, on the other hand, did not inquire at all about the literary scene in Leipzig.

signed IM

Comments

The IM attended the reception, as instructed. The reporting has not been checked; there is no reason to doubt its veracity.

Protection of the [*confidential*] source must be guaranteed.

On March 9, the next day, a shorter version of the above report was sent as a telegram to the Ministry for State Security in Berlin. The telegram is addressed as follows:

Sender: Regional Headquarters Frankfurt (O),
                                 Department XX

Recipients: Ministry for State Security Main
                                 Department XX,
                                 Director, and Ministry for State Security Main
                                 Department XX/7, Director

While the information in the two reports is basically the same, the conclusion of the telegram is different; it mentions the informant Fries by name.

> Plenzdorf and Fries were unable to figure out the objective of the reception; both were amazed by the invitation on short notice and the superficiality of the evening.

MORE REPORTS ON THE RECEPTION AT CYNTHIA MILLER'S RESIDENCE

In my file there are four reports on the March 7, 1985 reception in my honor at cultural attaché Cynthia Miller's residence. Two of these reports, both dated March 9, 1985, are similar in content and clearly based on the information IMB "Pedro Hagen" communicated to his Stasi-handler Gerhard Hoffmann when they met on March 8, 1985. The other two provide some new information and insights that probably came from the other informant present at the party, Eberhard Scheibner, who is referred to as "die Quelle" (the source). The longer of the two reports dated March 9, 1985, appears below. Note that Scheibner plays a much more prominent role than he did in the report Fries made on March 8, as he takes me to task and vigorously defends the

GDR and the practices of its Writers' Union. Much of this is fictional, but it certainly makes Scheibner look like an ultra-loyalist functionary, exactly how he wished to be perceived by the Stasi and his supervisors.

File   Zipser   March 9, 1985

Regarding the reception of the Press and Culture Counsellor of the Embassy of the USA in the capital city of the GDR, Cynthia Miller, on 3/7/1985 at 6:00 p.m. in her residence, 1110 Berlin, Platanenstrasse 98.

[...]

As became known unofficially, some of the invited persons were, among others

Hermann Kant   President of the Writers' Union of the
                       GDR (WU)
Rudi Strahl   Member of the Executive Committee
                       of the WU
Eberhard Scheibner   Secretary of the Writers' Union
Fritz Rudolf Fries   Member of the Executive Committee
                       of the PEN Center of the GDR

and the operatively known writer, Ulrich Plenzdorf.

Zipser had already met and conversed with Plenzdorf on the evening of his arrival in Hotel "Metropol" in Berlin.

The names of other persons who received invitations could not be determined as yet.

Eberhard Scheibner, Fritz Rudolf Fries and his wife, and Ulrich Plenzdorf and his wife accepted the invitation.

The unofficial source was unable to discern other persons from the literary domain of the GDR.

In addition to the parties named above, 5 other persons not known to the source attended this reception.

After ca. 1 ½ hours another married couple came to this reception; they were introduced simply with the comment that they are old friends of Mr. Zipser.

In his personal conversation with Zipser, the source asked Zipser to explain what has become of his scholarly work on GDR literature. Zipser claimed back then—1977/78—that he wanted to write a comprehensive book on GDR literature and GDR writers. He spent several months in the GDR, but up to now no one has read even one printed line written by Mr. Zipser, which is very strange indeed.

As a result of this questioning, which obviously was embarrassing for Zipser, he attempted to explain in a very roundabout way that the American publishing house planning to bring out his work had changed owners several times and, despite assurances during the interim, his manuscript was not published. According to Zipser's statements, this has to do with the American Nordland Publishing Company. (No information on this publisher is available to the source.)

Zipser indicated further that his book will be readily available in May 1985 and he will have a complimentary copy sent to all participating GDR authors as well the Writers' Union. This scholarly work is going to be published in 3 volumes, 2 volumes of which will contain the texts from the 45 GDR authors and 1 volume the interviews he conducted with GDR writers.

Zipser mentioned in passing that he is well aware that there will also be people in the GDR who will not be pleased with his book, but he is an American and wrote the book from this point of view.

Zipser stated additionally that the actual reason for his visit to the GDR is that he has been appointed and installed as director of the USA booth at the Book Fair in Leipzig. He stated, with regard to what the USA would display at its booth, that he did not yet know any details about this. However, the USA would not be putting political books on display, but rather fiction primarily, children's books, history and science books.

Zipser attempted to attack the Secretary of the Writers' Union of the GDR, Scheibner, by questioning why the writer Helga Schütz was not permitted to accept his invitation to visit Oberlin.

Comrade Scheibner countered, telling Zipser that it looks very odd and Zipser has lost his credibility as regards his integrity of purpose vis-à-vis the GDR, since up to now after 8 years there is still not one line written by him to be read on GDR literature and its writers, and since in the past he only invited writers—with one exception—who established themselves through oppositional types of behavior vis-à-vis the GDR, and that if Zipser is seriously striving to have good relations with the GDR he has to respect certain principles that are in force in the GDR; for example, how the GDR does not allow someone to dictate which writers it has to send somewhere, since the delegation principle prevails in the Writers' Union.

This reply made Zipser very uncomfortable and he tried in turn to explain why he would have to persist with the invitation to the writer Helga Schütz. Zipser then indicated that there is a foundation at his institution, Oberlin College, which is governed by a "democratic" committee. This committee, he said, has decided to invite German-speaking writers from both German states. Thus, they have invited (among others) the FRG writer Gert Hoffmann and the Swiss writer Adolf Muschg, and now the governing committee wants just to bring Helga Schütz to the USA and no other writer. If the GDR does not permit Helga Schütz to travel, Zipser asserted, the GDR is not going to be represented.

At that point Comrade Scheibner told Zipser that nobody in the GDR would be upset by this. Zipser's institution must adjust to the fact that the Writers' Union makes such determinations in the GDR or it is senseless to continue dealing with one another.

On top of that, Comrade Scheibner once again pointed out to Zipser that he had contact with 45 writers during his last stay in the GDR, some of whom were far more important and more representative than Helga Schütz.

At that point Zipser repeated once again, stubbornly, that he will renew the invitation to Helga Schütz with a concrete deadline for permission to make the trip, since he could not afford to have another cancellation on short notice, otherwise he would not receive funding approval for any more GDR authors.

Comrade Scheibner pointed out to Zipser that he would not influence or alter the position of the Writers' Union through his stubbornness. As long as no printed line written by him is available, he remains noncredible. When his books have appeared in print, it might be possible to continue the conversation.

As also became known unofficially, Zipser spoke with Plenzdorf about another longer research residency in the GDR. Specific details on that could not be obtained as yet.

At the conclusion, as goodbyes were being said, Zipser approached Comrade Scheibner and told him that he had thought about his arguments and the Writers' Union ought to give him suggestions as to which writers he could invite to the USA. Then Comrade Scheibner replied that he would take note of that and present it to the executive committee of the Writers' Union.

Zipser also mentioned that he intends to remain in Leipzig until 3/16/1985 and plans to start his journey back to the USA from Berlin on 3/17/1985.

BOOK FAIR IN LEIPZIG: MARCH, 1985

On March 8, 1985, Cynthia Miller and I were chauffeured in a US Embassy automobile to Leipzig, where arrangements for the exhibit of the best books published in the US during 1983-1984 were already underway. That evening I met US Ambassador to the GDR Rozanne Ridgway, who invited the book fair team from the embassy to a gala dinner. Ambassador Ridgway also invited Cynthia Miller and me to ride with her to the restaurant in her US Embassy vehicle. It was a black four-door Cadillac sedan, long and luxurious, with American flags fastened to the sides of the front headlights. As we drove around Leipzig's Ring Street with the flags fluttering proudly and attracting lots of attention, people stopped what they were doing and stared at the Cadillac. Undoubtedly, most of them had never seen an automobile like that. Another nice memory!

The next morning Ambassador Ridgway, Cynthia, and I attended the book fair's opening ceremony and the reception that followed; there I met Klaus Höpcke, the powerful Deputy Minister of Culture in the GDR. Also present at the book fair was Eberhard Scheibner from the GDR Writers's Union. Over lunch one day we continued our discussion of Helga Schütz, the German writer-in-residence program at Oberlin College, and the "Delegierungsprinzip" (delegation principle) I had been instructed to follow when we wanted to invite a writer from the GDR.

While in Leipzig I stayed in the drab, somewhat dilapidated Interhotel am Ring, which was just a short walk away from the Trade Fair House on the main market square, the multi-storied home of the Book Fair. When reading the file report on my activities in Leipzig, I noted without surprise that my telephone had been bugged: "As could also be determined operatively,

ZIPSER attempted several times to make telephone contact with the holder of phone number: 32 39 43 Leipzig." The file also reminded me that I had met (for the first time) with outspoken dissident writer and poet Lutz Rathenow, who was not permitted to publish his work in the GDR. After publishing his first book in West Germany, a collection of short texts critical of the GDR (*Mit dem Schlimmsten wurde schon gerechnet / Already Prepared for the Worst*), Rathenow was arrested in December 1980 and imprisoned for a month. Although he was under close surveillance by the Stasi, he and his friends managed to smuggle manuscripts into West Berlin and West Germany, to be published there. We had a dinner meeting that lasted several hours and were joined by Hans-Jürgen Schmitt, an editor with the West German Fischer Taschenbuch Verlag who had published several anthologies of GDR literature. For some odd reason, Schmitt is not mentioned in the file report.

> As a result of the additional operative surveillance, it was determined that on 3/11/1985 ZIPSER met and had a several hour conversation in Leipzig with operatively known Lutz RATHENOW.
>
> It was learned unofficially that ZIPSER characterized his conversation with RATHENOW, on which he took detailed notes, as very useful. According to comments ZIPSER made, their conversation had to do with books. RATHENOW expressed the view (among others) that more books by writers such as BUKOWSKI and UPDIKE [*20th-century American authors, Charles Bukowski and John Updike*] needed to be translated in the GDR. RATHENOW assured ZIPSER that on the part of GDR citizens there is great interest in the USA booth at the Leipzig Book Fair.

Before we parted company, Rathenow gave me an unusual present, a hand-made book containing typewritten texts by eight younger oppositional writers who were unable to find a GDR publisher for all or some of their works.

In the GDR and elsewhere in the Soviet bloc, banned authors reproduced censored and underground publications by hand and passed the documents from reader to reader. This clandestine self-publishing practice was known as *samizdat*; it was a key form of dissident activity, the purpose of which was to circumvent official state censorship. It was not without danger, as harsh punishments were imposed on persons caught possessing or copying censored materials. I considered it an honor to be given an authentic *samizdat* literary anthology by Lutz Rathenow.

I had meetings with a number of other East German writers while in Leipzig, but these are not recorded in my file. I met Wolfgang Hilbig for the first time, had dinner with him and his significant other in the HOG "Paulaner" restaurant. Like Rathenow, Hilbig was a poet and prose writer who had remained staunchly defiant in the face of the oppression he experienced in the GDR. He, too, had been imprisoned for a short time in 1970, and later in 1985 he was granted a visa that enabled him to move to West Germany, where his career would flourish. Had I met Hilbig and Rathenow a year earlier, I would have been able to include them in *DDR-Literatur im Tauwetter*, but by March 1985 that book was finished and ready for the printer.

The report covering my activities at the Leipzig Book Fair begins with my arrival in East Berlin on March 6, 1985. This seven-page document is dated March 29, 1985 and labelled top secret. As one reads the report, it becomes apparent that the Stasi and the GDR authorities were interested most of all in ascertaining the "real" purpose of my visit to Leipzig. Other topics covered are the March 7 reception in my honor at Cynthia Miller's residence; my insistence on again inviting Helga Schütz to be writer-in-residence at Oberlin College and my stubborn refusal to involve the GDR Writers' Union in the selection process; and, surprisingly, my view of President Ronald Reagan's arms buildup. Excerpts from the March 29 report are cited below.

Main Department XX	**Berlin, March 29, 1985**
Top secret	**5 copies made**

No. 252 / 85

Information

On the GDR stay of the operatively known American Germanist
Dr. Richard ZIPSER

As a result of the operative surveillance of Dr. ZIPSER initiated
during his stay in the GDR, in the period from 3/7 until
3/17/1985, the following activities and operatively relevant
behavioral patterns of Dr. ZIPSER were observed. (personal
data known)

[...]

As was learned privately and confidentially, ZIPSER made the
following assertion regarding the purpose of his stay in the GDR:
The actual reason is not his official assignment to serve as the
person in charge of the USA booth at the Leipzig Book Fair, but
rather the transferal of his contacts with GDR writers to staff
members at the USA Embassy in the GDR. Over and above that,
he is supposed to use his position as presider at the US fair booth
to facilitate forging new contacts to GDR writers and introduce
these persons at once to a staff member of the USA Embassy or
make the writer aware that the Embassy is interested in having a
conversation with him/her. And so, for example, ZIPSER asked
an unofficial source directly if he/she would be interested in
continuing their conversation with the American contingent. If
so, he would then notify Embassy Counsellor Cynthia MILLER.
Ms. MILLER would then get in touch in the near future and
they could make whatever arrangements they wish. But ZIPSER
would recommend that the source not visit the USA Embassy,
which he says is guarded like a fortress. He would suggest that

the source arrange to get together with MILLER and meet her "by chance" in a café. The source let ZIPSER know that this decision would be his/hers to make.

Since the time span of the Leipzig Book Fair, where he [*Zipser*] is relatively tied down, is not sufficient for the transferal of all the contacts he has to GDR authors, he is contemplating paying another much longer visit to the GDR this year, probably in the summer. He plans to combine this with the expansion of his own personal knowledge of GDR literature and writers. In his opinion there have been all sorts of changes in the GDR literary scene since his last stay. Writers who at that time were well known and played a major role, he says, are no longer there and have left the GDR.

In the meantime a new generation of writers has come of age; he would like to get to know them through their literary works as well as personally.

[...]

Unofficially, it was possible to learn the following about the nature of ZIPSER's activity and this college in Oberlin. At the college in Oberlin, according to ZIPSER's account, there is a foundation that is governed by a committee. ZIPSER is chair of the German Studies Department and has five colleagues. His department has also been assigned to teach Soviet literature. For this reason, two of his colleagues are said to be Slavicists. Each year they are able to invite guest writers from German-speaking countries. In accordance with this possibility they are interested not only in having German-speaking authors from the FRG, Austria, and Switzerland among their guests, but also GDR authors. Up to now that had always worked well, he says. So there were no difficulties with invitations and residencies of GDR authors Volker BRAUN, Ulrich PLENZDORF, Jurek BECKER. [*Volker Braun was never German Writer-in Residence at Oberlin College. The initial reference should be to Christa Wolf.*]

[...]

Privately and confidentially, it became known that ZIPSER— after consultation with USA Embassy representatives (presumably Cynthia MILLER)—commented in the presence of an unofficial source that, whether he wants to or not, he would again have to invite GDR writer Helga SCHÜTZ to visit the college in Oberlin because the committee insists on it, even if it involves provoking the GDR.

In case SCHÜTZ is denied permission to travel by the GDR, he says, this would constitute proof that writers in the GDR are restricted in their personal freedom, that the GDR is thereby violating human rights and forcing the college to fall back on just the GDR writers living in the West and former GDR writers.

The restriction and hindrance of travel by GDR writers and other creative artists would then provide conclusive and convincing arguments for the supposed proof of human rights violations in the GDR at the European Cultural Forum to be held in Budapest, Hungarian People's Republic, in November 1985. [*This gathering was linked to the Helsinki Accords or Helsinki Declaration, the final act of the Conference on Security and Cooperation in Europe held in Helsinki, Finland, on July 30 and August 1, 1975. Thirty-five countries, including the US, the Soviet Union, the Federal Republic of Germany, and the German Democratic Republic, signed the Declaration in an attempt to improve relations between Communist bloc and Western nations. Ten years after the signing of the Declaration it was Hungary's turn to host—for the first time a Soviet bloc country—the European Cultural Forum in Budapest, a gathering of delegations from the countries that had signed*] *the Declaration. This conference and earlier conferences held in Belgrade and Madrid were designed to monitor compliance with the Helsinki commitments. The theme of the Budapest event was freedom in culture and art, which formed the third "basket" of the Helsinki Accords. The conference promised to be an interesting one, since the censorship that was practiced overtly or covertly in the Communist bloc countries was contrary to the principles of the Helsinki Accords, thus offering an easy target for the Western delegations.*]

[. . .]

In connection with a statement by members of the PEN Center USA, who in the beginning of this year spoke out against the space armament of the Reagan administration, ZIPSER was asked by a source for his opinion on the position of these USA writers as well as on Reagan's arms policy in general.

With regard to that question, ZIPSER said it might well be that some writers or professors at his college are involved in this way. But there is nothing organized. He personally is not concerned about this issue. He is an academician and trusts that his government will ably solve the problem.

ZIPSER left the GDR on 3/17/1985.

The report concludes with four recommendations on how to control and monitor my GDR-related activities in the future, which are cited below.

For the purposes of reconnaissance and precautionary prevention of ZIPSER's hostile plans and intentions connected with possible further stays in the GDR and the deepening or the addition of contacts with GDR writers, the following measures are being recommended:

1. Since ZIPSER emphasized, during his conversation with Comrade SCHEIBNER, that even in the future he does not intend to coordinate with the GDR Writers' Union when inviting GDR writers to visit the USA, one should check and see to what extent on the part of the Writers' Union the Ministry of Foreign Affairs can be informed about this issue, in order to prevent additional official stays in the GDR by ZIPSER.

2. Through the Main Directorate for Reconnaissance one needs to check and see to what extent conclusions can be drawn about the nature of Oberlin College in Ohio/USA, ZIPSER's place of employment, in connection with possible undercover activities of this institution as well as about ZIPSER's role there.

3. During ZIPSER's possible further stays in the GDR, private or upon invitation of the USA Embassy, operative control measures will be activated and carried out.

4. In connection with ZIPSER's assertions that he is not interested in questions of disarmament and in this regard has complete confidence in the Reagan administration, one needs to check and see if--through appropriate targeted comments by unofficial collaborators and in the Writers' Union of the GDR-- ZIPSER's reputation can be so damaged that even adversarial forces will avoid further contact with him.

In an attachment to my file from the central archive, labelled Ministry for State Security, Main Department XX, 2 staff members, No. 976, Z i p s e r, Dr. Richard, 2nd card, there is an interesting note regarding the "real" purpose of my March 1985 trip to East Berlin and Leipzig:

Main Department XX/7/Info. 462/85, from 6/10/1985: Z. presided over the USA publishers' collective book stand at the spring 1985 Leipzig Trade Fair; while doing so he was supervised by Cynthia MILLER. ZIPSER's assignment was to renew his personal connections and contacts with GDR citizens and introduce these individuals to MILLER. Furthermore, he was to siphon off persons from the cultural sphere and gather information on alleged violations of human rights by GDR state agencies, which is needed for the European Cultural Forum in Budapest where delegations from the countries that signed the Helsinki Accords will gather. (Central Archive 9721)

Clearly, the Stasi and the GDR authorities had concluded that I was working for a branch of the US secret service, but that was simply not the case. However, it is true and certainly understandable that Cynthia Miller was eager to meet some of the East German writers and artists I knew, and of course I was eager to reestablish contact with as many writers as possible during this short visit. While in Leipzig I had dined (separately) with two East Germans who worked at the US Embassy and were helping Cynthia Miller at the book fair, as recorded in the file report dated March 29, 1985, but this was not an attempt to siphon them off, as stated in the above note. Also, the assertion that I was gathering information on alleged human rights violations by GDR state agencies is based on an assumption that is not grounded in fact, but bold leaps of this sort occur throughout my file.

FINAL REPORT IN THE FILE LABELLED "PEDRO HAGEN": MARCH 18, 1985

In this document, which is based on information Fries communicated orally to his Stasi-handler Gerhard Hoffmann, there is further speculation about the reason for my presence at the Leipzig Book Fair as well as the nature of my association with John Wiley & Sons, the publisher of my textbook edition of Ulrich Plenzdorf's *Die neuen Leiden des jungen W.* (*The New Sufferings of Young W.*, 1979). At the conclusion of the report, which appears in its entirety below, Hoffmann specifies the next steps that needed to be taken by way of follow-up.

Department XX/7 Frankfurt (O), 3/18/1985
ho-ri

Source: IM

<u>Prof. ZIPSER, Richard</u>

During his stay in the GDR from 6/03 to 17/03/1985, Zipser planned to attend the spring Leipzig Trade Fair, the Book Fair in particular at the same time.

A short note with information about Zipser was enclosed with an invitation to a reception in his honor on 3/07/1985 at the USA Embassy in the GDR. This note indicates that Zipser received the Ph.D. in German studies from the

JOHNS HOPKINS UNIVERSITY

in 1972. At the present time he is working in the German Department at

OBERLIN COLLEGE.

The note also indicates that he is associated with

JOHN WILEY AND SONS
PUBLISHERS
NEW YORK.

The term "associated" is taken verbatim from the note and cannot be construed clearly in the translation. There is the possibility that ZIPSER is employed by the publishing house that is named, which would explain his participation in the Leipzig Trade Fair. On the other hand, a connection to this publisher would be inconsistent with his needing to offer the publication of "DDR-Literatur im Tauwetter" to a Swiss publisher. Thus, it is not possible to say with certainty what assignment brought ZIPSER to the GDR and especially to the spring Leipzig Trade Fair.

signed IM

Comments

Information was provided by the IM as an addendum to the report he gave on 3/08/1985. A precise interpretation of the term "associated" was not possible, not even with the aid of its context. The above-mentioned information about ZIPSER also revealed that he had numerous publications on GDR literature in the USA and has invited many GDR authors to visit the USA.

Evaluation

The information is meaningful inasmuch as it names specifically the entity that may have made ZIPSER's stay in Leipzig possible. If ZIPSER was in Leipzig as a representative or assignee of the publishing house named above, that explains why he did not launch into any additional activities.

Measures to be taken

- Evaluation of Trade Fair reporting by XX/AI

- Addendum for evaluation in monthly report

- Information as a copy to Main Department XX/7 for operative evaluation

Hoffmann
Capt.

RE-ENTRY BAN: JUNE 11, 1985

In connection with the three measures cited at the conclusion of the report above, there is a short but extremely important memorandum in my file with some handwritten notes bearing different dates. The first note, dated April 29, 1985, indicates that the Stasi was considering not allowing me to re-enter the GDR; the second note, dated June 11, 1985, provides evidence of their decision not to permit me to enter the GDR again and explains why; the third note confirms receipt of this memorandum on July 9, 1985 presumably for filing. The typewritten heading on the memorandum appears below, followed by the notes.

Comrade Lieutenant Colonel B u h l

Comrade Generalmajor Kienberg requests consultation.

Consultation took place

with Comrade Colonel [*Karl*] Brosche
arranged by XX/7
consultation with Main Directorate for Reconnaissance
in order to consider what specifically
can be initiated against Zipser
possibly entry ban
response sent by XX/7
4/29/85 Buhl [*signature*]
memorandum Comrade Colonel Brosche
Z. is considered enemy of the state by XX/7
entry ban will be initiated
6/11/85 Buhl [*signature*]

received 7/9/85

FINAL COMMENTS ON INFORMANT/WRITER FRITZ RUDOLF FRIES

Fritz Rudolf Fries was outed as a Stasi informant in 1996. He began working as an informant for the Ministry for State Security in 1972, initially as an IM, then as a trustworthy IMV, next as an even more trusted IMS, and finally as a totally reliable IMB, one of the highest levels in the ranks of Stasi informants. He worked for the Stasi until at least 1985, under the code name "Pedro Hagen" and under the watchful eye of his handler, First Lieutenant/Captain Gerhard Hoffmann. Fries informed on other authors and persons of interest like myself; he passed along information gathered at receptions in embassies and gatherings in private homes, and he dutifully carried out his assignments both at home and abroad. His main reward, as far as I can tell, was the privilege of travelling to non-socialist countries; he was a passionate traveller, so this perquisite was particularly important to him. In *Alle meine Hotel Leben: Reisen 1957-1979* (*All My Hotel Lives: Travels 1957-1979*, 1980), Fries reflects in short impressionistic prose texts on his travels to faraway places such as Cuba, Argentina, Albania, Poland, Slovakia, Barcelona, Bruges, Paris and Normandy, as well as to some destinations close to home, such as Leipzig and Zwickau. In each of these fifteen prose pieces, his love of travel is on full display. His carefully crafted texts bring to life places in foreign countries that most GDR citizens would never have been able to visit.

In his 320-page memoir, *Diogenes auf der Parkbank* (*Diogenes on the Park Bench*, Berlin: Das Neue Berlin, 2002), Fries uses humor, hyperbole, sarcasm, and even self-pity to rationalize his decision to work for the Stasi and downplay its importance. In a section titled *Operativer Vorgang "Autor"* (*Operative Activity "Author"*), he compares himself to Faust who entered into a pact with the devil. Fries's devil, of course, is his Stasi handler. In an effort to defend himself and his despicable actions in the presence of real and imagined accusers who ask "How could you?", he writes about himself in the third person, unable to use the personal pronoun "I" as he does in other sections of the book. Perhaps he is trying to distance himself from Fritz Rudolf Fries, the informant.

Was war es, dass er den "Pakt mit dem Teufel" unterschrieb, nach fast zehnjähriger Verweigerung, und sich, zum Jux, mit Faust verglich? Nun hatte er gestundete Zeit, und er würde sagen und schreiben können, was er wolle—sofern (und daran dachte er zunächst kaum) er den Teufel mit kleinen Brosamen zufriedenstellte. Er würde endlich reisen können, Spanien war sein Ziel. Von schleichender Krankheit bedroht (er weist auf seine Krücken) seien diese Jahre die einzigen, die ihm noch grössere Reisen erlaubten. Und: Was genau wollte denn der Teufel? Er wollte Auskunft über die Verhältnisse in Spanien nach Francos Tod. Das zu liefern sei kein Vergehen gewesen, diente es doch dazu, die diplomatischen Beziehungen zwischen der DDR und Spanien aufzubauen. Etliche seiner Kollegen und Verwandten konnten daraufhin privat und dienstlich nach Spanien reisen . . . Und je mehr die DDR diplomatische Anerkennung fand, desto mehr wurde sie ein Opfer ihrer Widersprüche. [. . .] Wem konnte es schaden, wenn er nach einer Reise seinem Führungsoffizier einen Bericht gab, mündlich, den er schriftlich dem Schriftstellerverband oder dem PEN Zentrum zu geben verpflichtet war. (238)

What led him to sign the "pact with the devil" after refusing to do so for almost ten years and, in jest, to compare himself to Faust? Now he was on borrowed time and would be able to say and write what he wanted—provided that (and initially he hardly thought about it) he satisfied the devil with little breadcrumbs. He would finally be able to travel, Spain was his objective. He was threatened by an insidious disease (he exhibits his crutches) that would make these years the only ones in which he would be capable of longer journeys. And: What precisely did the devil want? He wanted information on the state of affairs in Spain after Franco's death. Providing that would not have been an offence; after all it served to build up diplomatic relations between the GDR and Spain. A number of his colleagues and relatives would later on be able to travel privately and on business to Spain . . . And the more diplomatic recognition the GDR would gain, the more it would become a victim of its inconsistencies. [. . .] Whom could it harm if he gave his case officer a report, orally, after returning from a trip, the report he was obliged to give in written form to the Writers' Union or the PEN Center.

Fries's effort to present himself as innocent of any real wrongdoing is not convincing, and it is clear that he too is not convinced of his innocence. The final section of the book, *In einem anderen Land* (*In Another Country*), finds him on vacation in Sri Lanka. The last paragraph, in which he may indirectly be admitting that he erred and asking for forgiveness, reads:

> Die Buddhisten glauben an eine Wiedergeburt. Je nach der Schuld, die wir in diesem Leben angehäuft haben, erreichen wir im nächsten Leben eine höhere oder niedrigere Daseinsform. Es ist eine grosse Geste des Verzeihens in dieser Lehre, und die Mahnung, sein Leben in jeder Stufe bewusst zu leben.
>
> ENDE (318)
>
> The Buddhists believe in reincarnation. Depending on the sins that we have amassed during this life, we will attain a higher or lower form of being in the next life. There is a grand gesture of forgiveness in this teaching, and the reminder to live every stage of one's life consciously.
>
> END

Fries, who died in December 2014, never apologized for his career as an informant and probably did not have any real regrets, except for being outed and this: despite the fact that he was an accomplished fiction writer, essayist, and editor, one will always think of him as an informant first and then as a writer. That is a punishment he most assuredly earned and deserves.

KARL-HEINZ JAKOBS IN OBERLIN: FEBRUARY – MAY, 1986

In the fall of 1985, the German faculty at Oberlin College again invited Helga Schütz to be German Writer-in-Residence, just as I had said we would do in my March 1985 conversations with GDR Writers' Union functionary Eberhard Scheibner. We proposed that she spend approximately three months in Oberlin during the spring 1986 semester, from mid-February to mid-May, and asked her to let us know by no later than the end of October if she would be able to accept the invitation. Predictably, her application for a visa to travel to the US was again denied, so I proceeded to contact Karl-Heinz Jakobs, a prominent GDR prose writer who had been living in West Germany since 1977.

Jakobs was one of the more vociferous of the writers and intellectuals who protested the expatriation of dissident GDR writer/singer Wolf Biermann in November 1976, and his hardened criticism of the ruling SED Party led to his dismissal from the Berlin Writers' Union as well as from the executive committee of the GDR Writers' Union, and finally to expulsion from the SED Party in 1977. Because of his deteriorating relations with the GDR authorities, he was given a three-year "visa" and asked to leave the country for that period of time. The visa was extended for four more years; when it expired in 1984, Jakobs decided not to return.

Although restricted in some ways by this special arrangement, just as Jurek Becker had been after moving to West Berlin, Jakobs increased his commitment to confront the problems of the communistic GDR directly. He maintained that the typical path of an East German writer led to schizophrenia, because one always had to paint the details but leave the whole out of sight. Early during his years in West German limbo, Jakobs broke with this schizophrenic tendency and wrote *Wilhelmsburg* (1979), a novel that examined the dynamics of a provincial city in a nameless, German-speaking socialist state. The hero brings to mind the typical GDR citizen: he is a man who keeps his opinion to himself for fear of the consequences, a man who says "yes" even when he thinks "no." In 1983, he published a largely autobiographical book about the events that followed the revocation of Wolf Biermann's East German citizenship—*Das endlose Jahr: Begegnungen mit Mäd* (*The Endless Year: Encounters with Mäd*), another work critical of the GDR's government.

Our choice of Jakobs as a substitute for Helga Schütz most assuredly angered officials in both the GDR Writers' Union and the Ministry of Culture. For Jakobs, much like the two GDR writers in exile who preceded him—Bernd Jentzsch in 1982 and Jurek Becker in 1979—had evolved into an outspoken critic of the Honecker regime, the GDR state, and its brand of socialism. I like to think that the GDR authorities, when they realized that we had chosen Jakobs to be our German writer-in-residence in spring 1986, regretted their decision to deny Helga Schütz this opportunity. From their perspective, she certainly would have been a far better representative of the GDR than dissident writer Jakobs.

My memory of Karl-Heinz Jakobs's Oberlin residency is sketchy, but I can recall some things very well. He occupied the office adjacent to mine in Rice Hall and spent a lot of time there, so we had plenty of contact and now and then I was able to observe him at work. He was an unusually disciplined worker, spending many hours writing every day. I was surprised to see that he wrote the first draft of his prose texts with the electric typewriter, not by hand. He would draft a short story, essay, or chapter of a novel from beginning to end, then would proceed to revise the pages in a really unique way. He would begin this process by making handwritten changes within the text and scribbling notes in the margins. Using scissors, he would then cut the pages into sections, each one a full paragraph or more. These he would reassemble on his desk and then scotch tape them to the wall. While the strips of paper were hanging on the wall, Jakobs would review and rearrange some of them, thus creating a new whole. This "collage" technique of writing and editing is very common today, now that we work on computers with cut-and-paste features.

The picture of Jakobs in the photo galleries reminds me that he was a good-natured and sociable person, very laid back, someone with whom you would enjoy having a beer and casual conversation. He came to our house and joined us for dinner frequently, and my wife Ulrike and I always enjoyed his company and our conversations. I recall that he was somewhat lonely that semester, and there were understandable reasons for that. His English was quite poor, something that limited his ability to engage socially with persons outside the tiny German-speaking community in Oberlin. Also, apart from mealtimes in the German House, he did not socialize with students. The downsized German faculty was not large enough to offer him adequate companionship, but Ulrike and I did our best to provide him with a social life.

NEW HAMPSHIRE SYMPOSIA FOR THE STUDY OF THE GDR

The first International New Hampshire Symposium for the Study of the German Democratic Republic was held in June 1975, at the 320-acre World Fellowship Center in Conway, situated in the scenic White Mountains. This annual week-long conference, which brought together scholars from the humanities and social sciences with an interest in East German studies, continued without interruption for twenty-five years. The goal of its founder and principal organizer, Lutheran pastor Dr. Christoph Schmauch, was to have a gathering of scholars—primarily from North America, West and East Germany—who would discuss and present papers on themes such as "Das Menschenbild in der modernen Literatur der DDR" (The Image of Human-kind in Contemporary GDR Literature), 1975; "Images of Revolution in the Culture of the GDR," 1976; "The Role of the Writer in the Socialist Society of the GDR," 1977; and "Human Needs and Wants in the Socialist Society of the GDR," 1978. The overarching objective was to promote world peace and achieve greater understanding through the formal and informal exchange of ideas in this pastoral setting. From 1981 on, the conference proceedings were published each year in the series *Studies in GDR Culture and Society*

(Washington University Press of America, 1980-1996), edited by symposium co-organizer Dr. Margy Gerber, who was a professor of German at Bowling Green University.

I, along with a small number of other scholars with a serious interest in GDR studies, shunned this conference, even though I was invited many times to present a paper there. The reasons for my boycott were as follows: I thought the symposium was helping to promote the socialist GDR state and society in inappropriate ways, for ideological reasons embraced by those in charge and some of the attendees, and that it was not critical of the SED-regime's oppressive cultural policies and human rights practices. My other main criticism of the event was related to the "Delegierungsprinzip" (delegation principle), which the symposium organizers allowed the SED to practice in a way that was mutually beneficial. By permitting the GDR cultural officials to designate a number of participants each year, the organizers ensured that they would always have persons from the GDR on the program, such as writers, literary and other scholars, and even various types of government officials. These persons, who were handpicked and uncritical representatives of the GDR, had an important assignment to carry out at the Conway symposium: they were expected to deliver a pro-GDR message and try to transform as many attendees as possible into friends of the GDR. Their main targets were what one might call "naive" symposium participants, professors from the US with little direct experience or knowledge of the GDR. The GDR propagandists and apologists hoped these professors would come away from the symposium with a positive view of socialist East Germany that was unrelated to reality. And, they further hoped that the "naive" professors would carry that positive view back to their home campus and into their classrooms, where it would be communicated to their students. It was a very efficient and effective strategy, inexpensive as well.

In the spring of 1986, when Karl-Heinz Jakobs was the German Writer-in-Residence at Oberlin College, I experienced an instance of what I consider to be compromising behavior on the part of one organizer of the Conway symposium, an illustration of how eager those in charge were to please the architects and administrators of the GDR's cultural policies. Here is what happened. I received a call from a Germanist colleague who had a keen scholarly interest in Jakobs and his writings. He asked me if Jakobs might be interested in attending and participating in the Conway symposium that had been scheduled for June 20 – 27. I checked with Jakobs, who indicated that he would indeed like to participate, information I passed along to the colleague who had inquired about this possibility. This professor then approached the organizer of the symposium and proposed that they invite Jakobs to attend. The request was denied. The professor reported to me that he was told that inviting an oppositional writer like Jakobs would amount to waving "ein rotes Tuch" (a red cape) in the face of the GDR cultural officials; it would be an unnecessary provocation.

The program for the Twelfth International Symposium on the GDR (1986) lists five participants from the GDR, one of whom was writer Wolfgang Kohlhaase (German Film Academy-Berlin). The others were Lothar Bisky (SED Academy for Social Sciences), Alfred Loesdau (SED Academy for Social Sciences), Karl-Heinz Röder (GDR Academy of Sciences), and Reiner Saupe (Humboldt University). They all presented papers, including one by Bisky on "Aspekte der Kulturpolitik der DDR" (Aspects of GDR Cultural Policy), and some served as discussants or session moderators as well. Why, one might ask, was a repressive state like the GDR invited to send delegates of its choosing to the Conway conference, persons (and here I exclude Kohlhaase) who would present and defend the SED-regime's point of view on various issues? Why was the GDR given this opportunity to get its message out within the US, not only at the symposium but also in the pages of the conference proceedings?

The Ninth International Symposium on the GDR was held from June 17-24, 1983. The "Call for Papers" lists the topics of twelve seminars that comprise the program and the names of the professors serving as seminar organizers. It offers some additional information that should be of interest, namely: "Registration fee, Room and Board for the whole week, all-inclusive: $170 (This fee includes a $10 charge for a GDR participant's travel fund.)"

Given the low all-inclusive charge for a one-week stay, it seems likely that some anonymous organization was subsidizing the conference. Also troubling, at least to me, is the $10 each participant was being charged to support the participation of one or more unnamed persons from the GDR.

I cannot move on without adding that most participants in the Conway conference were not GDR apologists or sympathizers. For many, it simply provided an opportunity to learn more about East Germany while interacting with colleagues who were also interested in GDR studies; for some it was a place to present one's research in the form of a paper and receive feedback; and others viewed it as an unusual kind of vacation with swimming, hiking, and cycling in a resort-like New England setting, even if one had to endure the pro-GDR propaganda.

FINAL REPORT IN MY STASI-FILE: AUGUST, 1986

The subject of the last report in my file, according to its heading, is "Activities of American Germanists vis-à-vis GDR Writers." Two professors from the US are mentioned, Thomas Fox (Washington University, St. Louis, Missouri) and Otmar Drekonja (St. John's University, Collegeville, Minnesota), both of whom had participated that summer in a seminar for Germanists held in East Berlin and Leipzig. The information in the report came from an unofficial source, probably an East German informant who also attended the seminar. At some point, Fox and Drekonja were asked for their opinion of my book, *DDR-Literatur im Tauwetter*, and both gave a positive response. Excerpts from this document appear below.

> The American Germanists
> Prof. Fox, Thomas
> [*personal information omitted*]
> Dr. Drekonja, Otmar
> [*personal information omitted*]

made use of a stay in the GDR, the purpose of which was to attend an international seminar for Germanists that took place in Berlin and Leipzig, in order to contact GDR writers.

[…]

F. und D. were aware, among other things, that operatively known

> Dr. Z i p s e r, Richard
> Oberlin/Ohio
> University Oberlin

has published his book "GDR Literature 1971 to 1978" [*the reference is to "DDR-Literatur im Tauwetter"*] as a three-volume edition in Switzerland. Zipser had conducted extensive investigation for this project in 1976 and established connections to GDR authors, in particular to those who had strong reservations about the GDR's cultural policies.

This publication was adjudged to be important by F. and D., since it presents an enormous amount of material.

Unofficially, there have been no references as yet to writers having received complimentary copies.

Furthermore, up to now there have been no references to reviews that pertain to this publication.

REVIEW OF *STUDIES IN GDR CULTURE AND SOCIETY 6*: AUGUST, 1987

In the fall of 1986, the book review editor of *THE GERMANIC REVIEW (GR)*, a prestigious scholarly journal edited by the Department of Germanic Languages at Columbia University, asked me to review *Studies in GDR Culture and Society 6. Selected Papers from the Eleventh International New Hampshire Symposium on the German Democratic Republic.* Edited by Margy Gerber et al. Lanham, New York, and London: University Press of America, 1986. vii + 206 pp. My review of this volume, which I submitted in August 1987, appears below. For reasons that I will later explain, it was never published.

This volume contains 14 papers that were presented at the 1985 New Hampshire Symposium on the German Democratic Republic. With one exception, the contributions are informative and of interest to scholars who wish to keep abreast of more recent cultural, economic and sociopolitical developments in the GDR. As the editor points out in the preface, this volume is more slender than previous ones in the series (e.g., volume 5 contained 25 papers and had a total of 361 pages), which may be attributed to the program structure of the 1985 Symposium. It is also unfortunate, in the opinion of this reader, that so few of the contributions are concerned with GDR literature per se—and in these, as in most of the other papers, the use of sociological approaches and discussion of social issues predominate.

If you are short of time, I would recommend that you read the following two essays first: "The Abrogation of Politics: Pseudo-Marxism in the GDR and Eastern Europe" by Lyman H. Legters and "Changing Patterns of Male and Female Identity in Recent GDR Prose" by Christiane Zehl Romero. Both are well-researched and well-written articles that offer intellectual analyses and new insights as well as factual information. At the other end of the spectrum is a short speech by Karl-Heinz Röder, the GDR's delegate to the conference, which is entitled "The Perception of the United States in GDR Policy and Society: Preconditions and Possibilities for Dialogue." If you have time to read it, you are likely to wonder (as I did) how Dr. Röder came to participate in this conference and, more importantly, why the editor decided to publish this obvious piece of propaganda.

In addition to the above-mentioned, the volume contains two articles on the GDR economy, one evaluating the GDR's economic performance, the other explaining the position of the GDR economy between East and West; an essay on the role that traditional German authoritarianism has played in the development of socialism in the GDR; a discussion of scientific-technical progress and humanization-of-work schemes in the 1970s and early 1980s; an analysis of the social situation of (working) women in the GDR today, some 40 years after World War II; a piece on the current attitudes and practices of young people with respect to marriage and family; an essay on fictional depictions of illness and disability in GDR literature and the relevance of the classical concept of the "socialist personality;" an assessment of the state of literary criticism and research in the GDR today, as opposed to the 1950s, 1960s, and 1970s; an article on the attempt by GDR critics to come to terms with modernism, postmodernism, avantgardism, and other "bourgeois" –isms and to relate them to recent GDR literature; and, finally, essays on two individual writers, Richard Pietrass, whose name and poetry are not widely known in the West, and Wolf Biermann, whose status and success as a "GDR writer in exile" are examined.

By way of conclusion, I would like to make three general observations: 1) Most of the papers in this collection would have profited from the thorough rewriting that is generally needed to transform a talk into an article suitable for publication. 2) The editor(s) should reconsider the apparent policy of publishing all papers presented at the Symposium; some pruning must be done, if quality is to be maintained. 3) An effort should be made to increase both the total number of papers and the percentage treating literary topics in future volumes. If these changes are made, the texts in <u>Studies in GDR Culture and Society</u> will become indispensable rather than interesting reading for students of the GDR.

In September 1987, I received a letter from the book review editor, acknowledging receipt of my review for publication in *THE GERMANIC REVIEW*. She wrote: "I've attached a list of revisions for the review, to which we're hoping you'll agree, and we look forward to receiving the final version when you've had time to incorporate them." The revision list, which was almost as long as my book review, appears below:

1. p. 1, 2nd para.: Text would read better if the following 2 phrases were omitted: "If you are short of time" and "If you have time to read it."

2. same para. as above: "At the other end of the spectrum. . .": What spectrum is meant here? If, for example, a political spectrum is being described, it needs to be stated at which end Legters/Zehl Romero stand, and how their stance is to be differentiated from that of Röder.

3. top of p. 2: " this . . . propaganda": the reader needs to be told in what way (s) it is propaganda, ideally with specific examples.

4. p. 2, full para.: this para. needs to be expanded in two ways: 1) much more needs to be said about the content of the essays, both as regards the specific essays and the larger context of the directions this collection takes, whether they point to new areas of investigation, etc. It would help if at least a couple of the outstanding contributions could also be described in some detail, with your commentary as to why they stand out; 2) for each essay mentioned, the author's name needs to be mentioned. This para. could easily expand into a 2-3 page discussion.

5. the final para. needs several types of revision, as follows: 1) these points raise some puzzling questions, to wit: re point 1: is it necessary that symposium proceedings be rewritten? You might explain what problems arose from the lack of rewriting in this collection; re point 2: why the "(s)" after editor? The "et al." after Gerber's name would point to multiple editorship. Also on this point: the title says "selected": is this not the case? re point 3: how can you increase the number of contributions to a conference, or force a literary angle? 2) phrase "indispensable rather than interesting" needs rewriting.

6. a general problematic point that recurs several times is your complaint that too much was included in the volume, yet at other points the weakness of the volume is attributed to the paucity of material in this book. This point needs to be stated consistently: does the book need less or more?

When I received this long list of proposed revisions, which I clearly would have had to make in order to have my review published, I surmised that someone on the editorial board—not the book review editor, Dr. Shelley Frisch, who was merely the messenger—did not like my implicit criticism of the Conway symposium. The list of revisions amounted to a tedious home-work assignment designed to discourage me and alter the thrust and tone of my review. The *GR* was not going to reject my review outright; they would just keep giving me revisions to make until I got it right or gave up. I did not want to play this game, which was a favorite tactic of publishing houses in the GDR so as to avoid being accused of editorial censorship. The matter was complicated by the fact that I had previously embarked on a major project with the *GR*, the preparation of two special issues under my guest editorship on "Literary Censorship in the German-Speaking Countries." This project was extremely important to me, and I did not want to do anything in connection with the book review that would jeopardize it. Hence, I decided not to protest or do anything further with the review, and predictably the book review editor did not contact me again.

DDR-STUDIEN/EAST GERMAN STUDIES

In the fall of 1985, around the time that *DDR-Literatur im Tauwetter* finally appeared in print, I contacted Dr. Jay Wilson, Editor in Chief at the New York office of Peter Lang Publishing. I wanted to explore the possibility of establishing a series of scholarly monographs, published in English or German, on topics in the humanities and social sciences pertaining to the GDR. Wilson supported the idea and in 1986 I became General Editor of *DDR-Studien/ East German Studies*, the only monograph series in the US focusing exclusively on the GDR. The first volume, published in 1987, was not a monograph but a *Handbook of East German Drama: 1945 – 1985* by well-known theater specialist Herbert Lederer. Over the years, we published books on important GDR authors such as Jurek Becker, Peter Hacks, Wolfgang Hilbig, Irmtraud Morgner, and Christa Wolf, and on topics such as *Science Fiction Literature in East Germany, Searching for a New German Identity, Protokolliteratur in der DDR* (Protocol Literature in the GDR), *Heinrich von Kleist in der Literatur der DDR* (Heinrich von Kleist in GDR Literature), and *Unvollendete Trauerarbeit in der DDR-Literatur* (The Unfinished Process of Grieving in GDR Literature). I remained general editor of this series until 2014, the year in which I retired.

FINAL ENTRY TO MY STASI-FILE: MARCH 17, 1988

The very last entry to my file is on an index card, dated March 17, 1988. At the foot of the card, the last line states "Ministry for State Security, Department X/Backofen General Repository for Individuals 2877/88 restricted," indicating that very few people had access to the file.

FALL OF THE BERLIN WALL: NOVEMBER 9, 1989

From time to time we witness events of a historic and very public nature, and of such magnitude and importance that we remember forever exactly where we were when we experienced or learned of them. I have experienced four such events in my lifetime. The first was the assassination of President John F. Kennedy in November 1963. I was a senior in college, and I heard the devastating news while listening to the radio in my dormitory room. The second was Neil Armstrong's moonwalk in August 1969. I was vacationing in Athens and watched that unbelievable event through the window of a department store where countless televisions were broadcasting it to a large, fascinated sidewalk audience. The third was the fall of the Berlin Wall on November 9, 1989. I was in my office at the University of Delaware that afternoon, preparing for a department meeting, when my wife called and said excitedly "they are tearing down the wall." Incredible! I, like so many others, had thought the detested "Mauer" was there to stay at least through my lifetime, if not forever. Finally, I remember watching CNBC's daily business program on 9/11/2001 while getting dressed for work. It was approximately 9:40 a.m., and the New York Stock Exchange had just opened. As the co-anchors were puzzling over what had just happened to one of the World Trade Center towers that had been hit by an airplane, I saw another plane come out of nowhere and smash into the second tower, causing the huge explosion, death and destruction we all remember. Four colossal and unforgettable events, two of them horrifying, the other two uniquely uplifting.

The collapse of the Berlin Wall profoundly affected the lives of many Eastern Europeans, who had been living since the end of World War II behind the so-called iron curtain, sealed off from the West and non-communist countries. During this period, 1945 to 1989, Germany had been divided into two states, the pro-Western Federal Republic of Germany and the German Democratic Republic, a communist state occupied and controlled by the

Soviet Union. In October 1990, the world witnessed the reunification of the two Germanys, another momentous historical event I never expected to see in my lifetime.

The period leading up to the Berlin Wall's collapse was one of unprecedented turmoil in the GDR, marked by mass demonstrations against the government and the system, first in Leipzig and then throughout the GDR. On August 23, 1989, Hungary opened its border to Austria, and thousands of East German tourists took advantage of this opportunity to escape to the West. The SED leadership underestimated the seriousness of the situation and failed to make changes that might have calmed things down; nor, fortunately, did they use force to restore order. On October 18, 1989, Erich Honecker resigned unexpectedly as General Secretary of the SED Central Committee and was replaced that day by Egon Krenz. Krenz, a hard-liner like Honecker, was responsible at the time for security issues in the SED. He spoke vaguely of wanting to introduce a "Wende" or change in direction within the GDR, but did not initiate reforms or do anything else to improve the situation.

By sheer coincidence, GDR writer Helga Schütz was our house guest in October 1989, precisely when the change in the SED party leadership took place. She had come to the US to give lectures and readings at several universities, including the University of Delaware. We watched with fascination as events in the GDR unfolded, and it was incredibly interesting to hear Schütz's commentary. Her presentation to a German-speaking audience was a very special occasion, since she was able to give us an insider's perspective on what was occurring in the GDR.

On November 9, 1989, the Berlin Wall came down. It happened suddenly and took everyone by surprise. Thousands of East Berliners had gathered at the border crossings that day and demanded that the crossing points be opened. In the evening, the crossing at Bornholmer Strasse was opened peacefully and soon thereafter other border crossings were opened as well. East Germans from all over the GDR rushed to East Berlin, and from there they streamed into West Berlin. On TV one saw East Germans standing on top of the Wall and talking to border guards, who did nothing to stop what was happening. In the days and weeks that followed, the Wall would literally be torn down, and on TV I watched people from both Germanys chipping away at the Wall with pickaxes, eager to help tear it down and obtain a concrete piece of history. The fall of the Berlin Wall was not only the high point of Germany's "peaceful revolution," it was one of the greatest moments in German history!

PROJECT ON LITERARY CENSORSHIP IN THE GERMAN-SPEAKING COUNTRIES: 1987 – 1990

A topic that would come up frequently in my conversations with GDR authors, especially those who were writers in residence at Oberlin College, was the existence of literary censorship in their country, how it functioned and impacted their writing. Through these conversations I came to understand the various forms and subtleties of literary censorship, and I also came to appreciate the dilemma it posed for every writer living in the GDR. These writers were not able to address any topic of their choosing in their works, and they were expected to exercise restraint and remain within the parameters of what was permissible. The ultimate goal was to have the writers censor themselves, so that official censorship would not be necessary, and self-censorship was more prevalent in the GDR than most writers wanted to admit. In other words, the system worked well. Not all GDR writers cooperated, of course. Some tried to widen the parameters and wrote critically about taboo topics, such as the Wall, the Stasi, the SED party, socialism as it existed in reality, and major problems prevalent in GDR society. The highly critical writers, such as Stefan Heym, Wolf Biermann, Reiner Kunze, and Thomas Brasch—to name just a few, were considered subversive and not permitted to publish any or many of their works in the GDR. Some were able to publish their writings in West Berlin or West Germany, and in the late 1970s and 1980s many dissident writers had to emigrate to the West, where they would be more able to earn a living.

In the mid-1980s, Professor of German Inge Halpert, who was Executive Editor of *THE GERMANIC REVIEW*, announced that the editorial board was soliciting interesting topics and guest editors for special issues. I contacted Halpert and proposed preparing a special issue on "Literary Censorship in the German-Speaking Countries." Halpert and the editorial board liked my proposal, which eventually culminated in the publication of two special issues of *THE GERMANIC REVIEW* (spring 1990 and summer 1990) on that topic.

The two-part series, for which I served as guest editor, explored the problem of literary censorship in the major German-speaking countries, focusing on the period following World War II. Four Germanists contributed to the project: Tamara Evans (Switzerland), Paul Haberland (Austria), A. Leslie Willson (Federal Republic of Germany), and I (German Democratic Republic). We began with Switzerland and Austria in the first issue, then continued with the FRG and GDR in the next issue. Each contributor wrote an essay discussing the various forms and consequences of literary censorship within a particular country. Each of these essays, designed to introduce readers to the general problem of literary censorship in that country, was followed by a companion article in which contemporary writers addressed the topic of censorship.

In order to gather firsthand information, the contributors asked a large number of writers from each German-speaking country to respond to a set of four questions (in German) on the topic of censorship.

1. Is literary censorship practiced in your country? If so, in which form (e.g., self censorship, state or juridical censorship) and to what extent?

2. Has one of your works ever been censored? If so, please describe the occurrence.

3. If literary censorship is practiced in your country, does it have any impact on the way you or the way your colleagues write?

4. Is censorship practiced when a selection of books is made for public libraries and bookstores?

The contributors solicited responses to these questions from authors of different generations and varying degrees of prominence, either in a personal interview or by letter.

In the fall of 1987 and the spring of 1988, I sent a censorship question-naire to twenty-five former GDR writers, persons who had left the GDR to live and work in the West. I had decided not to contact any authors living in the GDR, as I felt that sufficient and perhaps more accurate information on literary censorship in that country could be obtained from those who would seemingly have less reason to fear the possibility of reprisals.

In time, I heard from seventeen of the twenty-five writers I had approached. Some wrote lengthy letters explaining why they could not answer my questions on censorship; two agreed to respond at first, then decided not to later on. I received responses from nine authors, six of whom provided me with very detailed and insightful information on censorship in the GDR. A few writers chose to discuss their experience of censorship in both Germa-nys, and one described a unique form of censorship in the FRG that affected only former GDR writers who were overly critical of the GDR. The writers who cooperated by responding to the censorship questionnaire or providing other material were Wolf Deinert, Gabriele Eckart, Jürgen Fuchs, Wolfgang Hegewald, Karl-Heinz Jakobs, Frank-Wolf Matthies, Stefan Schütz, Joachim Seyppel, and Gerhard Zwerenz. Their responses, written in the first half of 1988, constituted part two of my contribution to the special issue, "Literary Censorship in the German Democratic Republic. The Authors Speak."

At the conclusion of my May 1989 essay on "The Many Faces of Censorship in the German Democratic Republic, 1949-1989," which was part one of my contribution to the special issue, I stated:

> As the 1980s draw to a close, ideological restrictions on artistic freedom have again been relaxed and we have entered another period of "thaw" in the GDR. One can only hope that the cultural climate will remain warmer throughout the 1990s and into the next century. (Summer 1990, Vol. LXV, No. 3, p. 116)

About six months later we witnessed Honecker's resignation and the fall of the Berlin Wall, followed by momentous political changes in the GDR. However, my essay and its companion piece did not contain information on the situation that had developed during the six-month period after the fall of the Berlin Wall and before publication of the second special issue in the summer of 1990. And due to publication deadlines for this project, it was not possible to do the extensive rewriting and revising that would have been necessary to bring the material up to date. However, in an effort to reflect the dramatic changes that had taken place in the area of censorship, I decided to include letters I had received in the spring of 1990 from GDR writer Helga Schütz and stage director Heinz-Uwe Haus. Their keen observations on the disappearance of state censorship in the GDR, on the insecurity of GDR authors at that point in time, and on the uncertain fate of writers whose work would no longer be censored or supported by the state, provided an appropriate conclusion to "The Authors Speak."

LAST TRIP TO EAST BERLIN: JULY, 1990

In the 1970s and 1980s, I made countless trips to West Berlin and East Berlin, shuttling back and forth via Checkpoint Charlie. My last visit to East Berlin was in July of 1990, about eight months after the Berlin Wall had been opened. I spent a week in West Berlin, and from there I twice drove into East Berlin without the inconvenience of having to pass through Checkpoint Charlie. Yet, for some strange reason, I missed that border crossing and the inconvenience that was part of it. I spent some time just driving around East Berlin, surprised and pleased to see how much of the central Mitte district was still familiar. On my second visit, I met Ulrich Plenzdorf for lunch in a trendy new restaurant in the Nikolaiviertel, and he told me about some changes that had taken place in the GDR's literary scene and everyday life as well. The appearance of East Berlin had also begun to change as the two Berlins were gradually being forged into one gigantic city. Gone were the barriers that had rendered the Brandenburg Gate, the Reichstag Building, and the Wall inaccessible from East Berlin.

The Berlin I first visited as a student in June 1963 was already a divided city, and for me that was part of its charm and mystique. In the 1970s, I actually enjoyed the experience of shuttling back and forth between East and West Berlin, experiencing immediately the sharp contrast between the two cities, one bustling with life throughout the day and night, the other its polar opposite. I liked and was intrigued by both Berlins, and I relished the eerie tension that one felt in the two Berlins of the Cold War era, which John le Carré captured perfectly in spy thrillers like *The Spy Who Came in from the Cold* (1963).

REUNIFICATION OF GERMANY: OCTOBER 3, 1990

In 1990, the German Democratic Republic joined the Federal Republic of Germany, thereby creating a unified German state, and East and West Berlin were also reunited into a single city. The process of transforming the GDR into a democratic state and unifying the two Germanys began with the "Wende" (change in direction) in November 1989 and culminated in a Unification Treaty, which was signed by officials of both German states on August 31, 1990. This treaty, the result of intense negotiations between the GDR and the FRG, provided for the accession of the GDR to the FRG. The end of the unification process is officially called "Deutsche Einheit" (German Unity) and is celebrated annually on October 3, a national holiday in Germany.

In accordance with Article 23 of the Basic Law of the FRG, which took effect on October 3, 1990, five of the GDR's newly created federal states (Bundesländer)—Brandenburg, Mecklenburg-Western Pomerania, Saxony, Saxony-Anhalt, and Thuringia—became states of the FRG. The 23 boroughs of Berlin formed Land Berlin, which became one of Germany's 16 constituent states. Berlin was again designated as the capital of united Germany and, after the establishment of German unity, it also became the seat of the parliament and government. The socialist German Democratic Republic, founded after World War II on October 7, 1949, was no longer a satellite state of the Soviet Union and no longer a nation by itself.

Helmut Kohl, who died at age 87 on June 16, 2017, served as Chancellor of the Federal Republic of Germany from 1982 to 1993, then as Chancellor of unified Germany from 1993 to 1998. He witnessed the fall of the Berlin Wall and, following that momentous event, was a major force behind German reunification as the Cold War came to what many people thought was its end. He has been called, and he deserves to be called, the "architect of German unity." When he perceived the possibility of forging the two Germanys into one, he moved decisively and through skillful diplomatic negotiations helped press forward in that direction. Another leader, one with less courage and experience, might have hesitated and lost the opportunity to reunite Germany. But Kohl—like Otto von Bismarck who, after uniting all the states of Germany, became the first Chancellor of the German Empire in 1871—was determined to build a stable and prosperous German republic with a unified national identity. He succeeded and, in so doing, secured his place alongside Bismarck in German history. Today, Germany is the most economically powerful and politically influential country in the European Union.

The reunification of Germany took me very much by surprise. I, like almost everyone else, did not see it coming. And as with the collapse of the Berlin Wall, I never thought an event of such momentous historical-political significance would ever happen or be permitted to happen in my lifetime. Many persons in the GDR, as well as in the governments and populations of Western and Eastern European countries, were opposed to German reunification. But happen it did, to my utter amazement, and I am pleased that the German nation was reassembled and that it is once again intact!

I would like to make two additional observations on the subject of German reunification. First, one must acknowledge the important role that Soviet leader Mikhail Gorbachev played in reuniting the two Germanys after the Berlin Wall fell in 1989. Without his cooperation and goodwill, East and West Germany could not have come together. Second, the Unification Treaty was just the beginning of a long and difficult process of the two Germanys coming to a territorial and political union. There were many obstacles to overcome and no one, including Helmut Kohl, could possibly have foreseen what this process would entail. In order to achieve his goal Kohl hurried the East Germans into unification by promising them "blühende Landschaften" (blossoming landscapes), an unrealistic vision of the economic prosperity the West could provide. But today, over thirty years later, wages and pensions in the eastern states of Germany still are not equal to those in the states of former West Germany; also, the rate of unemployment is much higher. Many of the former East Germans feel forgotten and, understandably, are resentful. For these reasons mainly, there is still a wide divide between the states and populations of former East and West Germany.

FRAGEBOGEN: ZENSUR / QUESTIONNAIRE: CENSORSHIP

My first sabbatical leave at the University of Delaware was in 1992-1993, and I decided to do more work on the topic of literary censorship in the GDR. The project I conceptualized in 1991 involved interviewing a large number of former GDR writers, a process that again was carried out with the help of a questionnaire and the postal system. My efforts culminated in a 341-page book entitled *Fragebogen: Zensur. Zur Literatur vor und nach dem Ende der DDR* (*Questionnaire: Censorship. On Literature Before and After the Demise of the GDR*), which the prestigious Reclam Verlag Leipzig published in the fall of 1995. In the foreword to the book, I provided some background information, set forth my objectives, and explained my methodology:

> This book is linked to a project I undertook in the late 1980s, together with three co-authors. At that time our purpose was to examine the problem of "Literary Censorship in the German-Speaking Countries," focusing on the period following World War II. We completed this study in the spring of 1989—six months before the so-called "Wende" (turn in direction)—and it was published in two special issues of *THE GERMANIC REVIEW* (spring 1990 and summer 1990). In addition to serving as guest editor of both issues back then, I contributed the two articles that comprised the section on the GDR.
>
> [...]
>
> In the period following the "Wende," I decided to prepare a more comprehensive, book-length study that would just document aspects of literary censorship in the GDR. The focus this time would be predominantly on writers who had lived and worked in the GDR until it collapsed in 1989, and they would be given an opportunity to express their views on censorship. Beginning with the academic year 1992-1993, I was at last able to dedicate myself totally to this project.
>
> My book focuses primarily on a period of time encompassing the last twenty-five years [*1945-1990*] and is comprised of two major sections. In the first section, which is titled "Continuity in Change: Literary Censorship in the German Democratic Republic," readers are introduced to the general

problem of literary censorship in the GDR. The following issues, among others, are discussed here: Why was the practice of state censorship deemed necessary? What legal basis did the constitution of the GDR provide for it? What forms did censorship assume during the forty-year history of the GDR? How was it carried out, officially and unofficially, by various branches of government and other institutions? How did some writers contrive to circumvent censorship? In addition, the book delves into the sensitive and particularly difficult problem of self-censorship, the impact that censorship had on literary creativity and productivity (positive as well as negative aspects), and—last but not least—the question of how the writers perceive the censorial climate in unified Germany.

The second and much larger section of the book, which is titled "The Writers' Responses," gives the reader an insider's view of how literary censorship functioned and how it impacted the writings and lives of the affected writers. In order to acquire firsthand information, I wrote at the end of 1992 and beginning of 1993 to approximately 240 GDR authors of varying ages and prominence. These writers represented the entire political spectrum that existed in the GDR, from the party loyalists to the so-called dissidents. I asked them to answer the following six questions, directly or in essay form:

1. How and to what end, in your opinion, did the various forms of literary censorship (e.g., state, ideological, juridical, and self-censorship) function in the GDR?

2. Did the practice of literary censorship influence your use of language, subject matter, or aesthetic position?

3. Has one of your works ever been censored? If so, please describe the occurrence.

4. Have you ever practiced self-censorship? If so, under what circumstances and what motivated you to do that?

5. Which forms of censorship have you experienced since your departure from the (former) GDR or since reunification?

6. On the topic of literary censorship, do you have additional experiences or information that you would like to communicate here?

The reaction to my request was overwhelming. I received letters from over half of the authors I had contacted, and in the end more than 70 writers agreed to participate in my project. Some writers referred in their responses to texts they had already published on the topic of censorship (which are cited in the appendix to this book). However, a larger number of the contacted writers declined to collaborate on the project. The reasons for this were diverse. One could name, as an example, the somewhat understandable desire not to say anything that might contribute to further damaging the already tarnished image of the GDR. At times the suspicion was also voiced that my book would have to turn out very one-sided, since the GDR and its writers would appear in a bad light. Many reactions also reflected the fear that the publication of an honest description of experiences with the GDR censorship could prompt former GDR publishers (especially those who had employed censorship abundantly in the past) to distance themselves from the authors in question. In some cases a publication also failed to materialize due to the plain and simple fact that I was unable to pay them an honorarium. On the other hand, some writers did not want to participate simply because they were angry about the developments that had led to the rapid demise of the GDR and then to the swift unification with the FRG. Many were bitter about the fact that they still had not found a publisher for their works in the new, unified Germany. Every letter that I received was informative [. . .]. (7-10)

The significance of this book, and in my view the same thing can be said of *DDR-Literatur im Tauwetter* (*GDR Literature During the Thaw*), is that it documents an important aspect of the GDR's literary life and literary history. Also, it presents insiders' views on how literary censorship actually functioned and affected writing in East Germany, at a point in time when all of this was still fresh in the writers' minds. I was fortunate to be able to do a study that no one else will ever be able to do and produce a book that scholars interested in GDR literature and/or the topic of literary censorship should find increasingly interesting and useful.

Originally, a new and very small German press, Forum Verlag Leipzig, founded in 1989 as the GDR was collapsing, was going to publish *Fragebogen: Zensur*. In 1994, I sent them the completed manuscript, which the publisher assigned to a young freelance editor from West Germany, Thomas Gallien, who was working on several book projects for the Forum Verlag. In December 1994, Gallien was kind enough to inform me that the Forum Verlag had been experiencing serious financial difficulties and was likely to declare bankruptcy early in the next year. He was able to have me released from the contract, so that my book would not be tied up in the bankruptcy proceedings, and I would then be free to negotiate with another publisher. Gallien also worked on special projects for the venerable Reclam Verlag Leipzig and proposed that we try to place the book with them. He presented the project to the chief editor and executive officer, who were in favor of publishing my book, but it also had to be approved by the editorial board of the other Reclam Verlag in Stuttgart, which was in the process of acquiring Reclam Leipzig. The final decision was to be made at a joint meeting of chief editors and executives in late January, which was going to be held in Leipzig. One can imagine how happy I was when Gallien called me in late January and said jubilantly, "Reclam macht's!" ("Reclam's going to do it!") Reclam hired

Gallien to work on the book with me and he did a magnificent job. I was and remain deeply grateful for his intervention on my behalf at the Forum Verlag, for his advice and assistance, and for the support he gave me at every stage leading up to publication.

In October 1995, the Reclam Verlag sent each author who had contributed to *Fragebogen: Zensur* a copy of the book. I received letters from many of these former GDR writers, most of whom were pleased with the outcome of my project. However, one writer—the Halle poet, Heinz Czechowski—was angered by the complaining and whining some of his colleagues had done in their essays about the difficulties they had been experiencing as writers in the market-oriented publishing world that existed throughout unified Germany. On October 11, 1995, he had this to say in the first paragraph of a letter addressed to the Reclam Verlag Leipzig:

> Liebe Kolleginnen und Kollegen des Reclam Verlages,
>
> heute erhielt ich das Buch FRAGEBOGEN ZENSUR, das ich begierig – dabei Puccinis TURANDOT hörend – verschlang. Leider, leider ist mein Eindruck mehr als zwiespältig – müsste ich es rezensieren, würde ich es in satirischer Form tun. Diese armen Unschuldshäschen, die nun an der Marktwirtschaft scheitern. . . Ich glaube, verzeihen Sie mir bitte, das Beste ist noch mein Gedicht NACHTRAG, weil es in alle möglichen Richtungen offen ist und keine Antwort weiss auf all diese Fragen.

> Dear Colleagues at Reclam Publishing,
>
> Today I received the book QUESTIONNAIRE: CENSORSHIP, which—while listening to Puccini's TURANDOT—I eagerly devoured. Sadly, sadly, my impression is more than ambivalent— if I had to review it, I would do it in a satirical form. These poor innocent bunnies who now are struggling as a result of the market economy. . . I think, you will excuse me please, that the best is my poem ADDENDUM because it is open in all possible directions and offers no answer to all these questions.

The poem "Nachtrag" ("Addendum"), dated November 26, 1994, which Czechowski references immodestly in his letter, has censorship as its theme and serves as a splendid conclusion to his contribution to *Fragebogen: Zensur*. It summarizes the entire dilemma in which writers in the GDR found themselves and recalls one of the worst aspects of GDR cultural policy.

NACHTRAG

Ich bin aus dem Kontext genommen. Wieder
Stelle ich mir die alten Fragen: doch
Weder ich noch Gott weiss eine Antwort.
Der alte Wein in neuen Schläuchen?

Es fällt mir schwer, mich auf das Eigentliche
Zu konzentrieren. Was aber ist
Das Eigentliche? So fragte ich mich schon
Vor wievielen Jahren . . . Ach.

Es gibt keinen Fortschritt für einen,
Der sich verinnerlicht hat. Mein Leiden
An der Natur ist kontinuierlich: Ich
Habe vor der Zensur nichts zu verbergen.

Doch die Zensur existierte und existiert.
Keine Antwort ist auch eine Antwort.
Die Dinge haben sich sublimiert. Wer alles
~~sagen kann,~~
~~Sagt überhaupt nichts. Stundenlang~~

Schreie ich gegen die weisse Wand, doch die
Gibt keine Antwort. Ein echoloses
Schriftstellerleben, wer
Erträumte es nicht? Jeden Morgen

Stehe ich auf, um das weisse Papier zu beschreiben.
Doch wer
Kauft mir ab, was ich schreibe? So
Verzweifle ich letzten Endes doch
An meiner Fähigkeit, die Natur

Zu begradigen, und
Zensiere immer noch mich. Jeder Schritt
In meine mir immer fragwürdiger
werdende Zukunft
Ist begleitet von Wörtern, die mir

Immer fragwürdiger werden. Und meine Fragen,
Die ich an meine Freunde richte,
Harren noch immer der Antwort. Allmählich
Verklärt sich mein Blick in der Verzweiflung.

Niemals eine Antwort bekommen zu können.
Noch immer
Zensieren sich meine Freunde selbst.
Für ihre Vergangenheit, der sie brachgelegt haben,
Finden sie, wie auch ich, keine Sprache. Das

Ist es, was mich verzweifeln lässt
An meinem sich abwärts neigenden Leben,
In dem ich keine Antworten mehr finde auf Fragen,
Die längst verjährt sind, denn auch die Zensur

Hat ihre Sprache verloren. Geblieben ist aber
Immer noch diese vergebliche Suche
Nach einer Stimme, die sagt, was sie meint,
Und die dennoch gehört wird . . . (82-83)

ADDENDUM

I have been taken out of context. Again
I ask myself the old questions: but
Neither I nor God knows an answer.
The old wine in new vessels?

It is difficult for me to concentrate
On the essence. But what is
The essence? I already asked myself that
How many years ago . . . Oh.

There is no progress for someone
Who has internalized himself. My suffering
From the natural world is continuous. I
Have nothing to conceal from censorship.

But censorship existed and exists.
No answer is also an answer.
Things have been sublimated. Whoever can
say anything,
Says nothing at all. For hours on end

I scream against the white wall, but it
Does not give an answer. An echoless
Writer's existence, who
Did not imagine it? Every morning

I arise to fill the white paper with words. But who
Is going to believe what I write? So
I despair in the end after all
Of my ability to straighten out

The natural world, and
Keep on censoring myself. Every step
Into my ever more uncertain future
Is accompanied by words that to me

Become increasingly questionable. And
my questions,
That I pose to my friends,
Are still awaiting answers. Gradually
My vision is transfigured in the despair.

Never being able to receive an answer. My
Friends still continue to censor themselves.
For their past, which they have left fallow,
They, as well as I, find no language. That

Is what causes me to despair
Of my downward trending life,
In which I find no more answers to questions
That long ago became invalid, for censorship

Has also lost its tongue. Still remaining though
Is this futile search
For a voice that says what it means,
And that nevertheless will be heard . . .

THREE LETTERS AND A RESPONSE FROM UWE BERGER: 1993–1994

In 1993 and 1994, following the collapse of the Berlin Wall and the reunification of the two Germanys, I received three letters from the poet and cunning Stasi informant, Uwe Berger (IMV "Uwe"). All three are related to my request for information on his experience and perception of censorial practices in the former GDR, which I eventually received and published in *Fragebogen: Zensur* (*Questionnaire: Censorship*). Bear in mind that at this point in time I did not yet know that Berger had been an informant and, more importantly perhaps, Berger probably did not think I would ever discover his dark secret.

In his letter of January 7, 1993, just as in the 1976 and 1977 reports from IMV "Uwe" that are in my file, Berger's hypocritical and opportunistic nature are on full display. There is an exaggerated attempt to flatter me in the first paragraph, as he makes reference to the "pleasant conversation" we had when I visited him at his home in June 1976, then some positive comments about US citizens in general ("openminded interest" and "absence of petty-mindedness"), and finally the evocation of Ronald Reagan's phrase "a meeting place" ("Ort der Begegnung") and its symbolic extension—first to the US Embassy in East Berlin and then to all of Berlin as meeting places of East and West. He also mentions that he visited the residence of the US Ambassador to the GDR on Independence Day in 1986, 1987, 1988 and 1989, possibly in an effort to establish himself as a "friend" of the US. Now, what is Berger trying to accomplish with this overly complimentary letter, what does he want from me? His next letter, dated August 5, 1993, provides the answer: my assistance.

He begins this letter by wishing me much success with my project on literary censorship in the GDR, to which he is going to contribute without honorarium. He then makes reference to the cultural situation in Germany, where financial support for publishing is hard to come by. Due to this "situation," he says, he has not been able to place his manuscripts with any German publisher. So he asks if I see a possibility, even a slight one, to get them published in the USA. The texts in question are poems from the years 1989 to 1993, he notes, which he does not want to have "put on ice." This is very important because he wants to prove that his work did not begin and end with the GDR.

On the day after Christmas 1994, Berger wrote another letter to his "friend" in Delaware, Richard Zipser. This time he expresses gratitude for the opportunity to contribute to *Fragebogen: Zensur* and, with incredible hypocrisy, indicates that he was pleased to have life in the GDR behind him ("was Gott sei Dank hinter mir liegt" / "which thank God lies behind me").

To round out the portrait of IMV "Uwe" in the post-Wall period, I am presenting without commentary his reponse to the last of six interview questions I sent him in connection with *Fragebogen: Zensur*.

Question: On the topic of literary censorship, do you have additional experiences or information that you would like to communicate here?

Answer: On 11/1/1989, hence still before the huge Alex-demonstration (11/4) and the collapse of the Wall (11/9), I called into question in the Cultural Association [of the GDR] the "leading role," that is to say the monopoly on power of the SED. My statement, a consequence of my experience with the GDR and not just its literary censorship, was broadcast that same evening on the television program "Aktuelle Kamera"/ "Current Camera".

[The Alexanderplatz demonstration on November 4, 1989, in the center of East Berlin was a demonstration for political reforms and against the GDR government. With more than half a million protestors, it was one of the largest mass meetings in GDR history and a milestone of the peaceful revolution that led to the fall of the Berlin Wall and German reunification. This was the first demonstration in GDR history that was organized by private individuals and permitted to take place by the authorities. The protestors did not demand the opening of the Berlin Wall or possible German reunification. Instead, they concentrated on the democratization of the GDR with references to guaranteed freedom of speech and freedom of assembly.]

["Current Camera" was the flagship television newscast of Deutscher Fernsehfunk, the state television broadcaster of the GDR from 1972 to 1990.]

IN SEARCH OF MY STASI-FILE (1)

With German reunification on October 3, 1990, a new government agency was founded, Der Bundesbeauftragte für die Unterlagen des Staatssicherheitsdienstes der ehemaligen Deutschen Demokratischen Republik (The Federal Commissioner for the Records of the State Security Service of the former German Democratic Republic). It was informally called the Gauck-Behörde (Gauck Agency) for short, after Joachim Gauck who served as the first Federal Commissioner from 1990 to 2000. The agency commonly refers to itself and is also known as the Stasi-Unterlagen-Behörde (Stasi Records Agency).

This office was responsible for preserving the records of the Ministry for State Security of the GDR, including files the secret police had compiled on individuals and stored in archives. There was a debate about what should happen to the files, whether they should be opened to the people or kept closed. The fate of the files was finally decided under the Unification Treaty between the German Democratic Republic and the Federal Republic of Germany, which allowed access to and use of the files under certain circumstances. Along with the decision to keep the files in a central location in the eastern part of Berlin, they also decided who could see and use the files, and to permit individuals to see their own files. Following a declassification ruling by the German government in 1992, the files of the Ministry for State Security of the GDR were opened, leading people to seek access to their files. Between 1992 and 2011, around 2.75 million individuals, mostly former GDR citizens, requested access to their own files. The declassification ruling also gave people the right to acquire copies of their documents.

In March 1993, I decided to join the ranks of those seeking access to their Stasi-files and sent the Gauck Agency a letter expressing my desire to see any documents they might have related to my person. The letter described in detail my scholarly work on GDR literature, my professional and private contacts with prominent GDR authors, some of whom I had hosted as guest writers in residence at Oberlin College. It provided a list of my publications and editorial work on various aspects of GDR literature. I also mentioned my many trips to the GDR and stays there, as well as my contact with the Writers' Union and the Humboldt University. Finally, I inquired about the possible existence of a Stasi-file containing information on me and, if one did exist, how to go about gaining access to that file.

In April I received a response to my inquiry, indicating that I needed to submit two items to the Agency: a file inspection application on a special form and a proof of identity certificate. I dutifully completed the uncomplicated application form, dated it April 20, 1993, and returned it to the Agency along with a photocopy of my passport. In early May, I received a letter acknowledging receipt of the documents I had submitted and assigning a registry number for my application. The letter concluded with a vague and somewhat discouraging message indicating that, due to the large number of inquiries the Agency was receiving every day, the processing of my application would take some time. It also asked me to refrain from making inquiries in writing or by telephone. I did not expect that the processing of my application would take several years, but that is in fact what happened.

In June I received another letter from the Gauck Agency, this time requesting a notarized proof-of-identity certificate. I was told that the search for documents containing information on my person could not be initiated until that certificate was on hand. According to my records, I sent a notarized photocopy of my passport to the Agency on August 9, 1993, and after that I received no more communications from them.

JOACHIM WALTHER'S *SICHERUNGSBEREICH LITERATUR /*
SECURITY ZONE LITERATURE

In 1996, former GDR author Joachim Walther published his landmark study, *Sicherungsbereich Literatur: Schriftsteller und Staatssicherheit in der Deutschen Demokratischen Republik* (*Security Zone Literature: Writers and State Security in the German Democratic Republic*, Berlin: Ch. Links). This 888-page book documents and analyzes how the Stasi went about implementing and enforcing the SED Party's cultural policies in the realm of literature, how it monitored and tried to influence and control GDR writers. Walther, who worked as an editor for the publishing house Buchverlag Der Morgen Berlin from 1968 to 1983, had been forced to resign from that position due to his opposition to censorship and related issues. He began working on this meticulously researched documentary study shortly after the "Wende" (change in direction) and was given full access to the files of all former GDR writers. In brief, his assignment was to use these documents to determine the nature of the relationship and level of collaboration between GDR writers and the secret police agency.

In the introduction to *Sicherungsbereich Literatur*, Walther comments on the reasons why GDR writers and artists were willing to work with and for the Stasi: "A special factor in the readiness of writers and artists to collaborate with the Ministry for State Security was the belief in utopia, along with ignoble reasons like careerism, envy, craving for power, and need for recognition."(10) He confirms my own conviction that high-level SED Party officials and Stasi officers overestimated by far the importance of literature in their society and the power of free speech; and that explains why they went to extraordinary lengths to suppress freedom of expression.

When *Sicherungsbereich Literatur* was published in 1996, I immediately purchased a copy and spent a couple of hours browsing through it. At one point, I skimmed through the index from A to Z, looking for the names of writers and other persons I knew. When I reached Z, I found "Zipser, Richard 533, 544, 546, 589, 598." Five references to me, incredible! And then I proceeded to read the following reports from or about these informants: Uwe Berger, Fritz Rudolf Fries, Anneliese Löffler, and Paul Wiens. The first of these is meant to illustrate the form and content of an unofficial collaborator's report.

[Uwe Berger: IME "Uwe"]

1) The lyric poet Uwe Berger, alias "Uwe," handwritten on August 11, 1976: "June 22, 1976. In accordance with instructions, I called Sarah Kirsch. I told her that Dr. Richard Zipser had mentioned

her twice in his conversation with me. Specifically, he said she had recommended me, and that she and I are GDR authors of the literary genre that is his favorite. Sarah Kirsch answered cautiously. 'When he was at my place, I gave him a number of names; yours was also one of them. He had asked me whom else I might be able to recommend.' We then exchanged a few unimportant sentences. I tried to find out about her opinion of Zipser. But she only agreed with me when I said it might become a very valuable book. She thanked me for my call and waited for me to end the conversation. The motivation for my call was weak. Further initiatives of this sort could make Sarah Kirsch suspicious. My friendly rapport with her remained intact." (533)

[Fritz Rudolf Fries: IMV "Pedro Hagen"]

In 1978 monthly meetings were held. [*Stasi officer Gerhard*] Hoffmann noted that the collaboration had become significantly more trustful; the IM would occasionally report "of his own accord," for example about Sarah Kirsch and the American literary scholar Richard Zipser. In 1979 "Pedro Hagen" was re-registered as an IMV [*a higher level of informant than IM and IME*]. Report on meeting of March 6, 1979: "The IM was open-minded, interested, also provided information unreservedly on the issues that were raised." (544)

At the next meeting on March 12, 1981, "Pedro Hagen"—who in the meantime was re-registered as an IMB [*a higher level of informant than IMV*]—received the cover address "Käthe Martin," to which he was supposed to send a postcard from every place he stayed in the USA. In addition, he was handed 500 West German marks in an EG-container and given instructions on how to go about opening and destroying the container. The IM acknowledged receipt of the 500 West German marks in writing. After his trip it says in the evaluation meeting report of May 19,

1981: "He initiated activities in the USA that enabled him to proceed as instructed and demonstrated perseverance, e.g., in the efforts he made to contact Dr. Zipser." (546)

[Anneliese Löffler: IMS "Dölbl"]

After "Dölbl" had written reader's reports in the summer of 1978 on Günter Grass ("Der Butt" [*"The Flounder"*]) and Klaus Poche ("Atemnot" [*"Shortness of Breath"*]) and delivered reports on the USA Germanist Richard Zipser as well as Franz Fühmann and on some of her students, her report file breaks off abruptly with the reader's report dated August 13, 1978 on Poche's novel, without any reference to archiving or completing that piece of work. This would suggest that the remaining parts have been destroyed, so that it is not possible to make a reliable statement about the duration of IM "Dölbl's" informant activity beyond the year 1978. (589)

[Paul Wiens: IMS "Dichter" / *"Poet"*]

According to the name index of his report file, he provided information from 1967 on about (among others) Bella Achmadulina, H.C. Artmann, Amfried Astel, Rudolf Augstein, Jurek Becker Wolf Biermann, Heinrich Böll, Nicolas Born, Volker Braun, Heinz Czechowski, Hilde Domin, Adolf Endler, Hans Magnus Enzensberger, Efim Etkind, Konrad Franke, Fritz Rudolf Fries, Barbara Frischmuth, Franz Fühmann, Lew Ginsburg, Peter Gosse, Peter Härtling, Stephan Hermlin, Stefan Heym, Walter Janka, Uwe Johnson, Gustav Just, Heinz Kahlau, Rainer Kirsch, Sarah Kirsch, Lew Kopelew, Ludvik Kundera, Günter Kunert, Reiner Kunze, Alain Lane, Jurij Ljubimow, Erich Loest, Frank-Wolf Matthies, Christoph Meckel, Karl Mickel, Irmtraud Morgner, Heiner Müller, A. W. Mytze, Bulat Okudshawa, Fritz Pleitgen, Ulrich Plenzdorf, Boris Polewoi, Hans Werner Richter, Andrej Sacharow, Klaus Schlesinger, Christoph Schlotterer, Peter Schneider, Hans Georg Soldat,

Alexander Solshenizyn, Erwin Strittmatter, Klaus Wagenbach, Joachim Walther, Berta Waterstradt, Christa Wolf, Gerhard Wolf, Richard Zipser and other German, French, Hungarian, Yugoslavian and Soviet authors. Moreover, the poet was also an informant in his private life: In his IM-file there are private letters from the year 1972 to Irmtraud Morgner, to whom Paul Wiens was married from 1971 on, with the notation: "from 'Poet,' hand over at meeting." (598)

US GERMANISTS IN THE INDEX TO JOACHIM WALTHER'S BOOK

One day, as I was thinking about *Sicherungsbereich Literatur* (*Security Zone Literature*) and what a magnificent contribution it makes to our knowledge and understanding of one of the darkest aspects of GDR history, it occurred to me that I should look for references to other US Germanists in the index to Walther's book, just out of curiosity. In the 1970s and 1980s, the number of US Germanists with a serious interest in GDR literature was not too large, and over the years I had become acquainted with most of them. With the help of US publications such as *Studies in GDR Culture and Society*, collections of papers presented at the annual New Hampshire symposia on the German Democratic Republic, *GDR Bulletin*, and *GDR Monitor*, I made a list of colleagues who had been active in the area of GDR studies in the 1970s and 1980s. When I completed that exercise, the list had more than thirty names on it. I then proceeded to look up each of those names in the index to Walther's book, hoping to find references to some of them. To my surprise and bewilderment, only one US Germanist is cited in that index: Richard Zipser. I have done a great deal of thinking about that and have come to this conclusion: There was only one US Germanist who had engaged in what the Stasi considered to be subversive activities in the GDR, only one had been considered an enemy of the

GDR state. Today, as before, I am proud of the fact that the vast majority of the GDR writers I knew and worked with on various book projects in the 1970s, 1980s, and 1990s viewed me and my work on GDR literature in a very different light.

IN SEARCH OF MY STASI-FILE (2)

The informants' references to me in five sections of *Sicherungsbereich Literatur* (*Security Zone Literature*) gave me the excuse I needed to approach the Stasi Records Agency again, this time with evidence that I in all likelihood did have a Stasi-file. Since more than four years had elapsed since my initial inquiry in March 1993, I wrote a more forceful letter to which I attached photocopies of the relevant passages that appeared in Joachim Walther's book (see Part 106). In this letter, which is dated June 30, 1997, I asked about the status of my application to gain access to my Stasi-file, assuming that one existed. In the concluding paragraph I wrote:

> The mention of my name several times in Joachim Walther's book strengthens my suspicion that Ministry for State Security documents related to my person exist. I would therefore like to ask you, on the basis of the new information that has surfaced, to process my application as soon as possible and advise me as regards the existence of files containing personal information about me and, if applicable, grant me permission to inspect those documents. I would be grateful for a reply.

My letter had the desired effect; it got the process of locating the reports and other documents that comprise my file underway—at last! In September 1997, I received a letter from a case worker at the Agency, Ms. Eckert, indicating that the preliminary search for documents had met with success. In the letter Ms. Eckert stated that, due to the relatively small size of my file, they would be willing to make a photocopy of it and send that to me. She invited me to call her at the Agency and let her know how I wanted to proceed.

I was delighted to learn that I would not have to travel to Berlin, in order to inspect my file. I called Ms. Eckert and expressed interest in receiving a photocopy of the file and, when asked, affirmed that I was prepared to cover the photocopying and shipping charges. She did not say when I could expect to receive the file, just that it would take a while to gather all the documents and then process and photocopy them.

ARRIVAL OF MY STASI-FILE: JANUARY 22, 1999

After sixteen months had passed, the Stasi-file arrived without any forewarning on January 22, 1999, one day before my 56th birthday. What a surprise and unusual birthday present that was!

In the package containing my 396-page file, I found a six-page cover letter from Ms. Jabs, a Stasi Records Agency case worker. The letter is dated January 15, 1999, and makes reference to my application to gain access to my file, which the Agency had received on April 20, 1993. Ms. Jabs addresses and explains a number of important matters in her letter, most of which have already been discussed in the "Introduction" to this book.

Ms. Jabs points out that the information I have received comes from Stasi records that have been compiled to date. One cannot rule out the possibility that additional documents related to my person will be found as the ongoing organizational work continues at the Agency and other repositories. But due to the large number of applications she has to process, she is unable to inform individual applicants when new documents have been discovered. Therefore, I should consider contacting her again in about two years with regard to supplemental information. Moreover, she also recommends that I submit a renewal application to the central Stasi Records Agency in Berlin.

COMING FULL CIRCLE

We have now come full circle, back to my starting point, the day when my Stasi-file showed up unexpectedly in my mailbox. The file has enabled me to relive some important stages of my life and my academic career in ways that would not have been possible without such a document. It also enabled me to rediscover the person I was in the 1970s and 1980s, and I learned a great deal about myself through the eyes and observations of others. I also realized that my experiences in the GDR and interactions with East German writers, bureaucrats, and regular citizens—especially in the 1970s and 1980s—transformed me gradually into a different human being, into a more compassionate and politically-aware person with a more comprehensive and conservative world view. And, I think the process of reading my file and the Fries/Zipser file, assimilating and reflecting on the contents of those unusual documents, and then writing this memoir, has been transformative as well.

By sharing much of the file with readers of this book, I hope to provide them with unique insights into cultural-political, literary, and everyday life in the GDR. Few if any Americans have experienced the GDR as I did, and I am pleased to share some of my experiences and memories so others can gain a better understanding of what life was like in the actually existing GDR, the country with a forty-year history that no longer exists.

IN SEARCH OF MORE INFORMATION IN THE STASI-FILES OF OTHERS

In the concluding paragraphs of her letter dated January 15, 1999, which accompanied the shipment of my Stasi-file, Ms. Jabs addresses my inquiry about the possibility of checking the files of some other persons for more information about me. She indicates that the Stasi Records Law provides for this particular type of access which is regarded as a third-party request. To help initiate the search process, the applicant has to furnish the names, addresses, and other pieces of information about the persons whose files are to be inspected. After further correspondence on this subject, she gave me a deadline for submission of the information needed to narrow and facilitate the search—September 30, 1999. I called Ms. Jabs in mid-August and let her know that I would be sending her the information she had requested to conduct further research on my behalf. In early September 1999, I sent her a long letter in which I provided the names of five GDR writers, a professor, a publisher, a GDR Writers' Union functionary, and a married couple whose Stasi files—assuming that they existed—might contain reports or other information on me.

I never received a response to this letter, which might have gone astray in the mail or been misplaced at the Agency. Or, it is possible that Agency officials decided it would be too time-consuming to do the amount of research my additional request would have involved. From my first attempt to gain access to my file in 1993, which began a process that took almost six years to conclude, I expected that the search for more information on me in the files of others would take a very long time. Hence, I was not concerned when I did not hear anything more from Ms. Jabs, who had been very helpful to me. In November 2002, I received a package containing 44 pages from Fritz Rudolf Fries's Stasi-file, which came as quite a surprise. It had not been sent to me by Ms. Jabs or in response to the letter mentioned above. After reading and incorporating some of that material into my memoir, I had what one might call file fatigue. As the years went by, I decided to be patient and not make further inquiries. One day, perhaps, I will find another package from the Stasi Records Agency in my mailbox, another surprise. But if that package never arrives, I will not be disappointed. Again, and especially after writing this memoir and then translating it into English, I have a serious case of file fatigue and am eager for closure.

IN RETROSPECT

Reading my Stasi-file closely while preparing this memoir was a bitter-sweet, emotionally draining experience, painful at times—e.g., when I came across unexpected deception or outright lies about my person; pleasurable at other times—e.g., when the file confirmed that none of my closest friends had informed on me, something I had come to fear. Much of what I read intrigued me, and it was particularly interesting to see how most of my informants tried to make themselves look good to their handlers by distorting or omitting certain facts or even fabricating things in their reports. In the end, I realized that none of them had done me any real harm, but that realization did not make me feel better about them. The file also reacquainted me with Richard Zipser of the 1970s and 1980s, a person I realized I no longer knew; it brought back many memories, good ones and bad ones.

In his eloquent memoir, *The File* (New York: Vintage Books, 1998), Timothy Garton Ash tells us

> how a Stasi-file opens the door to a vast sunken labyrinth of the forgotten past, but how, too, the very act of opening the door itself changes the buried artifacts, like an archaeologist letting in fresh air to a sealed Egyptian tomb. For these are not simply past experiences rediscovered in their original state. Even without the fresh light from a new document or another's recollection—the opened door—our memories decay or sharpen, mellow or sour, with the passage of time and the change of circumstances... But with the fresh light the memory changes irrevocably. A door opens, but another closes. There is no way back now to your own earlier memory of that person, that event. It is like a revelation made, years later, to a loved one. Or like a bad divorce, where today's bitterness transforms all the shared past, completely, miserably, seemingly forever. Except that the bitter memory, too, will fade and change with the further passage of time. (108-09)

ADDENDUM

April 7, 2012. Today, to my surprise, I found another communication from the Stasi Records Agency in my mailbox. I thought to myself: What is this about? The envelope contained six pages, including a one-page cover letter from the assembler, Ms. Doris Gorsler, the text of which appears in a slightly modified form below.

SUBJECT	**Notification about the use of documents for the reassessment of activities of the State Security Service, in accordance with § 32a of the Stasi-Records-Law (StRL).** **Here: Central Evaluation and Information Group, Edition 1977 / Logbook-No. 006269/93Z**
REGARDING	Items of Information from the Year 1977
DATE	3/30/2012
ATTACHMENTS	Excerpt from the Item of Information: K 3/13 from June 28, 1977

Dear Dr. Zipser,

Since 2009 the research department of the Stasi Records Agency has been publishing the Ministry for State Security's reports to the political leadership of the GDR as a reference book. The volumes of the edition for years 1961, 1976 and 1988 have already appeared under the title "The GDR from the Perspective of the Stasi. The secret reports to the SED Leadership." At present the annual edition for the year 1977 is being prepared for publication.

Among the reports to be edited for this year's publication is "Item of Information" K 3/13 from June 28, 1977 "Regarding Some Problems Related to Hostile-Negative Activities of Groups of Persons in the Area of Art and Culture."

The report contains information about your person that was collected by the MfSS. According to § 32 a of the Stasi-Records-Law individuals from this time period, public office holders, and political functionaries are to be notified in advance when information about them is going to be published. Enclosed are the relevant sections from the report that I am sending for your information.

We will be grateful for annotations, corrections, or addenda to the information that is contained in the reports. If applicable, you will be acknowledged in the footnote commentary. [...]

The first page of the attached document is a handwritten distribution list with the names of high-ranking SED party officials and Stasi officers who received the report, as shown below.

K 3/13

CEIG 5530 [CEIG = Central Evaluation and Information Group]

Distribution List

~~Com. Hager, Kurt [Member, Politburo of the Central~~ Committee, SED]

Lamberz, Werner [Member, Politburo of the Central Committee, SED]

Mittig, Rudi [Deputy Minister of the Stasi]

Kienberg, Paul [Lieutenant General, Director of Main Department XX, MfSS]

Fischer, Karl [Member, Department of Agitation, MfSS]

Schorm [Colonel Bernhard Schorm, Deputy Director of Department I, MfSS]

Original Dept. VHA 190/7.7

MDS [Main Department Stamp]

The subject of the report appears on the next page, by itself, with a handwritten date, as follows:

6/28/77

Comments

about some problems in connection with hostile-negative activities of groups of persons in the area of art and culture

Next comes the report itself; the segment with references to me is three pages long and appears in a slightly modified form below. Astonishing to me as I read these pages is the high level of paranoia and irrational fear of activities perceived as hostile—on the part of regime-critical writers in the GDR, outsiders living in or visiting the GDR, such as journalists and publishers from the West, individuals like myself, and even the embassies of some non-socialist countries. For the Stasi, enemies of the GDR state, its brand of socialism, and its cultural policies are everywhere.

Active "Contact Persons" at present (among others) are especially

Schwarz	- Correspondent for the "Spiegel" [*German weekly news magazine*]
Nöldechen	- Correspondent for the "Westfälische Rundschau" [*German newspaper*]
Sager	- Correspondent for ZDF [*Zweites Deutsches Fernsehen, German public service television broadcaster*]
Schulz	- Correspondent for the DPA [*Deutsche Presse- Agentur, German news agency*]
Nette	- Correspondent for the ARD [*Arbeitsgemeinschaft der öffentlich-rechtlichen Rundfunkanstalten der Bundesrepublik Deutschland, consortium of regional public broadcasters in Germany*]
Menge	- Correspondent for "Die Zeit" [*German national weekly newspaper*]
Vickers	- Correspondent for the BBC [*British Broadcasting Corporation, public service broadcaster*]
Johnson	- Correspondent for the BBC
Sudau	- Correspondent for the "Frankfurter Rundschau" [*German daily newspaper*]
Barkow	- Correspondent for "Stern" [*German weekly news magazine*]

Employees of FRG publishing houses systematically seek out writers who were signees of the "protest petition" [*a reference to the GDR writers' declaration of protest against the government's expatriation of oppositional writer/singer Wolf Biermann in*

November 1976] and conduct lengthy "discussions" with them. (Take, as examples, Ingrid Grimm/Bertelsmann-Publishing, Elisabeth Borchers/Suhrkamp-Publishing, Ingrid Krüger/ Luchterhand-Publishing.)

The intent and purpose of these contacts, especially with writers, is above all to strengthen their misgivings and their negative attitude as regards the cultural policies of the GDR. At the same time, detailed advice is provided on personal problems related to the "creation of literature" and the publication of their "works" in the FRG.

To be integrated into the totality of hostile activities are the growing attempts to make contact and exert influence on the part of the embassies of non-socialist countries, particularly the Permanent Mission of the FRG in the GDR. Since the beginning of December 1976 a marked increase has been detected in reciprocal visits and discussions between employees of the Permanent Mission of the FRG in the GDR, as well as employees of the Embassy of the Republic of Austria, and persons from groups within the GDR of negative creative artists and persons engaged in the cultural sector; (to be singled out are the Leader of the Permanent Mission, *[Günter]* Gaus, and the Speaker for Culture and Sport, Winfried Staar). *[After the creation of the German Democratic Republic in 1949, the Federal Republic of Germany did not recognize the GDR as a separate and independent state with sovereign authority. It therefore did not have an embassy in East Berlin, which the GDR maintained was its capital city. Instead, the FRG established a Permanent Mission of the FRG to the GDR, which was situated in East Berlin. This enabled it to conduct whatever diplomatic activities it deemed necessary within the GDR.]*

Western embassies and the FRG mission systematically issue invitations to writers and persons from the cultural sector of the GDR to participate in receptions, dinners, and discussions in their quarters—without giving notification in every instance, in compliance with the diplomatic conventions of the MfFA [*Ministry for Foreign Affairs*]—and in private dwellings with [*authors*] Heym, Jurek Becker, Hermlin, Schlesinger, Kunert, Schneider and others participating.

(According to information on hand, this group of persons accepts the invitations on a regular basis and comes up with their own initiatives to obtain invitations.)

At such gatherings, especially the ones in private dwellings, advice is provided on essentially the same "problems" that were mentioned earlier.

An integral part of the adversarial efforts aimed at converting, manipulating, disrupting, as well as creating an "inner opposition" among persons from the cultural sphere and writers in the GDR are notably also the activities of such persons as, for example,

> SCHWENGER, Hannes
> President of the West Berlin
> Writers' Union and Secretary
> of the so-called "Freedom and
> Socialism" Committee

and

> Dr. ZIPSER, Richard
> Professor of German Studies at
> Oberlin College/USA

[...]

The MfSS has known for some time that Dr. Zipser is a contact partner to hostile-negative GDR writers who willingly provide him with detailed information about the state of affairs within these groups of persons. In June 1977 he again had several face-to-face meetings with signees of the protest declaration ([*Sarah*] Kirsch, Plenzdorf and others).

What I cannot understand after reading the paragraphs above, which reveal that the Stasi believed in June 1977 that I was engaging in subversive activities, is why the GDR authorities permitted me to return to that country as an IREX scholar in the fall 1977 and spring 1978. Perhaps, since the agreement with IREX was relatively new (established in 1975) and important to the GDR in their effort to gain international recognition, they did not want to do anything that might strain relations. Also, I had been awarded the IREX fellowship several months before this report was written and distributed.

The final paragraphs of the report, cited below, provide further insight into the psychosis that pervaded the Stasi and a reminder that it was one of the most hated and feared secret police agencies the world has ever known.

In recent months the most active hostile-negative forces among writers and persons from the cultural sector of the GDR increasingly organized get-togethers in private dwellings of varying types and modes of concealment (birthday celebrations, so-called farewell parties for persons relocating to the FRG, and so forth), mostly with the participation of diplomats from embassies of non-socialist states within the GDR, journalists, writers and employees of publishers from non-socialist states, in particular the FRG and West Berlin.

FRG writer Günter Grass has participated in a number of these gatherings lately.

The purpose and intent of these gatherings apparently consists of "emerging from their isolation," to encourage each other as regards their negative and wavering stance, to discuss their situation and give advice on their modes of behavior and actions vis-à-vis Party sanctions, government bodies, and social institutions as well as during discussions with leading representatives of the Party and government; to inform Western contact partners especially about the state of affairs among the writers and persons engaged in the cultural sector of the GDR and their intentions; to exchange and spread half-truths, unsubstantiated reports and allegations of reputed sanctions of the Party and security agencies imposed on the so-called signees, so that a certain psychosis against the Party and security agencies will be fomented.

These forces intend to continue being active literarily, in the way they have been previously.

AFTERWORD

He, Who Thinks Differently, is an Enemy

I

More than two decades after German unification Richard Zipser, witness to a particular realm of the history of the division, that of "GDR literature," presents his memoirs. These are the memoirs of a researcher, teacher, and advocate for the literature that arose under the communistic Socialist Unity Party (SED) regime. Publications like *DDR-Literatur im Tauwetter* [*GDR Literature During the Thaw*] (1985), *Contemporary East German Poetry* (1980), as well as *Fragebogen: Zensur* [*Questionnaire: Censorship*] (1995) belong to the canon of American German Studies. Yet the reader does not need to know any of these works to benefit from reading this one. While *Von Oberlin nach Ostberlin* [*From Oberlin to East Berlin*] (2013) opens up a surprising historical context to those familiar with other works of Zipser's, the book can also stand alone, dealing as it does with the author himself. Just as every narrative invites the reader to take hold of the depicted reality, this one has something so provocatively radical that it is worth pursuing Zipser's retrospective.

It is in the nature of memoir literature that one can approach it via the whole or the individual components, whether of facts, incidents or constellation of participants: The reader himself is accountable!

II

The author, as the only American Germanist to be designated by the Ministry for State Security (MfSS) of the SED regime as an "operative," – this is documented in his Stasi file – had taken it into his head in the 1970s to research the thinking and working of writers all of whom were members of the conformist professional organization, and subsequently to publish his discoveries in the USA. In view of the touted socio-political "thaw" after the fall of Walter Ulbricht (1971) and Erich Honecker's renunciation of German unity, this did not seem a futile undertaking; quite the opposite, for the regime was craving international recognition.

The interview questions, approved in advance by the GDR Writers' Union, used the required vocabulary and were ideologically correct. Zipser was clearly confident that – even with self-censorship – differing personalities would bring to light differing views of newly decreed "flawed heroes." It was perfectly fine with this literary scholar, schooled as he was in Klemperer and Brecht, that the responses – in their essence – might provide an account of dissent, contradiction, incompatibility, in short of opposition to "top down infusion." At any rate, the "socialist hero" was passé and the "socialist human community" superseded by the "developed socialist society." Intellectuals and artists were given the prospect of "taboo-free zones," so long as they did not intend to shake the foundations of socialism.

Without doubt a "broad field," demonstrated by each of the 112 episodes, completely in character for the Germanist from Oberlin (Ohio), who wanted to gain his own knowledge on location through facts and in intimate, personal encounters with the writers. "Looking down from on high, one sees everything false." This heretical statement by the young Goethe might stand over Zipser's subversive search for knowledge. He saw himself on the track of changes that needed to be recorded. Since, in this project in the surveillance state, he came close to "hostile-negative actions," in keeping with directives, "continual political operative assessment, targeted scrutiny, and analytical processing of the information gained" were initiated. In the never-ending confusion of the Stasi operatives about how to categorize Zipser – whether as an academic simpleton or cunning CIA agent – it becomes clear whose child the "sword and shield" is, i.e., that of a party that knows it can keep itself in power only as an all-encompassing dictatorship. That someone can be interested in literature of their domain without being up to something seditious and of his own free will, as a foreigner, and takes the announcements of the SED 8th Party Congress seriously, sets off the usual alarm bells in the brains of their Chekists: Whoever thinks differently is the enemy.

III

Anyone who is even halfway socialized as a liberal democrat and no expert in or apologist for Marxist-Leninism can only shake his head in disgust over the appropriation of the literary scene by the secret service in the SED regime. Moreover, the shameless way many a writer in his reports celebrates his informant activity as the expression of a superior morality presenting itself as class struggle belongs to "GDR literature." As a reminder of the minefield on which Zipser had to acquire his investigations: of the 19 members of the Writers' Union Executive Committee, twelve had committed themselves to being informants. The local districts did not look any different: of the 39 Union writers in Halle, 14 were unofficial collaborators ("Inoffizieller Mitarbeiter").

How the system produced fear, cowardice and human duplicity was known to anyone who had been subjected to it. Without the general fear of arrest, repression, and degradation, the SED could not have existed. Zipser discovered little by little that with the 1973 World Student and Youth Festival, the "Woodstock of the East," the breakthrough to an unrestricted surveillance state was completed. (When Ulbricht was ousted in 1971, the MfSS had 45,500 full-time workers; when the SED regime fell, it had at its disposal 91,015 full-time workers and approximately 190,000 unofficial collaborators.)

In his interviews Zipser let writers speak from the generation that had started writing under these conditions and that in most cases accepted the postwar order as a space shaped "by the battle of the systems" (hence, many of them nourished the expectation of an "improvement" of circumstances; one of the illusions was called "socialism with a human face"). And in the course of encounters through the years, he discerned and documented their individual self-assertion and emancipation from the ruling ideology and indoctrination. Thereby a dialogue increasingly emerges in which the interviewer is drawn into the confidence of the interviewee. The memoirs reflect the growing power of resistance of a "different" way of thinking unleashed by him and radiating out – thinking committed to freedom, democratic identity, and the future of the society and of each individual.

More than facile expressions of "abhorrence and outrage," Zipser's book captures the structures and consequences of a "cradle-to-grave" dictatorship, because he does not compare the systems, but rather lets them speak for themselves. On the basis of encounters with artists like Ulrich Plenzdorf, Jurek Becker, Elke Erb, Sarah Kirsch and Bernd Jentzsch, he makes visible the contradictions of a society in which pronounced solidarity stands next to Stasi-terror, integration next to resistance, everyday pragmatism next to disappointed idealism.

It behooves later generations to exercise humility and take responsibility for life gained by the fall of the Wall in a free democratic society. Today it is scarcely imaginable that what Zipser documented was cruel daily life for decades between the Elbe and the Oder.

IV

At no point did Zipser ingratiate himself with the SED powers. One might not think it necessary to mention this. But the reality was different. A not insignificant number of American Germanists had elevated "GDR Literature" to their academic speciality. Often, however, it was impossible to determine whether they had chosen the literature or, rather, collaboration with the regime. Such at least was my shocked reaction in 1980 when a lecture and workshop tour took me for the first time to German Departments of universities on the East Coast and far into the middle and West of the US.

They spoke of their hatred of "predatory capitalism," were full of contempt for the "ugly American," wallowed lachrymosely in the belief in a "socialist alternative" and gave themselves up as willing partisans to the "other Germany." Thus, they selected mostly those texts that were "representative" of their good buddy. They preferred to seek out their contacts and tasks in the realm of "engineers of the human soul" rather than among those who described the gulag for what it was.

One of them nine years later, just a day after the Wall had fallen, argued unabashedly to me: "But the utopia! What happens to the utopia?" They knew very well how the regime was composed: "With the protection of the secured border we are building the better state." For anyone who wanted to know, it was obvious; solely by means of the death strip did the Wall maintain its political effect: whoever wanted to survive had to arrange himself – in the Party's "Hegelian" philosophical-ideological concoction; it was called understanding of necessity! In Zipser's memoirs they show up as well.

In the first weeks and months they held back, were on their guard about what and how much the Stasi files would reveal about their deliberate activity. Soon, however, they settled down, "historicized" the object of their devotion, and strutted again in public. When, for example, a critic held up to a prominent writer her onetime activity as an unofficial collaborator, 174 (!) faculty members of American universities got together to protest in a public letter (*Die Zeit,* June 18, 1993) that "positive social reform approaches in the

GDR had been disparaged." Regarding the author's legwork for the Stasi, they said sympathetically, "we don't have the comforting certainty that we would not have acted differently [...] in the same situation. Like many others at that time she may have seen in the GDR the only practical possibility of building a human alternative to capitalism. That she went astray when she got involved with the machinations of the Stasi, and deceived herself when she hoped for democratic reforms from the 'Unity Party,' one can recognize much more clearly today after the failure of this attempt than at the time in the GDR; however, it was not only the GDR that was characterized by calculated thinking or even political opportunism."

Whoever thinks this way has, to paraphrase Loriot, either a corpse in the cellar or is off his rocker.

Nevertheless, this type of dealing with the GDR dictatorship is not surprising. Too many intellectuals of the 20th century before them had already succumbed to the fascination of totalitarian systems contemptuous of the individual. Working together on the creation of a "new man" was always more enticing than really achieving equality, liberty, and brotherhood for all citizens through the workings of democracy.

V

Zipser's memories, awakened by the Stasi-reports, let the reader learn how the freedom and dignity of human beings and their right to "independent thinking and feeling" are the basic conditions for the creation and reading of literature. Because he regards with suspicion the totalizing view "down from above," during his stays in the GDR he looks at events from up close. The episodes recounted are like "an endless stream," moments that do not form a "constructed entity." Although he cites material from files, regulations, and "procedures," his book is not a documentary in the traditional sense, but rather a subjective examination of his achievement as an expert, scholar, and mediator of a certain chapter of German literature.

His portrayal comes at precisely the right time, in a situation in which – whether through thoughtlessness, ignorance, or intent – positions are increasingly spreading that relativize the injustice of the GDR regime (e.g., "... the GDR a small country with grey historic cities and green boulevards" the *Frankfurter Allgemeine Zeitung* of February 12, 2011 lovingly states).

Ultimately, all nostalgia also illustrates – among other things – the absence of knowledge and enlightening information. Thus, I hope that Zipser's contemporary testimony may find application in political and academic education. The responsibility to "think differently" must not come to an end!

Heinz-Uwe Haus

August 2012

Translated by Cecile Zorach

TRIBUTE

A Review and an Appreciation

Rarely do students follow so neatly in their professors' footsteps as I have been able to do. I took my first graduate independent study with Dr. Richard Zipser in the fall of 1987. Dr. Zipser had only recently taken up his position as Chair of the Department of Foreign Languages and Literatures at UD. He had come to Newark from Ohio after earning tenure and chairing the German Department at Oberlin College. I was a first-year MA student, somewhat unsure of my own purpose for studying German literature and, moreover, I had not yet spent any extended time in Germany. Through mentoring and teaching, Dr. Zipser helped me to clarify and pursue my goals. His unwavering support for study abroad made it possible for me to study and gain teaching experience in Bayreuth, both in winter-session programs and on a full-year's exchange.

Now, much later, I chair the German Department at Oberlin and can offer ample evidence that Richard Zipser's far-reaching scholarship, teaching, and administration have left a lasting mark on Oberlin, UD, and on our profession as a whole. Among his most outstanding legacies are the many East German authors whom he invited to Oberlin under the auspices of the Max Kade German Writer-in-Residence program. The tradition of (now former) East German authors at Oberlin is going strong. In the past several years, we have welcomed Uwe Kolbe, Irina Liebmann, Peter Wawerzinek, Susanne Schädlich, and Barbara Köhler.

By June of 2013, after fourteen years at Oberlin, including six years of chairing, I was convinced that I had a pretty good handle on international literary research and knew how to create rich opportunities for students fo learn from living authors. Yet Richard Zipser's "documentary memoir" humbled me and gave me an even greater sense of the risks and challenges he faced in building a bridge across hotly contested geopolitical borders. This unique book sheds light on the past and holds potential lessons for the future, offering valuable insights into *Germanistik* in the American academy and the enduring viability of academic and literary exchange.

Von Oberlin nach Ostberlin chronicles Dr. Zipser's scholarship on East German literature, research that, to Dr. Zipser's surprise, was monitored and scrutinized in over 400 pages of *Stasi* (secret police) files between 1973 and 1988. These secret records were made available to the public after 1991 by the Federal Commissioner for the Stasi Archives. *Von Oberlin nach Ostberlin* details the sweeping surveillance that pervaded East German life. Although this alone is not new information, it is nonetheless striking to learn that an American German professor was also so thoroughly targeted by intelligence operatives.

The book's attractive layout features an excellent glossary of terms and abbreviations, necessary for keeping up with the complicated taxonomy of informants and sheer number of East German acronyms. Dr. Zipser offers his own contextualizing remarks in fonts different from those used for Stasi reports, and he inserts comments in square brackets directly into the reports, where necessary, to correct factual errors or to counter the most outrageous claims. He could not always resist the impulse to correct spelling and grammatical errors within the Stasi files: "Schliesslich bin ich Lehrer" 'I'm a teacher, after all' (17).

Many entries reflect the efforts of informants to ascertain the purpose for Richard Zipser's work in East Germany and determine his credibility. At the time, Dr. Zipser was an Assistant Professor at Oberlin. He was writing a survey of East German literature published during the cultural-political thaw following Erich Honecker's assumption of leadership of the Socialist Unity Party. For his three-volume work, *DDR-Literatur im Tauwetter: Wandel, Wunsch, Wirklichkeit* (New York, Peter Lang, 1985), Zipser traveled frequently to the GDR and interviewed over forty-five publishing authors. The Stasi reports on this project make up the largest portion of *Von Oberlin nach Ostberlin*.

In addition to contextualizing commentary, Dr. Zipser generally lets the Stasi files speak—or misspeak—for themselves. Stasi informants were apparently unconvinced that Dr. Zipser did not work for the CIA. The paranoia of the IM reports is palpable, for example, when Dr. Zipser's manuscript is deemed "äusserst brisant" 'utterly explosive' (100) or when Dr. Zipser himself is characterized as a "Staatsfeind" or 'enemy of the state' whose "subversive" activities should be stifled (119). Informants report much consternation about Dr. Zipser's funding sources and posit conflicting explanations for why he has taken more time than (they believe) American scholars typically receive to complete a book. Dr. Zipser surmises in retrospect that had he not received a prestigious IREX grant, he would likely not have received further visas to enter the GDR after 1978 (101).

His Stasi files detail his serious—and for the GDR alarming—scholarship on such prominent writers as Christa Wolf, Sarah Kirsch, and Jurek Becker. Even early in his career, Zipser correctly judged that these GDR authors were producing works likely to earn a place in world literature. His good judgment is obliquely confirmed in Stasi files. Humboldt University literature Professors Eva Kaufmann and Frank Hörnigk were observed to regret that Richard Zipser was doing the work that they should be doing, but were not allowed to do (83).

Richard Zipser illuminates the contest between the GDR's internal need for control and its efforts to present a positive image abroad. *Von Oberlin nach Ostberlin* reveals how the self-image of the GDR was propagated by countless acts of personal hypocrisy and opportunism. It is by now well known that many once-respected authors collaborated with the oppressive system by working as informants. It remains devastating to read so many examples of how callously they could cast aspersions on their colleagues and manipulate the truth for personal gain.

Von Oberlin nach Ostberlin is a deeply personal book, a record of a notable career. The files testify to Richard Zipser's appreciation for and grasp of East German literature and accomplishments in bringing GDR authors to the United States. Dr. Zipser's scholarship in East Germany required courage and commitment on his part and now testifies to the strength of East German authors to create literature within the regime's oppressive confines. For these very reasons, the memoir sheds light on the security state in a world currently desperate for clear standards on privacy and the limits of surveillance.

Theater director and UD faculty member Heinz-Uwe Haus, himself a former citizen of the GDR, introduces the volume. Haus sees in it an antidote to mollifying recollections of East Germany that minimize the criminal, dehumanizing character of the totalitarian regime. Haus hopes that Dr. Zipser's book will find its way into educational as well as into political discourses, and I agree that it should. In fact, I am currently using the book this semester at Oberlin with advanced German majors in my Senior Seminar: Legacies of East German Literature and Film. This may seem to some to bring Richard Zipser's work "full circle," yet I hope that instead of closing the circle, I can carry on the work he began and did so well, furthering dialogue that is open and true.

Elizabeth Hamilton
Oberlin College